Labor of Innocents

LABOR OF INNOCENTS

Forced Apprenticeship in North Carolina

1715–1919

KARIN L. ZIPF

LOUISIANA STATE UNIVERSITY PRESS
BATON ROUGE

First printing

Designer: Melanie O'Quinn Samaha

Typeface: Centaur MT

Typesetter: G&S Typesetters, Inc.

Printer and binder: Thomson-Shore, Inc.

Library of Congress Cataloging-in-Publication Data

Zipf, Karin L., 1968–

   Labor of innocents : forced apprenticeship in North Carolina, 1715–1919 / Karin L. Zipf

    p. cm.

   Includes bibliographical references and index.

   ISBN 0-8071-3045-1 (cloth : alk. paper)

  1. Child labor—North Carolina—History.   2. Forced labor—North Carolina—History.

3. Indentured servants—North Carolina—History.   4. Apprenticeship programs—North Carolina—

History.   5. Family policy—North Carolina—History.   6. Social classes—North Carolina—History.

7. North Carolina—Race relations.   8. North Carolina—Social conditions.   I. Title.

   HD6250.U4N89 2005

   331.3′1′097560903—dc22

                     2004023426

For Jonathan

CONTENTS

ACKNOWLEDGMENTS / *ix*

INTRODUCTION / *1*

CHAPTER ONE

ORPHANS, BASTARDS, AND FREE BLACK CHILDREN
Colonial and Antebellum North Carolina Apprenticeship / 8

CHAPTER TWO

"JUSTLY ENTITLED" TO APPRENTICES
Race and Labor in Reconstruction / 40

CHAPTER THREE

FREE-LABOR IDEOLOGY, APPRENTICESHIP, AND
THE FREEDMEN'S BUREAU
Discontinuities in Law and Practice / 68

CHAPTER FOUR

RECONSTRUCTING "FREE WOMAN"
African American Mothers and Apprenticeship / 84

CHAPTER FIVE

PARENTS' RIGHTS OR CHILDREN'S BEST INTERESTS?
The Role of Judicial Discretion in Apprenticeship and Child Custody / 106

CHAPTER SIX

"THE DAY OF APPRENTICESHIP IS PAST"
The Demise of Apprenticeship and the Triumph of Child Welfare / 129

CONCLUSION / 153

NOTES / 157

BIBLIOGRAPHY / 179

INDEX / 197

Illustrations follow page 128

ACKNOWLEDGMENTS

This book has helped me fill a void left by my graduate study in nineteenth-century southern history. Although much of my coursework focused on the American South, little of it focused upon women and gender relations. While few of my professors specialized in these topics, they nonetheless influenced my scholarship. The most memorable of my professors was Eugene Genovese. Professor Genovese taught us to read intellectual history, and although I did not share his perspective on slavery and abolitionist thought, I learned how to read nineteenth century legal sources. This skill proved invaluable when I began to explore the world of free women and African Americans who lived on the margins of slavery. It was in Professor Genovese's seminars that I first became interested in apprenticeship law and its social implications.

Many thanks go to my dissertation adviser, Emory Thomas, who allowed me to pursue apprenticeship in his Civil War seminar and then as a dissertation topic. His support and encouragement helped me survive my encounters with a rather contentious dissertation committee.

Institutions also deserve special mention here. North Carolina Wesleyan College and the Thomas J. Harriott School for the Arts and Sciences at East Carolina University provided research support and encouraged me to explore apprenticeship in the classroom. A College Research Award from East Carolina University generously freed me from teaching duties for a semester to allow me to finalize revisions of this manuscript for publication. Staff at the North Carolina State Archives, the National Archives at East Point, Georgia, and Washington, DC, the Special Collections Department and the North Carolina Collection of the J. Y. Joyner Library at East Carolina University, the Southern Historical

Collection at the University of North Carolina at Chapel Hill, and the Special Collections Department at Duke University offered valuable assistance in locating and accessing government documents and manuscript collections.

Special thanks go to mentors and colleagues who read my work or engaged me in lively discussions about nineteenth-century southern and North Carolina history. Jane Turner Censer, Victoria Bynum, Janine Lanza, Elisabeth Hughes, Linda Kerber, and Laura Edwards all helped me gain perspective on women, race, and gender relations in the nineteenth-century South. Halcott Green, Peter Charles Hoffer, and Patrick W. McKee read the entire manuscript and familiarized me with a legal perspective. Leslie Miller performed services beyond friendship by reading the manuscript in its every incarnation. She and I spent several late nights examining page after page, and she spent many hours listening while I learned to articulate my arguments. Thanks to Heather White, who carefully edited the bibliography. I am also indebted to Karl Campbell, Nicola Creegan, Craig Fischer, Erica Kosal, Bill Owens, Cathy Parham, Sheila Phipps, Bob Trullinger, Rick Watson, and Kathy Wilson for their support over the years. At East Carolina University I benefited from the support and friendship of many colleagues, including Chuck Calhoun, Annalies Corbin, David Dennard, and Mike Palmer. I am grateful for the patience of the editorial staff at the Louisiana State University Press and for Joanne Allen's keen editing.

I must reserve a special mention for Paul D. Escott, who nurtured my interest in the history of the U.S. South during my undergraduate studies at Wake Forest University. His advice and guidance have helped steer me through my career, and his friendship is invaluable.

Amy and Kyle White, Susie and Dave Verrill, and Beth and Jesse Phifer supported me as I drove across the Southeast in search of research materials. RaShetta Chavis, Maria Honeycutt, Kim Sandhoff, and Tammy Warburton generously offered childcare to free me to write. My sister, Kristy Green, and her husband, Kevin, offered their advice and aid. I am deeply grateful to my parents, Bob and Nancy Zipf, and my husband's parents, Louis and Lulu Sarris, for their love, support, financial encouragement, and a place to stay during my research trips to the North Carolina State Archives and the National Archives in Washington, D.C. When I felt that I had reached a nadir in my graduate career and believed that I would never finish, my parents provided me with every emotional and material resource to help build my morale and keep me working.

Yet I am most indebted to my husband, Jonathan Sarris, who is my greatest confidant, closest friend, chief morale builder, most constructive critic, and former fellow graduate student. Without his support I never would have finished graduate school, probably continuing an earlier career in corporate law instead. Perhaps our sons, Robert and Theodore, will one day understand why we forfeited material wealth for relative austerity in our intellectual pursuits. For us, the emotional fulfillment far outweighs the sacrifices.

Labor of Innocents

INTRODUCTION

The autumnal equinox marked a time of change in eastern North Carolina, as it did everywhere else in the post–Civil War rural South. As the sun moved south toward the celestial equator and night lengthened to equal day, all classes of farmers — from the wealthiest planter to the newly freed family of former slaves — hastened to harvest ripened crops and slaughter livestock before the first frost. Night encroached upon valuable daylight hours, and the necessities of harvest required the labor of all able-bodied men, women, and children not only in the fields but also indoors, where preparations intensified as winter drew near. It was the approach of the equinox that prompted Daniel Russell Sr., a wealthy white planter and former judge in Brunswick County, near Wilmington, to scour the countryside in search of laborers to supplant his slaves lost to emancipation. On September 16, 1866, one week before autumnal equinox, Daniel Russell sent his son and two others to the home of Wiley Ambrose and Hepsey Saunders, two former slaves who lived as husband and wife. In broad daylight and without any warning to the family, the three men produced apprenticeship orders granted by the Brunswick County Court and seized the Ambrose daughters, Harriet and Eliza, aged fifteen and thirteen, respectively. After serving a brief time in jail with several other children who were in the same plight, the Ambrose sisters were transported to one of Russell's plantations to serve as apprentices.[1]

Russell's use of forced apprenticeship was not new. He was merely adopting the practices of an entrenched institution to overcome the political and economic turmoil caused by the Civil War. As early as 1715 North Carolina's elite had condoned involuntary apprenticeship. Like other North American colonies,

North Carolina had modified it from English common law to control indigent populations, secure an alternate source of cheap labor, and enforce a patriarchal and, later, white supremacist social order. To be sure, apprenticeship provided some very poor children with education and training in various crafts. However, involuntary apprenticeship, codified in law, was used by the state to control the composition and character of families. Local governments carefully scrutinized the families within their jurisdiction and indentured those children who lacked a white male patriarch. In an age when children provided essential labor to maintain households, apprenticeship threatened the very independence these families hoped to achieve.[2]

Thus, an examination of apprenticeship provides a rare opportunity to understand historical concepts of family and the realities that actual families endured. For example, the view of the ideal head of household, originally a white male patriarch, changed dramatically over the two-hundred-year history of apprenticeship. This study explains the source of that original view and explores the changing political and social climates that produced new standards of household and family. The study of apprenticeship helps to clarify the historical relationship between the family and the state. North Carolina used apprenticeship to undermine the authority of certain parents over their children. Single or widowed women who headed families faced the real and constant threat of losing their children to court-ordered apprenticeships. African American men experienced this threat as well. For generations, apprenticeship served as the state's justification for intervening in the affairs of families whose status it considered objectionable.

Yet apprenticeship was a fluid institution that underwent significant change over a period of two hundred years. In North Carolina, unlike in other southern states, substantive issues of apprenticeship surfaced in the North Carolina Supreme Court three times over the course of several decades. Sources reveal four major periods of change in apprenticeship law that seem to correspond to changing dynamics in race, gender, and class relations. The first significant period of change was in the 1850s, when, in an increasingly hostile racial environment, the state supreme court intensified its efforts to limit the rights of African American parents. Two North Carolina Supreme Court cases, *Midgett v. McBryde* (1855) and *Frolick v. Schonwald* (1859–60), show a change in doctrine specifying that unlike white women who bore white children, white women who bore "children of color" must see their children apprenticed. In 1865 and 1866, race again appeared to characterize apprenticeship as southern whites used the institution of apprenticeship to restore a white supremacist order in the South.[3]

The second period of change occurred in 1867, when legislators and the courts lifted racial restrictions that had not allowed African American men to keep their children but retained gender-based regulations requiring courts to apprentice all children of single women (both black and white) and certain widowed women. The third period of change began in the 1890s and ended in 1919. During this period, courts, legislators, and reformers harshly criticized the apprenticeship system because it failed to address children's rights, an increasingly popular concept among social reformers that had important consequences for gender relations. The year 1919 marks the fourth and most auspicious period, when the North Carolina General Assembly dismantled apprenticeship and in its place established the Child Welfare Act. Reformers, committed to protecting children's "best interests," initiated a wide-reaching child welfare program that included a juvenile courts system, a child labor law, and a compulsory-education law. In fact, it is this system that serves as the heart of modern governmental policies concerning children and families.[4]

These four periods are the heart of this study. The rich written record lodged in the North Carolina State Archives unmistakably reveals the nuances of change as ordinary women and men challenged prevailing legal definitions of apprenticeship. North Carolina Supreme Court cases, county court records, and other legal documents provide contextual details that bring to life the day-to-day technical and legal concerns related to the apprenticing of children. More than thirteen hundred apprenticeship indentures between masters and apprentices from selected county court records illuminate the institution's variability across the state and over time. Other sources offer valuable information as well. Federal records provide a vital perspective of apprenticeship. Fortunately, agents of the Bureau of Refugees, Freedmen and Abandoned Lands carefully documented apprenticeship for several years after the Civil War. These agents, some handpicked by Commissioner O. O. Howard to serve in North Carolina, frequently provided data, complaints and petitions by parents, and their own insights on postwar apprenticeship. Particularly compelling are the letters and reports of Eliphalet Whittlesey, assistant commissioner from 1865 to 1866, who found apprenticeship distasteful, and John C. Robinson, assistant commissioner from 1866 to 1868, who found the institution absolutely inhumane.[5]

These records show that the institution of apprenticeship remained complicated and fluid throughout its life. North Carolinians defined apprenticeship in
more than one way. The first type, court-supervised apprenticeships such as the
Ambrose indentures, were well documented and legally sanctioned. This formal indenture is the focus of this study not only because documents are so
widely available but also, and more importantly, because legal and court records
reflect the state's official approach toward controlling and maintaining children
subject to apprentice laws. Nearly all of these apprenticeships were involuntary
and ordered by the court. Parents had little say in their child's training, which
might be in the skilled crafts, domestic work, or field labor. Few parents willfully bound out their children through the court system. In fact, in the 1,317
apprenticeships studied in the seven counties surveyed from 1801 to 1860 only
nineteen fathers (1.5%) willingly bound out their children. Not surprisingly,
most fathers refused to apprentice through the courts for economic reasons.
A legally sanctioned apprenticeship transferred all power over the child's earn-
ings from the father to the new master.[6]

However, the role of apprenticeship is confused by the presence of a second
method of indenture. Fathers who sought skilled training for children yet
wished to retain control likely pursued an informal arrangement for their child
with a friend, relative, or acquaintance. Informal relationships ranged widely.
Some fathers hired their children out as field laborers or domestic workers and
controlled their wages. Others secured positions for their children as informal
apprentices to newspaper editors or lawyers. Governor John Morehead received
his legal training not in law school but as an informal apprentice to Archibald
D. Murphy. Since informal apprenticeships existed outside the court's jurisdiction, the parties involved lacked the protections outlined by the apprenticeship
code. Such relationships were matters of private contract; they were not registered with the court unless a dispute surfaced. Had Murphy encountered
trouble with his apprentice John Morehead, he would have been forced to seek
protection under state laws that governed contracts or master-servant relations.
The apprenticeship codes would not have applied. Needless to say, informal
apprenticeships exist in the written record only anecdotally and thus are not
addressed here. This study defines apprenticeship as an institution whereby the
courts assigned orphaned, fatherless, and certain African American children as
laborers to masters in various industries (including the crafts, domestic work,
and farming) not only to provide labor but also to preserve a social order rooted
in white male patriarchy.[7]

This book attempts to prove two interrelated points. First, apprenticeship was a constantly evolving system of social control. Over the course of its life in North Carolina, apprenticeship reflected different social perspectives on race, class, and gender. Second, power relations in apprenticeship law were not static but rather constantly contested and reinterpreted by white and black North Carolinians who shaped and challenged the laws. Winds of change in politics and society produced conflicts that forced new definitions and interpretations of race, gender, and class relations. These social categories — fluid and constantly contested — were produced and reproduced by changing relationships in society. In moments of crisis — times when the reins of power seemed most available for the taking — African Americans, single white women, and others contested the legal parameters of apprenticeship, sometimes altering the factors that defined apprenticeship law. In contesting the parameters, they challenged the basic formulations of gender, class, and race.[8]

Apprenticeship was not the primary labor system in North Carolina. It was easily overshadowed by slavery in the antebellum period and by sharecropping in the postbellum era. Apprenticeship's significance is more symbolic than numerical. The state-sanctioned apprenticeship system serves as a metaphor for power relations in nineteenth-century North Carolina. Power was not firmly entrenched in any single group, institution, or kinship network. In nineteenth-century North Carolina individuals and institutions claimed and contested power by constructing and reconstructing gender, class, and race relationships. The antebellum patriarchal elite, Reconstruction conservatives, and early twentieth-century reformers used apprenticeship to control certain groups — single women, free African Americans, and the poor — that lived outside the confines of slavery. Accordingly, apprenticeship law and custom reflected gender, race, and class discourses.

The focus of this book, then, is the impact of shifting constructions of gender, race, and class on the apprenticeship system in North Carolina. Chapter 1 explores the colonial origins of apprenticeship and antebellum apprenticeship patterns in both lower and higher courts. Chapter 2 examines southern whites' motivations in 1865 for instituting a race-based apprenticeship system as a substitute for slavery. Chapter 3 analyzes the Freedmen's Bureau's response to the apprenticeship of African American children from 1865 to 1866. Chapter 4 demonstrates that single black mothers resisted apprenticeship and claimed households of their own, but in 1867 state legal authorities redefined apprenticeship to recognize white and black men's rights as fathers yet deny white and black women's rights as mothers. Chapter 5 examines the rise of the "best interests of the child" doctrine and its impact on apprenticeship in the courts. Finally, Chapter 6 argues that apprenticeship met its demise in the Child Welfare Act in 1919, when reformers and legislators rejected apprenticeship as an archaic and cruel system that did not adequately serve children's welfare.

My interpretation emphasizes cultural and political developments in the apprenticeship system. Though I focus less on the economic value of apprenticeship, I call attention to it throughout the text. Parents depended heavily upon children's economic contributions to the family, and they engaged in heated battles with masters eager to acquire children's labor. Some scholars have noted that apprenticeship in northern states declined with industrialization because the institution failed to keep pace with the maturing market economy and the rising democratization of the polity. Others show that economic conditions in the North were diverse and that apprenticeship sustained labor markets in a variety of ways. In late nineteenth- and early twentieth-century North Carolina, textile factories marked the state's introduction to an industrialized economy. It is certainly possible that apprenticeship, used to provide labor to artisans and farmers, declined because it no longer served manufacturers' needs. But I contend that for more than two hundred years state authorities and other powerful individuals molded and shaped the institution to compensate for the changing times. Thus, apprenticeship could have been modified again to serve the needs of the twentieth-century economy. But it was not. Instead, changing cultural attitudes toward parenthood, children, and women made apprenticeship appear archaic and forced an end to the institution. While the economic conditions of apprenticeship are important, the cultural forces that shaped the institution are equally, if not more, significant.[9]

A brief explanation of terminology is necessary here. I have tried to preserve the spirit of the sources by retaining some original terms where appropriate. Legal terms, such as *in loco parentis* and *habeas corpus*, are italicized. The word *illegitimate* was frequently used in legal texts and general correspondence to describe the status of children born out of wedlock. County courts and practitioners of law used *illegitimate, born out of wedlock,* and *bastard* almost interchangeably. Thus, I occasionally use the word *illegitimate,* but not to express as a value-laden judgment of the children in question. In addition, I use the term *white supremacy* to refer to a doctrine held by certain individuals identified in the text who strongly believed in the natural superiority and rule of southern whites over southern blacks.[10]

This book refuses to accept apprenticeship as a nostalgic institution that trained children for a craft. The evidence shows that apprenticeship was an institution employed by the white patriarchal elite as a measure of social control. Lawmakers, courts, and other authorities denied women and African American men their right to guardianship of their children because of the enormous social consequences at stake. In preindustrial economies, children contributed labor that was essential for the maintenance of an independent household. Any man or woman with a house full of able-bodied children had a much greater chance of achieving independence. But without the protection of their parental rights, women and African American men suffered the loss of their children's labor and consequently lacked the opportunities of independence enjoyed by white men. Sustained as it was by North Carolina's elite, apprenticeship helped to ensure social conventions that relegated women and African American men to a dependent status at the same time that it fostered the perception of white men's independence. Independence and dependence, then, were the issues at stake that autumn night when Daniel Russell kidnapped the Ambrose children. Remarkably, his livelihood rested upon his claim to them as his apprentices.

CHAPTER ONE

ORPHANS, BASTARDS, AND FREE BLACK CHILDREN

Colonial and Antebellum North Carolina Apprenticeship

On June 24, 1824, in the *Raleigh Gazette*, James J. Selby, a tailor in Raleigh, North Carolina, offered a ten-dollar reward for the return of two runaway apprentice boys, William and Andrew Johnson. Selby promised the reward "to any person who will deliver said apprentices to me in Raleigh, or I will give the above Reward for Andrew Johnson alone." Selby did not explain why he valued Andrew Johnson over his brother. Perhaps he sensed some potential in the sixteen-year-old boy who would become president of the United States in 1865. More likely, Johnson had proved himself to be an efficient tailor's apprentice. In any event, the advertisement yielded no tangible returns. The Johnson boys eventually returned to their penniless mother and moved the family to Tennessee. In March 1827 Johnson opened a shop of his own, which he used as a steppingstone into Tennessee politics.[1]

The documents that bear witness to Andrew Johnson's apprenticeship serve as evidence of a small but significant social institution that existed on the margins of a society defined for the most part by slavery. In North Carolina, apprenticeship at once provided unpaid labor to artisans and taught young people, usually boys, the skills of a craft. Rooted in medieval and colonial practices, apprenticeship evolved in the shadow of slavery as another form of forced labor. North Carolinians enacted the first apprenticeship laws in 1715 to provide for orphaned and impoverished children. In the ensuing 150 years apprenticeship became an instrument used to control households headed by women and free blacks. By the time of the Civil War, lawmakers in North Carolina had designed an institution steeped in presumptions about gender, race, and class to deny single women, poor widows, and free blacks their rights as parents. Andrew

Johnson's mother, Mary McDonough, was one of these women who suffered the loss of her children upon the death of her husband. As a result of mandated apprenticeship laws, women and free blacks found it extraordinarily difficult, if not impossible, to maintain thriving households independent of white men.

North Carolina apprenticeship reflects many of the customs and practices of earlier forms of apprenticeship. English law defined an apprentice as "a young person bound by indentures to a tradesman or artificer, who upon certain covenants is to teach him his mystery or trade." Under apprenticeship law, the master assumed the rights and responsibilities of the child's father, and the apprentice became a member of the master's household. The earliest documentation of English apprenticeship dates to the thirteenth century, when the Chamber of the Guildhall recorded indentures and regulated the activities of London's guilds, or trade unions. Guilds recognized the value of taking apprentices. Apprenticeship provided crucial training for future craftsmen, who became either journeymen, who received wages from an employer, or masters, who could afford to open shops of their own, hire journeymen, and train apprentices. Apprentices served a master until they turned twenty-one. Upon completion of service, apprentices gained freedom and became citizens and members of the craft. Early records indicate that guilds regulated apprenticeship. For example, in 1466 the Tailors of Exeter limited masters to one apprentice. By the sixteenth century the Elizabethan government had assumed the power to supervise the institution. In 1563 legislators enacted the Statute of Artificers, which limited masters to three apprentices each, ordered minimal terms of seven years, and required written indentures. An act in 1597 allowed for the apprenticing of poor children. These statutes and others marked a new era in apprenticeship in which the government took control of the practice from the guilds.[2]

In New World colonies local governments, not guilds, retained control of apprenticeship. Early New England settlements used apprenticeship to provide education for poor and orphan children. Massachusetts Bay colonists criticized English apprenticeship and poor laws. The English Statute of Artificers required only the education of youths in industrial trades and neglected the training of poor youths who were indentured, or bound out, to masters in order to relieve the parish of their support. The Massachusetts Bay Act of 1642 empowered local authorities "to put forth apprentices the children of such as shall not be able and fit to employ and bring them up, nor shall take care to dispose of them themselves." In Philadelphia the training of apprentices sustained the rise of an artisan community. In the early 1770s more than 80 percent of the city's apprentices were bound to craftsmen. Eric Foner has shown that apprenticeship, along with other forms of bound labor, such as slavery and indentured servitude, accounted for a large percentage of Philadelphia's work force.[3]

Whereas in northern colonies apprenticeship provided the moorings of the artisan community, in southern colonies it tended to be more oppressive. Edmund Morgan has argued that "a servant in Virginia, as long as his term had not expired, was a machine to make tobacco for somebody else." In seventeenth-century Jamestown, apprentices were sometimes referred to as "Duty Boys," a name taken from the ship *Duty*, which transported some youths to the New World. The term of service for apprentices was typically seven years. After seven years as apprentices, they served seven years as tenants, unless they had committed a crime, in which case they were required to serve their masters as apprentices an additional seven years. Abuses proliferated, as masters bought and sold their servants almost indiscriminately. One Dutch sea captain reported in 1633 that planters gambled for servants at cards.[4]

Colonial records do not indicate that apprenticeship practices in North Carolina were as vicious as those Morgan found in early Jamestown. Nonetheless, North Carolina courts supervised several forms of servile labor during the colonial period. Planters used indentured servants (including apprentices) and slaves to compensate for a chronic shortage of labor. In 1715 the colony passed its first law governing servile labor. This act established basic protections for servants, such as a contract specifying the term of servitude, limitations on punishments, the master's obligation to provide "Competent Dyet, Clothing & Lodging," and a system for filing complaints. In 1741 the colony ratified the Act Concerning Servants and Slaves of 1741. This act provided further protections; for example, it limited punishment to thirty-nine lashings for both servants and slaves. The courts applied this act to various categories of servants, including those who voluntarily entered bound labor for a specified term to improve their lot or in return for passage, certain wage laborers, illegitimate and free black children, and slaves. Marvin L. Michael Kay and Lorin Lee Cary have concluded that white servants constituted from 23.82 percent to 29.3 percent of the colony's unfree labor force. They argue that by 1748 there were fewer servants than slaves, yet servants made up "a significant portion of the colony's work force until the Revolution." After the Revolution, adult indentured servitude declined as planters favored slavery and, occasionally, child apprenticeship.[5]

Apprenticeship and indentured servitude shared a few characteristics, but otherwise the two institutions were really quite different. Like indentured servants, apprentices were a source of unpaid labor for masters who provided food, clothing, and shelter until the term of service expired. Furthermore, officials commonly used the term *indenture* to describe the contract that bound servants to masters in either form of servitude. And as previously mentioned, certain protections and limits on punishment for both indentured servitude and apprenticeship were regulated under the Act Concerning Servants and Slaves of 1715 and that of 1741. But the similarities between the two institutions ended there. Unlike apprenticeship, indentured servitude was a contractual agreement between a master and a laborer. English and colonial North American law and practice recognized that white male adults owned and could freely sell their own labor. According to Robert J. Steinfeld, this concept, rooted in John Locke's theories of natural rights, is known as "possessive individualism." Steinfeld argues that the English and colonial North Americans freely accepted the view that an indenture was a "voluntary transaction between two autonomous individuals" and that "the hirer of labor had the legal right to control, use, and enjoy the other's personal energies for the term or purposes specified in the agreement." In North Carolina and other North American colonies laborers traded their labor in compensation for something else, such as passage to the colonies, or in repayment of a debt.[6]

Generally, contractual relations did not govern apprenticeships. To be sure, voluntary apprenticeships, in which fathers and children signed contracts binding children to masters, resembled the contractual nature of indentured servitude. However, a different sort of law governed court-ordered apprenticeships, in which courts bound out a minor's labor to a master with or without the consent of the child or its parents. County courts governed these relations in a series of acts "concerning Orphans," the first of which was passed in 1715. Eventually, North Carolina controlled apprenticeships by an "apprenticeship code," a body of statutes based upon judicial opinion and legislative acts that treated apprenticeship as an exclusive institution operating outside the parameters of accepted contractual relations. Indeed, apprenticeship required masters to sign contracts, but not with the child or the child's parents. Rather, masters signed contracts with the county courts, the self-appointed guardian of the child in question. In return for the labor of the child, masters pledged to raise the child in such a way that he or she would not become a burden upon the county. The difference, then, between indentured servitude and apprenticeship was really quite vast. Whereas indentured servitude marked a form of voluntary bound labor, court-ordered apprenticeships were involuntary and therefore subject to a different code of law.[7]

Documents illustrate that apprenticeship existed in North Carolina as early as 1695. In that year Albemarle County recorded the apprenticeship of "Wm ye son of Timothy Bead late of the County of Albemarle Decd being left destitute" to Thomas Harvey and his wife, Sarah. The indenture required Harvey to teach William Bead to read and to release him when he turned twenty-one. In 1715 the colony institutionalized the practice with the first apprenticeship law. Colonial law granted local courts the exclusive power to apprentice children to masters. The governor, proprietors, and General Assembly of the "Province of Carolina" stripped individuals of the right to contract, give, or bind "any children or Orphans." Only the colony's precinct courts possessed the ability "to Grant Letters of Tuition or Guardianship to such persons as they shall think proper for the care of bringing up Education of all Orphans & for the taking care of their Estates." This law centralized the apprenticeship system under the precinct courts and denied individual men the power to apprentice children.[8]

North Carolina colonial authorities passed the 1715 law to protect orphans' rights and to preserve and protect property that children inherited from deceased parents. The 1715 act entitled all orphans to an education "according to their Rank & degree." The law empowered the court to appoint guardians for those orphans who possessed estates with income sufficient to pay for their education. The law provided further protections for orphans who inherited personal property, such as livestock or slaves. Poor children fared differently. Colonial authorities reasoned that children with no estate must earn their keep through indenture. By binding out poor orphans to individual masters, colonial authorities reduced public expenditures for maintenance of the poor.[9]

The precinct courts possessed supervisory powers over all guardian and apprenticeship matters and disputes. Disagreements often involved a conflict between a master and a stepfather, who by law possessed no claim to his wife's children. Such a dispute arose in August 1716. That year the precinct court in Chowan County adjudged the case of John Fox, who had bound himself to John Avery in 1713. Avery complained that Fox, whom he had trained as a ship's carpenter and instructed to read and write, had abandoned his apprentice duties prior to the expiration of the term of his indenture. Fox, Avery argued, had gone to work for his "Father In Law one Cary Godby," who intended "to proffitt and advantage himselfe by the Labour and usefullness of ye said John Fox." Upon hearing Avery's complaint, the court ordered Fox to return and serve out the remainder of his term. The law protected the claims of the master to his apprentice, the "orphan" John Fox.[10]

Local governments carefully guarded the court's supervisory power over apprenticeship so as to prevent individuals from arbitrarily apprenticing children without the court's approval. Such an abuse happened two years before the colony implemented the 1715 law. In 1713 the Chowan Council ordered a "Capt Jenkins" to return a "Mellato Boy which he pretends was bound to him by his parents in order that he may be sent to his said parents againe." Captain Jenkins apparently had mistakenly assumed that he possessed the ability to apprentice a "mellato" boy. However, the Chowan Council restored the boy to his parents in order to protect its vested power. Such cases, though rare, suggest that the colonial court system, desirous of guarding its powers of indenture, restored children to parents of interracial unions. However, one cannot hastily conclude from the Jenkins case that colonial courts protected mixed-race couples' rights to children. In this instance the Chowan Council ruled only in its own interest. In fact, the council issued no statement at all concerning the rights of the "mellato" boy's parents.[11]

The 1715 Act Concerning Orphans functioned until the onset of the French and Indian War in 1754. Lawmakers trembled as the frontier erupted into violence, and they began to assess the colony's ability to fend off attack. On September 25, 1755, Governor Arthur Dobbs called an extemporaneous meeting of North Carolina's upper and lower houses to request immediate action in preparation for war with France. The French, he warned, had quietly dispatched troops to the colonies and planned not only to surround the colonies "by a Chain of Forts" but also to gain "all the Indians into their alliance and intimidat[e] those who were in Alliance with us." According to the governor, the French had promised the Indians "Premiums" to get them "to murder, massacre, scalp and carry away Captive all our settlers wherever they can surprize them."[12]

Governor Arthur Dobbs used the French and Native American threat as an excuse to wrest greater local autonomy from Mother England. The time had come, Dobbs argued, for North Carolina to assume more control over colonial matters, including orphan protection. He asked the legislators to revise the colony's laws in order to meet the demands of war. Dobbs urged the General Assembly to pass statutes that expanded colonial power at the expense of the British Empire. He asked for laws to strengthen paper currency, regulate exports, erect "County or Parish Schools for the education of your youth in the knowledge of religion and moral duties," and to strengthen the mutiny bill and the "Jayls," which he argued "are so weak without any Jaylor or person to guard them that no criminal can be secured." Fearing that the war would cause

tremendous scarcity of goods, Dobbs requested a more expansive apprenticeship law, one that reached beyond the orphan poor and forced "Planters who
have small Properties to bring up their children to industry, or to bind out their
children to necessary trades many of whom breed up their children to sloth and
idleness." Once properly trained, North Carolina's yeoman sons would produce
"the necessaries of life cheaper the excessive price of which at present is a great
discouragement to the Improvement of the Province." The General Assembly,
Dobbs anxiously implored, must increase its control not only over the colony's
finances but also over its youth in order to defeat the French.[13]

Dobbs's speech created apprehension among legislators, who immediately
set out to make the governor's recommendations law. The General Assembly
made many changes that expanded local power at the expense of the crown.
Among these changes was a new statute, An Act for Regulating Orphans, Their
Guardians and Estates. The new law did not require the apprenticing of
planters' sons, which Dobbs had requested, but it did place apprenticeship and
guardian issues under greater local control. This law transferred matters regarding orphans from the precinct courts to the county courts. The transfer
provoked controversy among colonial authorities. North Carolina Chief Justice
Charles Berry and Attorney General Thomas Child opposed the plan. In
March 1759 Berry and Child lodged a protest against the new orphan act on the
grounds that it placed matters of equity—issues involving orphans' estates—
in the wrong court system. "The Jurisdiction that is thereby given to the County
Courts," Berry and Child argued, "in Cases which are the peculiar objects of equity is not warranted by any similar practice or law in this country; and therefore this Act ought in our humble opinion to be repealed." The king agreed
with Berry and Child, and on April 14, 1759, the king's Privy Council repealed
several North Carolina acts, including the Act for Regulating Orphans, Their
Guardians and Estates and an act that established and enlarged the jurisdiction
of the county courts.[14]

The orphan law of 1755 had become one of many that suffered from the dispute over power between the king and his North Carolina subjects. The North
Carolina General Assembly nonetheless persisted in its struggle against the
crown. In 1762 the colonial legislature passed new acts that established the ju-
risdictions of North Carolina's superior courts of justice and inferior courts of
pleas and quarter sessions. Concomitantly, legislators passed An Act for the better Care of Orphans, and Security and Management of their Estates, which empowered the superior and inferior courts in all matters governing orphans. This

1762 act would serve as the basis for all succeeding apprenticeship legislation until apprenticeship was outlawed in 1919.[15]

The new law had an important effect on fathers' rights to their children. It established patriarchal guardianship and apprentice laws that denied women primary guardianship rights. Only a child's father possessed the right of primary guardian. Upon the father's death, the courts determined guardianship unless the father had already named a new guardian by deed or will. The law explicitly invoked patriarchal language in establishing the father's sole right as primary guardian. "It shall and may be lawful to and for the Father," the law stated, "to dispose of the Custody and tuition of such child or children for and during such Time as he, she, or they shall remain under the Age of Twenty-One Years, or for any less Time, to any Person or Persons other than the people called Quakers and Popish Recusants." The only limitation the colony placed on fathers was a religious one that prevented them from choosing Quakers or Catholics as guardians for their children. On mothers' rights the statute was silent.[16]

Thus the law implicitly defined an orphan as any child with no father. Courts were to select guardians for those orphans who had inherited estates. Orphans for whom "such Estate shall be of so small value that no person will educate and Maintain him or her for the Profits thereof" were to be bound out as apprentices. The court bound out all "free base born children," as well as "every such Female child being a Mulatto or Mustee, until she shall attain the age of Twenty One years." The law required all children to be bound until they reached the age of twenty-one, except white females, whose indentures terminated at age eighteen. Sometimes mothers, fearing the arbitrary court process, requested individuals whom they knew to agree to apprentice their child or children. In 1793 Mrs. Peter Clifton, apparently aware that her new husband was under no obligation to support her son from a previous marriage, asked a friend to inquire whether John Gray Blount, a North Carolina merchant, would serve as her son's master. "She is informed," her friend wrote, "that your Castle and Shipping enables you to furnish employment for a Number of Young Men and [she] would be glad to have him bound to you." Mrs. Clifton, who had relinquished her property to her new husband upon marriage, sought her son's apprenticeship to someone she knew and trusted.[17]

Though gender was the primary concern of the 1762 law, race also played a significant role. By law, free black men and women who bore children within marriage held the same parental rights as whites. However, colonial legislatures were less generous to free blacks who married whites or Native Americans. The law required apprenticeship of "every such Female child being Mulatto or Mustee, until she shall attain the age of Twenty One Years." No extant legal records explicitly justify the state's requiring apprenticeship of girls and not boys of interracial marriages. Some scholars have argued that colonial American legislators were more tolerant of interracial unions than their antebellum successors. In *The Free Negro in North Carolina, 1790–1860,* John Hope Franklin demonstrates that colonial intermarriages were legal, though discouraged. In 1741 the General Assembly enacted a law that required whites who married free blacks and the ministers or justices of the peace who joined them to pay substantial fines, but not until 1830 did the General Assembly declare that interracial marriages were illegal.[18]

The court apprenticed all children, including free African American boys, who were born out of wedlock. Masters compared their free black male apprentices favorably with their white counterparts. In 1787 William Blount, a North Carolina politician and a member of the enterprising Blount family, upon observing a "Nail Factory" in Philadelphia, resolved to train African American apprentices to smith nails. Blount observed that "Nail making" was a profitable business and "better calculated than any others for the Employment of Negroes." Blount hoped to train both white and black apprentices in nail making. Already he had "four boys" who "would as readily learn as the White boys I have seen here . . . I should suppose many white boys might be had prenticed [to us?] for seven years or more as their age might happen to be when bound by the Court."[19]

The 1762 act outlined the responsibilities of Blount and any other master or mistress to his or her apprentices. Masters stood *in loco parentis,* assuming a parent's responsibilities when courts bound children as their apprentices. The law required that masters and mistresses provide apprentices with "Diet, Clothes, Lodging, Accommodations, fit and necessary." The law further required them to "teach or cause him or her to be taught, to read and Write." Upon the expiration of the apprenticeship, the master or mistress must provide freedom dues, or an "Allowance as is by law appointed, for Servants by Indenture or Custom." Disgruntled apprentices could bring suit against their masters in court and, upon proving injury, recover damages. The court reserved the right to remove an apprentice and "bind him or her to such other Person or Persons" upon evidence of ill-treatment. These regulations limited masters' and mistresses' authority over apprentices and allowed the court to maintain a modicum of oversight throughout a child's indenture.[20]

The 1762 act also established the framework of North Carolina's antebellum court system, the institution primarily responsible for administering apprenticeship during the nineteenth century. Court documents provide a window through which scholars may observe the past. Though statutes illustrate society's rules of behavior, the courts offer evidence of people's real experiences with apprenticeship. In North Carolina counties, apprenticeship issues proceeded through the state's three-tiered court system. On the first tier stood the county court, the most local tribunal, which possessed the power both to bind out children and to annul indentures. According to the Revised Statutes of 1837, the county court, also know as the inferior court or the court of pleas and quarter sessions, collected the names of apprenticeable children from two sources. First, the warden of the poor was required to report the names of all fatherless children who had applied for poor relief. Second, the justice of the peace was obligated to submit names of orphans, free children of color in families "where the parents with whom such children may live, do not habitually employ their time in some honest, industrious occupation," and all illegitimate children. In addition, the county court had the power to apprentice any children who possessed property and did not live with their father if the court "thinks it improper to permit such children to remain with the mother." The responsibility of locating suitable masters, completing indenture contracts, and requiring payment of bonds fell to the chairman of the county court.[21]

Any complaints concerning apprenticeship proceeded to the second tier, the superior court. Should a master fail to fulfill his obligations to clothe, feed, or, in the case of white children, educate them in reading and writing, a parent or "next friend" could file a petition or complaint on behalf of the child. In 1833 the North Carolina Supreme Court ordered the Moore County Court to revise its method of binding out children so that the indentures specifically stated the child's form of employment and other requisites. A vague covenant prompted one apprentice, Lydia Burnet, to run away and seek assistance from Stephen Davis, who harbored her from her master. Judge William Gaston argued that all indentures must contain specifications for all duties required by law. Gaston asserted that the omission of these specifications "constitutes a very serious objection to the instrument." Parents who believed that a child had been wrongfully apprenticed could also file a complaint. Nancy Midgett did so in 1854, when she sued Willoughby McBryde for the return of her two children. Masters also used the superior court for relief. In 1852 William Hooks, the master of Thomas Artis, sued William T. Perkins for "enticing away and harboring" his apprentice. According to the court, William Perkins, unaware that Artis was under age twenty-one and still bound to Hooks, had employed the boy unlawfully. In such a case the superior court could force the county court to annul the indenture.[22]

At the final tier stood the North Carolina Supreme Court, the state's premier appellate body. The supreme court decisions established guidelines and set precedent for county courts and superior courts. Justices at the highest level could reverse decisions of the superior court. In addition, the supreme court determined the power and jurisdiction of the lower courts. In 1859 the North Carolina Supreme Court established the county courts' jurisdictional bounds in apprenticeship matters. Nine years earlier the Franklin County Court had apprenticed Alfred Prue, a "free boy of color," to Herbert H. Hight. In 1857 Prue had deserted his master and remained at large in Granville County until he was brought back to Franklin County Court and bound out again to Hight. Prue argued that since he was an inhabitant of Granville County, the Franklin County Court had no power to reapprentice him. However, Justice Thomas Ruffin opined that the court that originally bound an apprentice continued to hold jurisdiction of the child until the apprenticeship was properly discharged. Ruffin based his decision upon his own interpretation of a provision in the state apprenticeship code that required the court to collect a five-hundred-dollar bond from masters who assumed guardianship of free African Americans. The bond served as a promise that the master would not remove the child from the county. The General Assembly, Ruffin explained, had passed the law in 1801 to protect free black children from "being enslaved in remote places" and to provide a "strict police, so as to restrain their propensity to be idle and mischievous." The bond, Ruffin argued, "permanently vest[ed] the whole control of the free infant of color in the court which first legally takes charge of him."[23]

With the power to finalize jurisdictional and other substantive matters regarding apprenticeship, Ruffin and his colleagues on the supreme court bench possessed enormous power over North Carolina families. These justices fully embraced apprenticeship because it preserved the state's elite, white patriarchal political order. Thomas Ruffin, who joined the supreme court in 1829 and served as chief justice from 1833 to 1852, regularly articulated these views in court opinion. A plantation owner in Alamance County, he represented the state's elite and was one of North Carolina's most influential jurists.[24] Ruffin and other prominent state supreme court justices justified the elite's power in North Carolina society by regularly invoking paternalistic rhetoric. Ruffin upheld laws that preserved the husband's and master's rights as legal head of household. He favored an organic system that preserved the patriarch's rule and protection of his dependents. Ruffin did not advocate a society in which the patriarch possessed "the absolute power of a prince on his throne." Rather, he argued that a patriarch must exhibit benevolence and recognize his duties to his dependents. "Authority in domestic life," Ruffin asserted, "though not necessarily, is naturally considerate, mild, easy to be entreated, and tends to an elevation in sentiment in the superior which generates a humane tenderness for those in his power, and renders him regardful alike of the duty and the dignity of his position." Ruffin's court opinions reflected his view of authority. For example, he viewed any liberalization of divorce law as a threat to domestic stability. Divorce, he argued, violated society's sacred bonds of family and tradition. No challenge to patriarchal authority, including complaints of abuse, escaped Ruffin's patriarchal interpretation. In 1829 he upheld masters' right to beat slaves "because the power of the master must be absolute to render the submission of the slave perfect." In 1852 he ruled that husbands had the power to strike wives provided that they did not beat them from "mere wantonness & wickedness."[25]

Other antebellum chief justices, including Richmond M. Pearson, also defended North Carolina's patriarchal order. Pearson feared that free black men's and women's presence in society challenged white male patriarchy. In 1850 the state indicted a white man who assaulted a free black man. When the case, *State v. Jowers*, reached the supreme court, Pearson ruled in favor of the white man. Black "insolence" to a white man, he argued, "would be insufferable." Dismayed that free blacks made up a small yet healthy segment of North Carolina's population, Pearson argued that "it is unfortunate, that *this third class* exists in our society. . . . A free negro has no master to correct him . . . and unless a white man, to whom insolence is given, has a right to put a stop to it, in an extra judicial way, there is no remedy for it. . . . Hence we infer from the principles of the common law, that this extra judicial remedy is excusable." Pearson adamantly rejected African American men's right to claim domestic authority. Instead, he intimated, African Americans without "masters" required careful supervision and discipline from the white community.[26]

This paternalistic outlook in the highest echelons of North Carolina's court system penetrated local governments as well. Paul D. Escott has characterized North Carolina's local governments as "oligarchic" and "undemocratic." Though all white males voted for governor and representatives to the House of Commons, the state constitution prevented white men who owned fewer than fifty acres of land from voting for state senators. Other property requirements disqualified more than one-half of the male voters from running for the legislature. North Carolinians elected the sheriff and the clerk of court, but the governor appointed most court officials, including the justices of the peace. Justices of the peace, or squires, developed an oligarchic system in which they selected certain county officers, established local taxes, determined new road development, and established county policies on education and the poor. Their terms were for life. Some powerful families, such as the Hawkinses of Warren County, the Riddicks of Gates and Perquimans counties, and the Speights of Greene County, dominated the county court for decades. In fact, the slaveholding elite controlled a disproportionate number of seats in the legislature. Though the state's slaveholding families constituted 30 percent of North Carolina's population, they held 85 percent of the seats in the legislature.[27]

Thus the antebellum courts, fearing all challenges to elite white male patriarchy, used the 1762 apprenticeship act to regulate the freedoms of both African American parents and single mothers. In fact, legal theorists, lawmakers, and North Carolina Supreme Court justices not only upheld but also strengthened the racial and gendered legal constructions embedded in North Carolina orphan laws. The state guardian and apprenticeship laws were linked inextricably to gendered legal doctrines that governed women's lives. Southern states, including North Carolina, circumscribed white women's rights with coverture, a common-law doctrine of marriage that merged a wife's legal identity with that of her husband. Coverture limited a wife's right to own or manage property. Upon marriage a wife's property became her husband's. She could not claim her property or its profits, nor could she control her wages, make independent contracts, sue, or execute wills or sales. In return, the husband assumed her debts before marriage and provided a minimal level of support. Upon her husband's death a wife was entitled to dower rights, one-third of his estate for life. Unless a husband provided otherwise in a will, all other property passed to her husband's children or nearest heir. A wife's property in dower reverted to her husband's heirs upon her death.[28]

The state supreme court upheld a married woman's right to personal property only if her husband consented to a separate estate by covenant. The separate estate, if conveyed by deed, granted her restricted rights as if she were feme sole, or unmarried. In common law, justices resolutely restricted married women's right to property. However, North Carolina state legislators enacted several laws that more firmly secured married women's interests in property that they contributed to the marriage. Though husbands acquired ownership rights to their wives' property, the state forbade husbands to sell, convey, or mortgage that property without the wife's consent. The law, established in 1751, instructed county officials to obtain this consent by *privy examination*, or private examination, of the wife. (In 1848 legislators extended this law to cover leases as well.) In 1785, legislators secured married women's right to a separate estate or trust in cases where the husband consented.[29]

While coverture directly imposed restrictions on women's right to property, the doctrine indirectly limited their right to guardianship. Lawmakers recognized that married and widowed women lacked any legal right to their husbands' property. Thus, they reasoned that unless the husband had provided otherwise in a will, a widow probably did not possess the financial ability to maintain her children. To compensate for this circumstance, lawmakers freed mothers from primary guardianship responsibilities. Only the father was legally obligated to maintain and support the children. Though mothers and fathers both possessed rights as "guardians by nature," the law did not treat fathers and mothers equally in custody matters. This preconception of guardianship prevailed not only in North Carolina but throughout the nation. In *The Law of Baron and Femme, of Parent and Child, Guardian and Ward, Master and Servant, and the Powers of Courts of Chancery* (1846) Tapping Reeve argued that "the mother has no right to the person of her child, as the father has." At her husband's death she remained guardian by nature, but only until the court determined the child's permanent guardian. Then the court could remove her from guardianship of the child and (if the child was an heir) from guardianship of the estate as well. North Carolina legislators specified that county courts possessed the power "from time to time, to take cognizance of all matters concerning orphans and their estates, and to appoint guardians where none have been appointed by the father." Moreover, two antebellum state supreme court cases gave courts broad powers over guardianship appointments. Neither state statute nor common law endeavored to protect the guardianship rights of a mother who survived the father. With these restrictions upon mothers, lawmakers rested guardianship rights in the cradle of coverture.[30]

These restrictions on maternal guardianship persisted even when fathers abandoned their families. Fearing that deserted wives lacked the resources necessary to maintain their families alone, the 1796 General Assembly enacted legislation that allowed courts to apprentice children whose fathers had absented themselves for one year or more and left their families without sufficient support. "Great inconvenience and heavy charges arise to the citizens of this state," the General Assembly argued, "by persons deserting their wives and families, and leaving them burdens on the wardens of the poor." By indenturing these children, the General Assembly hoped to avoid greater expenditures for poor relief from county coffers.[31]

Limiting poor relief provided legislators and courts substantial motivation to apprentice children with absent fathers. But the poor-relief issue was only one factor that influenced North Carolina's involuntary apprenticeship law. Another factor was legislators' presumptions of women's character. Few legislators trusted women to raise children alone "in habits of industry and morality." Though the legislature stopped short of declaring women innately immoral, it implemented laws that prevented even self-sufficient women from maintaining their children and thus implied that women lacked the moral character necessary to raise children alone. This law had applied to single and widowed women as early as 1762. Then in 1800 the General Assembly addressed the growing population of married women who owned separate estates. As mentioned earlier, wives could own property, but only by their husbands' written consent or by legislative enactment. Yet their status remained uncertain. Coverture laws did not apply to married women granted this privilege. Feme sole, the status that governed single and widowed women, also did not apply, for the women remained married. Then how should the law apply to these women? And what should be done with their children if no father lived at home? In 1800, puzzled by an increase in the number of women with such an ambiguous status, legislators determined that children whose fathers had deserted and whose mothers owned separate estates would be apprenticed.[32]

Numerous petitions from men and women throughout the state likely spurred the General Assembly to enact this law. Distraught because of failed marriages, men and women found relief only from the General Assembly, which held the exclusive right to grant divorces and restore married women's feme sole rights to property. In 1800 the General Assembly considered seven divorce petitions from men (one man applied jointly with his wife) and twenty-one feme sole petitions from married women. While in most of the divorce petitions husbands charged their wives with adultery, in the feme sole petitions all of the women charged their husbands with abandonment. Many men left their wives indigent, having squandered their combined estates, and with several children. None of the women specifically requested a divorce, probably because they feared community exile or that legislators might reject such a request from a woman.

Instead, the women petitioned to restore their feme sole status, which included their right to all property they had earned or inherited and released them from their husbands' debts. In all twenty-one instances the General Assembly restored feme sole rights but specified that should the wife and husband subsequently cohabit, the wife's status would revert immediately to feme covert.[33]

The legislation could only have a positive impact, for many of the husbands had left their families in dire circumstances. Some women had contributed considerable property to their husbands' estates upon marriage, much of which was lost to their husbands' creditors. John Whitworth had squandered much of his wife's estate by "Gameing, Drinking & Contracting of Debts." Prior to her marriage with John, Elizabeth Whitworth had been a "Widdow with Two Children and was in affluent circumstances." According to Elizabeth, John had absconded in 1796, moved to South Carolina, and lived in "adultry" with another woman. Samuel Lawwell abandoned his wife, Elizabeth, and their child in 1797. Prior to his departure, Elizabeth saw her own possessions, including "a very likely negroe wench & other property" sold to pay her husband's debts. Because she expected to acquire more property upon her mother's death and more "by her Industry," Elizabeth was anxious to disentangle herself from her husband's financial problems. As if to endorse her cause, twenty-eight Warren County men supported her petition with their signatures.[34]

Ninety-three names accompanied Rachel Johnston's petition, including her own. In October 1794 Rachel's husband, Jacob, had left her in Rowan County with six small children "and in low circumstances." She hoped not only to restore her property rights but also to make a new life for herself and her children. In her own hand, Johnston informed legislators that she, "through her frugality and honest industry has brought [her children] up in honour and good fashion and in the fear of God." Having acquired some property since her husband's departure in 1794, Rachel desired to preserve it for herself and her children. She requested that the General Assembly grant her "Sole Right" to her real and personal estate as if she had never married, clear her from her husband's creditors, and grant her full power to sue in the courts. Her requests were common among women who drafted similar petitions. Elizabeth Whitworth and Elizabeth Lawwell requested nothing less.[35]

Legislation in support of all twenty-one women passed in December 1800. But bad news accompanied the good. These newly empowered wives, women who expected to make new lives for their families, suddenly realized that in gaining their rights to property they had lost their children. As if to remind these women that they could never attain full independence, legislators added a provision that specified that "in all cases" where women had their property and feme sole status restored, the children not living with the father were to be considered "orphans" and apprenticed "to some respectable person, whereby they may be raised in the habits of Industry and morality." Though no extant documents fully explain the General Assembly's intent for this provision, it is clear that legislators presumed that women, even those with sufficient resources, possessed no innate capacity to raise children "in the habits of Industry and morality." Yet in recognition of exceptions to this rule, legislators included a coda that allowed children "properly taken care of by the mother" to remain at home, but only at the discretion of the court. This arbitrary and vaguely written provision promised no significant protection to abandoned wives. In fact, these women faced no greater irony than that once they mustered the financial independence necessary to raise their children, courts stripped them of their parental rights.[36]

Widows experienced similar difficulties. Upon a man's death, courts classified his children as "orphans" regardless of the mother's condition. Courts appointed guardians for children who inherited estates from their fathers and apprenticed poor children if no one of wealth volunteered to serve as guardian. In 1822 this fate befell future president Andrew Johnson and his older brother, William. As a child, Andrew Johnson resided with his father, Jacob Johnson, his brother, and his mother, Mary McDonough, in Raleigh, North Carolina. When Johnson was three years old, his father died, leaving the family in poverty. Apparently, the court allowed Johnson's mother to raise her sons until they reached an age when they could learn a trade, when the court ordered both boys bound out and Andrew Johnson was apprenticed to a tailor. While Andrew Johnson's removal from his mother's custody is well known, most apprentices languished in obscurity, and it is impossible to know how many were forcibly removed from a mother's custody. Court records do not always distinguish between those poor orphans whom courts removed from their mothers and those orphans who had no parents at all. Only anecdotal evidence exists to indicate that courts willingly removed children from poor widows. Andrew Johnson's experience illuminates the practice because of his public stature later in life. To be sure, apprenticeship saved Andrew and William Johnson from poverty and provided them with an artisan's education. Only their mother, deprived of her sons' labor, was reduced to impoverishment.[37]

The law also denied single women the right to full custody of their children. The Revised Statutes of 1837 preserved the section of the 1762 act that required the apprenticeship of all "free base born" (illegitimate) children. North Carolina law defined an illegitimate child as *filius nullius,* meaning that he or she was related to no one. Lawmakers reasoned that the state should treat illegitimate children, whose mothers lacked full guardianship rights, as no different from other orphans and apprentice them posthaste. Some single women actively protested apprenticeship and the court's arbitrary selection of masters. In 1810 the Brunswick County Court denied Temperance Chavers the opportunity to maintain a productive household with help from her two young sons. Chavers argued that she had raised the boys from birth "with much difficulty and expense" and that just as they had reached the age "to remunerate her by plowing & other services," the court threatened to apprentice them. Chavers protested apprenticeship and called it "a great hardship." But realizing that she could not defy "the law of the State," she requested that the court apprentice her sons to "Genl Smith in whose justice to raise them properly and have them taught usefully trades she can confide." Unfortunately for Chavers, the court had declined to give her the chance to prove her independence and economic viability. Rather than give her the opportunity to raise her sons and become economically independent, the court decided to mandate her dependence by removing her children from her custody. By requesting that the court apprentice her sons to someone she knew, Temperance Chavers hoped to forestall a more arbitrary and possibly unacceptable indenture.[38]

Antebellum apprenticeship law was firmly rooted in assumptions about class and gender that denied poor widows and single women full rights to their children. The language of the law illustrates elites' biases and convictions. By 1837 the General Assembly had separated the orphan law into two chapters that clearly distinguished the rights of the rich and the poor. "Chapter 54: Guardianship" contained regulations for the care of children who had inherited estates or who had wealthy relatives willing to maintain them. "Chapter 5: Apprentices" contained regulations for the care of poor orphans. The presumptions of class and gender are immediately apparent in section 1 of chapter 5, which defines those orphans whom courts must apprentice. First, apprenticeship applies to poor orphans, namely, those "whose estates are of so small value that no person will educate and maintain him or her for the profits thereof." Next, it applies to all children with no father, including children "whose fathers have deserted their families"; children who have received property from their mothers and whom "the court, in its discretion, thinks it improper to permit . . . to remain with the mother"; and all children born out of wedlock. The 1837 definition of apprenticeship clearly demonstrates that North Carolina lawmakers lacked confidence in poor and single women's abilities to raise children.[39]

As the 1837 laws illustrate, the presumptions of gender and class that characterized the 1762 apprenticeship code persisted. But antebellum lawmakers increasingly incorporated regulations based on race into the code. From 1801 to 1854 the General Assembly enacted statutes that narrowly circumscribed free blacks' autonomy as parents. Moreover, a study of several North Carolina counties demonstrates that by 1860 the numbers of free black children apprenticed, often only a small percentage of indentures in 1801, equaled and in some instances eclipsed the numbers of white children apprenticed. Although presumptions of gender and class remained elemental characteristics of North Carolina's apprenticeship code, race increasingly influenced apprenticeship law both in theory and in practice.

Race became a more defining element of the apprenticeship code in 1801. At that time the General Assembly enacted a statute that required courts to take from masters and mistresses a five-hundred-dollar bond for each child as security against removing apprentices from the county where they were bound. In 1859 North Carolina Supreme Court Justice Thomas Ruffin upheld this statute after hearing *Prue v. Hight*, the previously mentioned case in which an African American boy was apprenticed in Franklin County and then removed to Granville County, where he was bound by a second indenture to another master. Ruffin argued that the boy remained an apprentice under the Franklin County Court's jurisdiction and thus the Granville County indenture was void. Ruffin argued that the framers of the 1801 statute had imposed the five-hundred-dollar security bond for two reasons. First, it provided some protection to free black children, who were constantly threatened by enslavement. Free black children, Ruffin explained, were unusually subject "to oppression and wrong, in being carried to remote parts and made the subject of traffic." Second, free black children required the strict supervision of police "so as to restrain their propensity to be idle and mischievous." The security bond thus prevented masters from taking free black apprentices outside of the jurisdiction of the county where the child was apprenticed and away from the watchful eyes of the county authorities.[40]

In 1826 the General Assembly expanded the parameters of apprenticeship to encompass, potentially, all free black children. Courts were to apprentice "all the children of free negroes and mulattoes where the parents with whom such children may live, do or shall not habitually employ his or her time in some honest, industrious occupation." The language was broad and vague; the definition of "honest, industrious occupation" was left to the discretion of the county courts. Another change to the law reduced requirements for the education of free African American apprentices. By 1837 courts no longer required masters to teach free black children to read and write. Often, Guilford County officials used a pen to strike out from African American children's indentures the printed provision that usually entitled children to some form of literacy training.[41]

The 1826 and 1837 statutes were the General Assembly's first legislated efforts to limit African American parents' rights, as had already been done to the rights of women. But an even greater transformation came in the 1850s, when legislators actually liberalized the law in certain respects for white women yet added new racial restrictions to the code. Over time the law eased requirements on the apprenticeship of illegitimate white children. By 1854 the General Assembly had modified section 1 of chapter 5, which specified which children in North Carolina were subject to apprenticeship. The act no longer required courts to apprentice "all free base born children." The new language of the act stated that county courts must require the apprenticeship of "all free base born children of color." This change allowed single white women, at least those who had financial means, to raise their white children without the threat of apprenticeship. Yet the General Assembly continued to require the apprenticeship of free black children regardless of their mother's means and poor children regardless of their mother's race.[42]

Two North Carolina Supreme Court cases—*Midgett v. McBryde* (1855) and *Frolick v. Schonwald* (1860)—offer perhaps the most compelling evidence for this change in legislators' and judges' attitude toward apprenticeship. Nancy Midgett, a white woman in Currituck County who had given birth to two "mulatto" children, challenged the new law in 1855 by demanding cancellation of her children's indentures to Willoughby McBryde. Since 1852 Midgett had lived in a house that her father had built for her near his homestead. Midgett's father had claimed responsibility for the children by educating and caring for them. To persuade the court, Midgett and her father invoked the language of the law. They stated that her father was "honest" and "respectable" and that Nancy Midgett herself had "during the last three years, behaved orderly and industriously." The court nonetheless upheld McBryde's right to the children. Supreme Court Justice Richmond M. Pearson argued that Midgett's and her father's good character was irrelevant because the law specified that "*all* free base-born children of color" were to be apprenticed irrespective of the mother's character or race. The new apprenticeship law thus applied to white women who bore "children of color."[43]

Racial standards prevented Nancy Midgett from maintaining her own children. But another white woman, Fanny Frolick, managed to keep her two children, who were white. Frolick knew that she could not maintain her illegitimate child, Eveleen, without help. To avoid Eveleen's impending apprenticeship, Frolick entered into a written agreement with Eveleen's father, a white man named James T. Schonwald. Schonwald agreed to pay Frolick ten dollars a month for Eveleen's support, and in return Fanny would educate and maintain the child. The contract further stated that if Frolick should die, or if Schonwald "became dissatisfied with the manner in which the said child is educated, treated or maintained," Schonwald could assume custody of his daughter. In 1859 Schonwald claimed dissatisfaction and demanded custody of Eveleen. Supreme Court Justice M. E. Manly upheld Frolick's rights to Eveleen because Schonwald failed to provide "reasonable cause, for dissatisfaction." Frolick, having secured the maintenance of her child through a valid agreement contracted with Eveleen's father, avoided the court-ordered apprenticeship of her daughter.[44]

Though both Fanny Frolick and Nancy Midgett were white, the courts applied the law in different ways for them because the fathers of their children were of different races. The court identified Fanny Frolick's daughter as white because both of her parents were white. Therefore, the courts could not apprentice her child if she had secured its maintenance, which she had. As previously mentioned, the General Assembly had removed the requirement that courts apprentice all "free base born children" in 1850. The new law required the apprenticeship, regardless of the mother's character or financial status, of all "free base born children of color." In 1855 Midgett lost her children to apprenticeship because their father was African American. These two cases demonstrate the racial transformations that began to take shape in the law during the 1850s.

North Carolina was not alone in its use of apprenticeship to control the free black population. Many southern states had adopted similar codes, which at first were used to control the children of single mothers but later were enhanced to restrict the rights of free blacks. Even states as far north as Missouri, Maryland, and Delaware and the District of Columbia possessed apprenticeship and child custody laws similar to those passed in North Carolina. The laws varied in some states. Maryland free blacks convicted of vagrancy risked losing their children to apprenticeship. Once indentured by the orphans' court, these children were subject to sale. In 1835 Missouri lawmakers required that all free blacks and mulattoes between the ages of seven and twenty-one be apprenticed. Unlike in the District of Columbia, where white and black apprentices worked side by side, mixing black and white apprentices in the workplace was prohibited in Missouri without the consent of the white apprentice's parent or guardian.[45]

A growing emphasis on controlling the black population characterized North Carolina apprenticeship. Throughout the state, black populations remained small but increased steadily before 1860. My seven-county study of apprenticeship bonds transacted between 1801 and 1860 demonstrates that North Carolina authorities became increasingly concerned with race. The counties selected here represent the diversity of North Carolina's geography and demographics. As table 1 shows, the free black populations in all seven counties never exceeded 10 percent during the sixty-year period studied. Robeson, Duplin, and Brunswick counties, which lie in the east, were rural and contained high percentages of slaves. In Duplin the free black community never exceeded 2 percent. However, in Brunswick and Robeson the free black population measured 6 percent in 1830. Mecklenburg and Wilkes counties, the westernmost counties in the study, were also rural but contained much lower percentages of slaves and free blacks (never more than 2 percent). Wake and Guilford counties are located in the North Carolina Piedmont. Large towns, such as Raleigh in Wake County and Greensboro in Guilford County, had dense populations of free blacks. In Wake the percentage of free blacks in the total population was a significant 4 percent in 1830 and 5 percent in 1860. The percentages of free blacks in Guilford were much lower, but the raw numbers remained high. In 1860 nearly seven hundred free blacks called Guilford County home. Table 1 demonstrates another important fact: between 1800 and 1860 the free black population in almost every county under study doubled (and, in some instances tripled) every thirty years.

All seven counties registered apprenticeships for the period under study. Authorities in those counties adopted distinctive styles and customs, but several procedures, often regulated by state law, remained constant. Each county apprenticed children, black and white, male and female, to members of the local community. Most "masters" were male. Few women became mistresses; those who did usually had a male relative or friend to cosign or provide bond. In Guilford County only 33 (or 4%) of 852. "masters" were female. In 1844 a Wake County white woman apprenticed two African American children,

TABLE 1

NORTH CAROLINA COUNTY DEMOGRAPHICS, SLAVE AND FREE, 1800–1860

POPULATION

County Surveyed	Total, Free and Slave			Free, White and Black			Free Black			Free Blacks as Percentage of Total, Free and Slave		
	1800	1830	1860	1800	1830	1860	1800	1830	1860	1800	1830	1860
Brunswick	4,110	6,516	8,406	2,496	3,409	4,775	163	408	260	4	6	3
Duplin	6,796	11,291	15,784	4,932	6,857	8,660	55	169	371	1	1	2
Guilford	9,442	18,737	20,056	8,537	16,143	16,431	40	382	693	0.42	2	3
Mecklenberg	10,317	20,073	17,374	8,386	12,927	10,833	15	140	293	0.15	1	2
Robeson	6,666	9,433	15,489	5,706	6,934	10,034	340	605	1,462	5	6	9
Wake	12,768	20,398	28,627	8,862	17,968	17,894	306	833	1,446	2	4	5
Wilkes	7,247	11,968	14,749	6,457	10,476	13,541	64	137	261	1	1	2

Sources: Fifth Census or, enumeration of the inhabitants of the United States (Washington, DC: D. Green, 1832), 90–92; *Return of the Whole Number of Persons Within the Several Districts of the United States . . . Second Census* (New York: Norman Ross, 1990); *Population of the United States in 1860; compiled from the original returns of the Eighth Census* (Washington, DC: GPO, 1864), 358–59.

Betsey Chavis (age 11) and John Chavis (age 14). In each case a male sponsor cosigned the apprenticeship contract. Courts almost never apprenticed children to white women without a male signatory. In one very rare instance Nancy E. Climer successfully had Bell Ashe, a free African American female, bound to her in 1856 without assistance from a male friend or relative. These few cases (fewer than 1%) suggest that the court approved apprenticeships to women only at its discretion.[46]

Apprenticeship contracts (or indentures) provide valuable information. All apprenticeship contracts provide the names of the master and child. Often the contracts list the child's age, intended trade or occupation, and terms of release. Masters frequently promised to provide the child with an allowance, tools, "freedom" clothes, and sometimes furniture upon his or her release from the indenture at twenty-one (or in the case of white females, eighteen). In 1820 Matthew Young, a Guilford County master, promised to give his apprentice, Betsey Pool, "one bed & furniture worth $30." He also promised "one spinning wheel, two suits of clothes, and learn her to read and write the clothes are as freedom dues." Not all masters were as generous as Matthew Young. Nonetheless, the law required masters to give apprentices at least one new suit of clothes, six dollars, and a Bible when they gained their freedom.[47]

Parents usually maintained watchful eyes to ensure that masters kept their promises. If they did not, parents sometimes protested and petitioned to have the court rescind their children's indentures. Rhoda Pollard, a white woman in Wake County, observed in 1838 that Berry Surls, the master of her child, John, had neglected her son. She petitioned the court and informed Surls that she had asked for her son's removal on the grounds that "his raising and education are neglected by you." Pollard argued that Surls had failed to instruct, feed, and clothe her son. He had neglected him, beat him, and degraded him "by obliging him or permitting him to sleep with Negroes and otherwise to make him a companion for them." According to Pollard, Surls had failed not only his statutory duties but also his customary duties to raise John Pollard alongside whites and not African Americans.[48]

Nearly all of the apprenticeships in the study were court ordered. Usually the court assumed the role of *parens patriae*, or custodian, and appointed children at its discretion. In these seven counties only a few fathers signed contracts willingly binding out their children to others. In the 1,317 apprenticeship bonds studied from these seven counties in the years 1801–60 only nineteen fathers (1.5%) willingly bound out their children. These numbers are probably low for two reasons. First, fathers may have preferred to hire out, rather than apprentice, children to others. Upon indenture, parental authority and the child's wages transferred from the father to the new master, who stood *in loco parentis*. John Robinson Sr., of Brunswick County, absolved himself of all right and responsibility as a father when he apprenticed his son, Jackson, to Steward P. Ivey "to learn the art, trade, and mystry of a black smith." Under the terms of the indenture, Jackson was to live with Ivey until he turned twenty-one, and Ivey promised to instruct him "and to faithfully provide good and sufficient meat, cloathing and lodgin and other necessaries fit and convenient for such an apprentice." Most likely, fathers preferred to hire out their children for designated periods of time, during which the father remained primary guardian and collected the child's wages until the contract expired. The apprenticeship bonds offer no records of fathers who hired out, rather than apprenticed, their children, as these were matters of private contract, not registered with the courts unless a dispute surfaced. Masters "apprenticed" slaves too. Yet, again, these arrangements fell outside the purview of apprenticeship law.[49]

Sometimes masters "apprenticed" their slaves by covenant to learn a profitable trade. In 1857 the Washington County Superior Court tried an action of covenant (not apprenticeship) in *James W. Bell v. Caleb L. Walker et al.* Sometime in the late 1850s James W. Bell had contracted with Caleb L. Walker and Jesse Herrington to "apprentice" his three slaves, Peter, Woden, and Abbott, as ship's carpenters and caulkers. The contract stipulated that Walker and Herrington would keep the slaves and provide for them and also pay Bell one hundred dollars annually for each slave. Apparently, Peter learned the trade of ship's carpenter well. However, Abbott and Woden learned little, if anything. Bell sued Walker and Herrington for failing to teach his two slaves the crafts. Walker and Herrington argued that they had made reasonable efforts to teach Abbott and Woden but that they had proved unwilling and obstinate. The court decided that despite the slaves' unwillingness to learn, the defendants had the right to coerce them to perform and thus there had been no breach of covenant. Though the court recognized that an informal apprenticeship relationship existed between the parties, contract law, not apprenticeship law, bound the conditions of service.[50]

Second, the law made it difficult for fathers to apprentice children voluntarily. In antebellum North Carolina fathers possessed a personal interest in a child. Though a father possessed a "right of property" in the child's services, he could not transfer his personal interest in the form of an apprenticeship to another without the child's consent. Thus, North Carolina law forbade voluntary apprenticeships for children under twelve and required the child's consent once he or she turned twelve. These provisions likely discouraged voluntary indentures.[51]

According to apprenticeship bonds, courts bound out greater numbers of free black children after 1830. The security bonds masters and mistresses signed when courts apprenticed free black children allow researchers to discern the ratios of free black to white indentures with some accuracy. The apprenticeship bonds indicate few apprenticeships in Duplin County, which reflects the low populations of free blacks in the east. Robeson possessed a significant free black community, but the records are sporadic because no bonds exist for the years 1831–50. The bonds from the 1850s are instructive, however, because they demonstrate an enormous increase in the percentage of free blacks apprenticed compared with the 1821–30 period. Between 1850 and 1860 Robeson County authorities witnessed a surge in population within the free black community and likely used apprenticeship as one means to control this growth.[52]

Nonetheless, table 2 indicates that apprenticeship was not a popular method of social control in eastern North Carolina counties. In the east, slaves accounted for a large percentage of the population, and apprenticeship never really caught on among either whites or blacks until the later decades of the antebellum period. In the 1830s, Brunswick County began a two-decade trend of apprenticing unequal percentages of free black (78% of children apprenticed in 1831–40) and white (22% of children apprenticed in 1831–40) children. By 1860 the raw numbers had evened out in Brunswick, but the percentage of free black children who were apprenticed far exceeded the percentage of white children who were apprenticed. The increase in free black apprenticeships in Brunswick after 1830 corresponds to the 1826 statutory change that required the apprenticeship of all children of color born out of wedlock and those whose parents were not employed in some "honest" and "industrious" occupation.[53]

Wilkes, Guilford, and Wake counties provide the most useful records for studying race and antebellum apprenticeship. In all seven counties white indentures remained high throughout the period 1800–1860. In Guilford the numbers of white male indentures surpassed those of any other group in nearly every decade. But beginning in the early 1830s the numbers of white male and female indentures declined, while the numbers of black male and female indentures increased. As in eastern North Carolina, the increase in free black apprenticeships in Guilford and Wake counties corresponds to the 1826

TABLE 2

EXTANT COURT-ORDERED APPRENTICESHIP BONDS, BY RACE AND SEX, 1801–1860

County Surveyed	1801–10 Black Male	Black Female	White Male	White Female	% Black	1811–20 Black Male	Black Female	White Male	White Female	% Black	1821–30 Black Male	Black Female	White Male	White Female	% Black
Brunswick	0	0	0	0	0	0	0	3	0	0	0	0	0	0	0
Duplin	1	0	0	0	100	0	0	0	0	0	0	0	0	0	0
Robeson	0	0	0	0	0	0	0	0	0	0	0	1	2	2	20
Guilford	1	1	0	0	100	6	4	41	12	16	15	9	161	45	10
Wake	3	1	17	1	18	8	6	12	2	50	4	0	8	1	31
Mecklenberg*	0	1	1	0		(3)	(11)	2(67)	1(16)	(14)	0	1	2	1	
Wilkes	5	0	25	9	13	1	0	6	2	11	3	2	9	6	25

County Surveyed	1831–40 Black Male	Black Female	White Male	White Female	% Black	1841–50 Black Male	Black Female	White Male	White Female	% Black	1851–60 Black Male	Black Female	White Male	White Female	% Black
Brunswick	9	5	3	1	78	6	4	6	1	59	5	3	7	1	50
Duplin	0	0	1	0	0	0	0	0	0	0	0	0	0	0	0
Robeson	0	0	0	0	0	0	0	0	0	0	20	3	14	0	62
Guilford	30	14	112	24	24	33	9	119	19	23	53	34	90	20	44
Wake	19	0	5	0	79	16	14	16	2	63	23	12	7	1	81
Mecklenberg*	(44)	1(32)	(82)	(22)	(42)						(13)	(12)	1(31)	(4)	(42)
Wilkes	16	6	20	8	44	5	7	8	2	55	0	1	6	5	8

Source: Apprenticeship Bonds, 1801–1860, Brunswick, Duplin, Robeson, Guilford, Wake, Mecklenberg, and Wilkes counties, NCSA.

Note: Number of court-ordered apprenticeship bonds in study = 1,298; number of voluntary apprenticeship bonds in study = 19 (data are not included in table); total number of apprenticeship bonds in study = 1,317.

*Data in parentheses are drawn from Minutes of the Court of Common Pleas and Quarter Sessions, Mecklenburg County, NCSA.

statutory change. The reason for the decrease in white male apprenticeships is unclear, though it is possible that over time courts were less willing to apprentice illegitimate white children whose mothers, like Fanny Frolick, could support them. Similar trends occurred in Wilkes County. The country disproportionately apprenticed free blacks in 1831–50. The data indicate that after 1830, courts in Guilford, Wake, and Wilkes counties increasingly used apprenticeship to control free black families. This inference seems reasonable, because all three counties experienced explosive growth within the free black community between 1800 and 1830.[54]

African American apprenticeship exploded in Mecklenburg County as well during the 1830s. Few apprenticeship bonds remain for Mecklenburg County, but county court minutes provide some evidence of change. The Mecklenburg County Court recorded ninety-seven apprenticeships in the years 1811–20. Fourteen percent of these apprentices were African Americans. But after the 1826 statutory change the numbers and percentages of African Americans apprenticed rose substantially. In 1831–40 and 1851–60 African Americans represented 42 percent of all children apprenticed in the county. However, Mecklenburg County's free black population never exceeded 2 percent of the total population. Authorities in Charlotte, which contained Mecklenburg County's significant urban population, maintained a watchful eye on the city's very small free black community. The data clearly demonstrate that the surveillance increased after 1826.[55]

In sum, the apprenticeship system was most popular in heavily populated areas such as Mecklenburg, Guilford, and Wake counties, where authorities used it primarily to control white children until the 1830s, when they shifted their attention to the apprenticeship of black children. In Wilkes County, located in the North Carolina foothills, apprenticeship also was used to control whites, though authorities increasingly used it to control the population's small free black community after 1830. Finally, apprenticeship was almost nonexistent along the North Carolina coast (Duplin, Brunswick, and Robeson counties) until the later decades of the antebellum period, when state authorities enacted greater restrictions on free black populations. Unlike the other four counties of the study, eastern counties rejected the large-scale use of apprenticeship to control white populations during the early nineteenth century.

North Carolinians never turned to apprenticeship as a primary source of labor, as the numbers in table 2 attest. Antebellum courts throughout the state probably never apprenticed more than a few hundred children per year. Slavery was the preferred mode of labor. However, some counties registered considerably more apprenticeships than others. For example, Guilford County, which contains the urban center of Greensboro, had far more apprenticeships than Wake County, in which Raleigh resides, during the decade before the Civil War. Though Guilford claimed a slightly smaller population (about two-thirds the size of Wake's population), county courts apprenticed 197 children there from 1851 to 1860; Wake county courts apprenticed only 43.

The explanation lies in the religious populations of the two counties. Wake County contained a high percentage of Baptists, Presbyterians, and Methodists, whereas Guilford had a sizable Quaker population. By the 1850s the Society of Friends had discouraged its members from owning slaves. Several Guilford Quakers, including members of the Coffin family, assisted escaped slaves on the Underground Railroad. Slavery violated the religious principles of many Quakers, who argued that every individual possessed an "Inner Light" that connected him or her with God. In protest of slavery, Quakers in 1814 established the North Carolina Manumission Society, which was supported by Friends in Guilford, Randolph, Chatham, Forsyth, and Orange counties. In the 1780s, Quakers adopted a policy of disowning members who used or traded slaves. To avoid discipline, some North Carolina slaveholding Quakers deeded more than seven hundred slaves to the Society of Friends, which eventually conveyed them to the North. Though some Quakers violated the policy and were disowned, others adhered to antislavery principles.[56]

For artisanal and enterprising Quakers, apprenticeship served as a substitute for slavery. Counties that contained sizable Quaker populations also experienced higher apprenticeship rates than other counties. A comparison of trade industries and apprentices' occupations suggests that Quaker artisans routinely apprenticed children for training in their crafts. Quaker David Beard established one of the largest hatteries in the state. Guilford Quakers, despite their pacifist ideals, also founded one of the largest groups of gunsmiths in the South. And when the market in long rifles suffered, gunstockers and gunsmiths turned to furniture making. Apprenticeships reflect the popularity of these same industries. Throughout the antebellum era white male youths of Guilford County were apprenticed as hatters, gunsmiths, furniture makers, and woodworkers. By contrast, Wake County courts apprenticed only a handful of children in the trades of hatting and cabinetry. No Wake County apprentices worked under the direction of gunsmiths. Other counties with substantial Quaker populations also had correspondingly higher rates of apprenticeship.

Guion Johnson counted numerous apprenticeships in Pasquotank, Carteret, and Orange counties, all of which contained sizable Quaker communities. North Carolina Quakers who were unwilling or unable to own slaves turned to apprenticeship as an alternate source of labor.[57]

Apprentices' occupations varied not only by county but also by race and gender. Masters trained white and black girls to become "spinsters," "seamstresses," and "housekeepers." A few African American girls encountered both gender and racial bias in their given trades. In the years 1841–50 four African American females in Brunswick County were trained to be servants. Masters provided males with a more diverse array of trades and occupations; nonetheless, race often determined a young man's craft. Masters designated white males for jobs as tanners, coopers, farmers, carpenters, merchants, blacksmiths, masons, coach or carriage makers, saddlers, harnessmakers, wheelwrights, confectioners, cabinetmakers, chairmakers, cobblers, clerks, machinists, bakers, pilots, hatters, tailors, painters, and bookbinders. As stated earlier, some white males in Guilford County were trained in gunsmithing and gunstocking.[58]

However, the trades masters designated for black males were narrowly circumscribed. Black male apprentices usually learned the trade of "farmer," though some became blacksmiths, tailors, masons, tanners, saddlers, cobblers, and coach makers. It was no accident that black male apprentices never learned the art of gunsmithing. In 1812 the General Assembly excluded free blacks from serving in North Carolina's militia, and in 1840 the legislature passed a law requiring free blacks to possess a license to carry a gun. During the 1850s several groups of citizens proposed bills to the General Assembly forbidding free African Americans to own guns. North Carolina whites seemed reluctant not only to allow free African Americans to carry arms but also to allow them to produce arms.[59]

John Hope Franklin suggests that antislavery agitators, increasing resistance from slaves, and growing communities of free African Americans prompted North Carolina whites to institute more restrictive race-based regulations in order to control free blacks in North Carolina. In 1829 David Walker published a proinsurrection abolitionist pamphlet entitled *An Appeal*. In 1831 Nat Turner led a rebellion against slaveholders in Virginia. These events, in conjunction with a rapidly changing economy, contributed to a general fear among whites of slave rebellions and encouraged them to restrict the movements and rights of free blacks. Southern whites' efforts intensified even further during the 1850s as political conflict between the North and the South escalated. By the decade before the war race had become a predominant concern of southern whites as they sought to secure white supremacy at the expense of the free black population. Southern whites found apprenticeship to be a useful method not only for controlling black parents but also for supervising black children's daily activities.[60]

For some of the women and children mentioned here apprenticeship continued to have an effect long after their indenture contracts had expired. Apprentices are difficult to trace in the largely rural environment of nineteenth-century North Carolina, but a few are documented in census records. The case of Andrew Johnson is well known. Although he never attained great wealth, Johnson's tailoring shop was a first step toward a role in Tennessee politics and the U.S. presidency. Arguably, he achieved more than any other child who was subjected to involuntary apprenticeship, but it should be remembered that Johnson and his family rejected the apprenticeship system. Johnson and his brother evaded North Carolina law by fleeing to Tennessee. His eventual success eclipsed that of most apprentices, who were generally less fortunate. None of the other apprentices or mothers traced in this study ever achieved a life of affluence or propertied independence. For example, the apprentices, Lydia Burnet (who ran away from her master, Cornelius Dowd), Thomas Artis, and Jackson Robinson, did not possess real estate in the ten years after their apprenticeships expired. Somehow the forty-one-year-old Burnet had forged a life for herself and four teenage children in rural Moore County by 1850. They probably worked as tenant farmers, though the census is silent on this matter. Surprisingly, Burnet's children, aged ten to nineteen, lived with their mother. Since they were perfect candidates for court-ordered apprenticeship, it is possible that Burnet managed some arrangement with a landholder to keep her children at home while they labored on a nearby farm. Having developed a distaste for apprenticeship in her own childhood, she likely hoped to prevent her children from having the same experience. Thomas Artis, a thirty-five-year-old free black farm laborer in Wayne County whose wife employed herself in "Keeping House," claimed a personal estate valued at one hundred dollars in 1870. That same year, Jackson Robinson, of Brunswick County, listed no estate or occupation at all.[61]

Tracing the lives of apprentices' mothers is more difficult. Since census research often depends on tracking surnames, it is a less reliable source for finding women who changed their names upon marriage. But women who kept their surnames do appear. Thirty-five-year-old Nancy Midgett, the mother who pursued her children's apprenticeship case all the way to the North Carolina Supreme Court, seems to have had a relatively lonely existence. After fighting hard, though unsuccessfully, against the apprenticeship of her two "mulatto" children to Willoughby McBryde in 1855, in 1860 she lived alone on Roanoke Island in remote Currituck County. There she claimed a personal estate of ten dollars. No record of her children remains. They did not live with Willoughby McBryde, who remained in Currituck County. McBryde, who possessed an ample estate, boarded with a family near the Currituck Courthouse. Perhaps census officials overlooked the children while they labored on one of McBryde's farms somewhere in Currituck County. What is clear is that apprenticeship, a system increasingly defined by race, destroyed Nancy Midgett's dream of maintaining a thriving, independent household.[62]

Antebellum racial anxieties produced a profound change in apprenticeship. Once an institution used to deprive certain poor women of their child-custody rights, apprenticeship became a tool of the elite white patriarchy. Yet the antebellum law clearly reflected vestiges of North Carolina's earliest apprenticeship regulations. Colonial law had provided the class and gender framework that denied poor women and single women rights to their children. But in the years 1801–60 the law and practice increasingly became defined by race. Apprenticeship threatened all free African American families, and the law freed masters from teaching African American apprentices to read and write. In the 1850s the threat of apprenticeship to free African American families or families of mixed race peaked. During that decade the state supreme court declared that courts must apprentice those white children whose mothers could not care for them and all children of color born of single mothers. Single white mothers who secured funding for their children escaped apprenticeship laws. However, the threat of apprenticeship loomed constantly in households headed by poor women and African American men and women. Some women, like Fanny Frolick, manipulated the system as best they could to maintain custody of their children. Many others could not. Although the Civil War would bring vast changes to the institution, many antebellum customs and laws would remain.

CHAPTER TWO

"JUSTLY ENTITLED" TO APPRENTICES

Race and Labor in Reconstruction

Colonel Eliphalet Whittlesey, assistant commissioner of the Bureau of Refugees, Freedmen and Abandoned Lands in North Carolina, criticized the postwar practice of binding out children. He said that he was "suspicious" of apprenticeship. The practice, he argued, "fosters the old ideas of compulsory labor and dependence" and resembled "slavery in the milder form of apprenticeship." Whittlesey perceptively captured the essence of postwar apprenticeship: southern whites had reshaped it to control North Carolina's African American population. County apprenticeship records suggest but do not conclusively prove that apprenticeship increased after the war. However, letters from white plantation owners and African American parents clearly illustrate that there were heated conflicts over the custody of former slave children. Postwar apprenticeship practices at once reflected southern whites' angst about labor scarcity and their assumptions of African American dependency. Embittered by defeat, humiliated by Union occupation, angered by emancipation, and distressed by the loss of slave labor, southern whites joined forces with politicians to transform apprenticeship into an institution they hoped would restore the prewar order.[1]

By 1865 apprenticeship had taken opposite trajectories in the South and the North. In northern states apprenticeship had begun a prolonged decline after the Revolution and had become almost nonexistent by the Civil War. As the industrial economy expanded, apprenticeship became outmoded. Employers favored the free labor system, which did not require them to meet the paternalistic obligations of other forms of bound labor. Free labor also promoted employees' personal autonomy, a freedom particularly welcomed by an increasingly politicized

TABLE 3
APPRENTICESHIPS, 1851–1864

County Surveyed	1851–60		1861–64	
	Total	One-year Average	Total	One-year Average
Brunswick	16	1.6	8	2
Duplin	0	0	U	U
Robeson	37	3.7	9	2.25
Guilford	198	19.8	41	10.25
Wake	43	4.3	10	2.5
Mecklenberg*	(60)	(6.0)	U	U
Wilkes	12	1.2	U	U

Source: Apprenticeship Bonds, 1801–1860, Brunswick, Duplin, Robeson, Guilford, Wake, Mecklenberg, and Wilkes counties, NCSA.
Note: U = unclear county bond records.
*Data in parentheses are from Minutes of the Court of Common Pleas and Quarter Sessions, Mecklenberg County, NCSA.

male youth inspired by the expansion of democracy. Even so, the transition to free labor was painful. As the American polity became more democratized, workers pressed politicians for legal changes to reduce their vulnerability to coercive labor. Employers responded by crafting legal codes that encouraged a ruthless free market economy. Young men and boys, once granted certain protections as a master's dependent apprentice, suddenly found themselves vulnerable to the vagaries of the labor market. In sum, northern apprenticeship succumbed to two forces, the market economy and workers' demands.[2]

North Carolina experienced a brief decline in apprenticeship during the war, but not for any of the reasons that it declined in northern states. Rather, wartime circumstances appear to have had a significant effect on apprenticeship. Table 3, a survey of seven North Carolina counties, shows that three counties, Robeson, Wake, and Guilford, experienced significant decreases in the numbers of children apprenticed. The one-year average number of indentures contracted per year fell from 3.7 (Robeson), 4.3 (Wake), and 19.8 (Guilford) during the period 1851–60 to 2.25 (Robeson), 2.5 (Wake), and 10.25 (Guilford) during the war years, 1861–64. Only one county, Brunswick, registered a slight increase. There, the one-year average number of indentures increased from 1.6 during the years 1851–60 to 2.0 in wartime. The decline throughout these years suggests that the Civil War had a measurable impact on apprenticeship patterns. Increasing casualties forced the Confederacy to reach into its population of young people in order to replace soldiers lost to battle and disease. Greater opportunities for employment in nascent war industries also provided alternatives for southern youth. And more men at the front meant that fewer masters remained behind to supervise free blacks.[3]

The Confederate government unwittingly discouraged apprenticeship by passing far-reaching conscription laws in 1862 and 1864. The laws potentially forced many young male teenagers who would have qualified for apprenticeship to enlist in the army instead. On April 16, 1862, the Confederate Congress passed the first conscription act. The act required conscription of all men aged eighteen to thirty-five. Two years later Congress reduced the minimum age limit to seventeen. The result was that potential masters were prevented from apprenticing male youths aged seventeen to twenty-one. Conscription tended to stimulate volunteering, and a disproportionate number of Confederate conscripts—nearly one-fourth—came from North Carolina. The conscription acts, not the onset of the free market or the factory system, contributed to apprenticeship's brief decline in wartime North Carolina.[4]

With so many men at the front, North Carolina rarely apprenticed girls and free blacks. Not only were there few masters to assume responsibility for them but state and federal governments preferred to employ adult workers rather than apprentice children. Throughout the South, girls and women from poor families labored as seamstresses, clerks, and semiskilled manufacturing workers. For example, in Augusta, Georgia, charitable organizations helped care for impoverished and unemployed women. There manufacturers reasoned that donations to the poor would deflect public criticism from affluent factory owners who profited off the inflationary wartime economy. Charitable organizations, likely seen by some authorities as serving a purpose by confirming women's dependence, may have viewed apprenticeship as unnecessary. Labor shortages required southern governments to employ free blacks as well. While some free blacks labored for the Confederacy, others joined the Union army. Early in 1863, free blacks enlisted as soldiers where the Union army had established a southern presence. The first three regiments of free blacks recruited in New Orleans included not only craftsmen but also former slaveholders and illiterate laborers. As slaves left plantations throughout the South, the labor market tightened further. Given the labor shortages that beset Civil War governments, apprenticing children to individual masters seemed illogical to southern bureaucracies that needed to mobilize workers for the Confederacy.[5]

Of course, apprenticeship was not the only labor system in North Carolina that suffered from the chaos of war. As Union troops advanced into the state,

North Carolinians, black and white, watched slavery crumble. In 1862 Union forces captured some of the islands making up North Carolina's Outer Banks. Union troops occupied Roanoke Island and towns such as New Bern and Goldsboro. The Union presence in these coastal areas spelled the end of slavery there. Northeastern areas such as Washington County experienced social and political upheaval. Meanwhile, slaves fled their masters and took refuge behind Union lines. Many black men enlisted as soldiers with the Union army, and even larger numbers obtained jobs as laborers; they dug ditches and canals, built breastworks, and served as guides for Union troops. Women and children also took refuge behind Union lines. Many of the soldiers' families settled on Roanoke Island. Nearly three thousand more settled on a swampy patch of land near New Bern later known as James City. At the war's end the camps were choked with refugees. The resulting impoverishment presented grave problems for the Union army and later for Freedmen's Bureau agents sent to manage the camps. Nevertheless, the freedpeople filled the camps beyond capacity. By leaving plantations, the freedpeople changed forever the state's labor economy. White plantation owners faced severe labor shortages once the freedpeople could negotiate the terms of labor.[6]

After the war, the scarcity of labor worried elite white women. Without servants or slaves the least desirous responsibilities in the household fell to white women. Former slaveholding women, accustomed to managing servants and slaves who performed the most tedious tasks, balked at performing menial labor in the household after the war. The Tillinghast sisters' letters from Fayetteville, for example, are replete with exaggerated complaints. Sarah Tillinghast, who lived with her sisters, Eliza, Emily, and Robena, asserted that white women should be freed from performing the most arduous tasks in the household. In May 1866 she informed her brother David that "God in his wisdom put the negroes in the south to do the menial work" because the climate of North Carolina "kills" white women. "Look at your own sisters," she argued, "we are fair examples." The four girls had once been strong and healthy, but menial labor had enfeebled them; the negative effects of housework had even forced Eliza into bed. "Emily's iron constitution," she complained, "was so taxed that it brought on a fever which has injured her almost irreparably." Sarah's morning duties wore her out so completely that she had to lie down and rest "nearly every day." "I did the cooking for a week in the winter," she informed David, "and I laid in bed another to pay for it." Sarah blamed emancipation for all these infirmities. "God intended these negroes" to do menial housework, she declared, "and I will live on bread and water and have this work done by them before I undertake to do it again." When domestic help grew scarce after the war, Eliza warned her brother Will that if he did not secure a young house servant for Sarah and Robena, "the consequences may be more serious than I can tell or you can imagine."[7]

Thus, white women and men, accustomed to slavery, sought to regain control of labor, and apprenticeship practices took new form. When agents of the Bureau of Refugees, Freedmen and Abandoned Lands arrived in late 1865, they found that local whites had sought to take matters into their own hands. Brevet Major H. H. Fisher reported to his supervisor, H. H. Beadle, that conditions in Duplin and Sampson counties had gone from bad to worse. The freedpeople had fled many counties, causing a severe labor shortage in the region. "To retrieve their losses," Fisher reported, the landowners had requested county courts to apprentice their former slaves' children "without respect to the wish of parents or conditions of the children." Local police routinely seized children in adjoining counties and whisked them back to Sampson County. Complaints came not only from parents but also from recent employers who had signed wage-labor contracts with parents for their children's employ. "As a necessary result of scarcity of labor," Beadle reported, "quarrels are arising between whites—the new masters by Indenture and late employers who were paying many of these minors good wages."[8]

Freedmen's Bureau agents elsewhere observed the growing popularity of apprenticeship. Masters throughout the South revived the antebellum practice of apprenticeship to secure labor once provided by slaves. Legislatures not only in North Carolina but also in South Carolina, Georgia, Mississippi, Arkansas, and Texas enacted special apprenticeship statutes, among many other laws known as the Black Codes, to control the freedpeople. For example, a South Carolina statute allowed local authorities to apprentice not only poor and orphaned children but also any children "whose parents are not teaching them habits of industry and honesty, or are persons of notoriously bad character, or are vagrants." In Monroe County, Georgia, one Freedmen's Bureau agent reported that by 1867 planters had apprenticed one-third of the black children living there. Some states, such as Mississippi, enacted further provisions that gave former masters first preference to children suitable for apprenticeship. Former slaves in Maryland, a state that had resisted secession, experienced the separation of families through apprenticeship. According to the historian Barbara Fields, an estimated 2,519 children were apprenticed between November 1864 and April 1867.[9]

Proceeding in lockstep with the courts in neighboring states, North Carolina county courts increased the number of apprenticeships significantly beyond antebellum levels. An analysis of county apprenticeship bonds and Freedmen's Bureau records demonstrate that across the state, North Carolina county courts apprenticed more children in 1865 than in any previous year. The seven-county study, which represents the diversity of North Carolina's geography and population, indicates some of these increases. Table 4 shows that three counties, Brunswick, Robeson, and Guilford, experienced increases during 1865. In Guilford County apprenticeships increased from an average of 19.8 a year in 1851–60 to 80 in 1865. Robeson County Court records and Freedmen's Bureau records demonstrate significant increases in 1865. Apprenticeship bonds show that the county court apprenticed at least 8 children that year, more than twice the one-year average of 3.7 for 1851–60. And Freedmen's Bureau records indicate that 125 apprenticeships contracted in 1865 through the Freedmen's Bureau or through illegal county court transactions were canceled by the bureau in 1867. The Robeson and Guilford increases demonstrate that apprenticeship grew substantially in more than one North Carolina region. Three other counties provided no data for 1865 but exhibited numerous indentures in 1866. In contrast, the apprenticeship bonds and Freedmen's Bureau records for Wake and Mecklenberg counties show almost no apprenticeships transacted in 1865 and 1866. Perhaps these apprenticeship bonds for 1865 and 1866 are lost. What is more likely, however, is that court-ordered apprenticeships did not occur there. In 1865 Wake and Mecklenberg counties, both urban areas, felt the effects of labor scarcity less than rural counties did. Also, the strong presence of federal military officers and Freedmen's Bureau agents and, in Wake County, the head of North Carolina operations, Assistant Commissioner Colonel Eliphalet Whittlesey, who despised the system and likened it to slavery, discouraged legal, court-ordered apprenticeships.[10]

Freedmen's Bureau records indicate that in the last months of 1865 whites turned to apprenticeship as one answer to their labor concerns. Former masters approached county courts and the Freedmen's Bureau, both of whom grappled for the authority to apprentice children. In Sampson County the court apprenticed 218 children during the 1865 November term alone. From September to December 1865 Freedmen's Bureau agents apprenticed 393 more children throughout the state. Southern whites, who hoped to shape African Americans into a steady agricultural work force, valued older children and boys, and they refused to apprentice many young children, who required years of nurture

TABLE 4

INCREASES IN ANTEBELLUM, WARTIME, AND RECONSTRUCTION APPRENTICESHIPS, 1851–1866

County Surveyed	1851–60		1861–64		1865		1866	
	Total	One-Year Average	Total	One-Year Average	Court Records	FBR Records	Court Records	FBR Records
Brunswick	16	1.6	8	2.0	14	—	—	—
Duplin	—	—	0	0	—	—	—	56
Robeson	37	3.7	9	2.25	8	125	26	—
Guilford	198	19.8	41	10.25	80	—	71	53
Wake	43	4.3	10	2.5	0	—	1	—
Mecklenberg*	1(60)	0.1(6)	0	0	—	—	1	5
Wilkes	12	1.2	0	0	—	—	—	—

Sources: FBR, extant apprenticeship bonds in North Carolina Division of Archives and History, Raleigh.

* Data in parentheses are from Minutes of the Court of Common Pleas and Quarter Sessions, Mecklenberg County, NCSA.

before they could perform productively. Analysis of indentures reported by the Freedmen's Bureau officials in the "Register of Indentures" reveals that during 1865–66 courts preferred to apprentice older children rather than younger ones, and masters requested that boys rather than girls be bound to them. To be sure, the register is not a complete listing of indentures in North Carolina. It encompasses only twenty-four counties and represents only a sampling of apprenticeship patterns. Nevertheless, it provides a window into the motives of whites who sought such indentures. The list contains the names of 326 children, 62 percent boys and 38 percent girls. The gender distinction is important because it indicates that although masters valued girls' work as domestics, they preferred to acquire boys to work in the fields. Of these 326 children, 247 (76%) were above age seven. Thirty-seven children had reached their seventeenth birthday, and some of these older children had reached their twentieth. That southern whites preferred older children as apprentices suggests that economic motives often drove apprenticeship.[11]

Freedmen and freedwomen frequently complained that planters had only the oldest children, those most capable of work, bound to them, leaving black mothers and fathers to raise the youngest children and no one to help with the work. Just before the war's close, Richard Boyle, a freedman, wrote to Abraham Lincoln informing him of the freedpeople's problems on Roanoke Island. Boyle inquired whether the Union troops had any right "to take our boy children from us and send them to Newbern to work." According to Boyle, U.S. military officials had requested that the freedmen send all of their older boys to claim their rations on a certain day. When the boys arrived, military officials "march [*sic*] them down to the head quarters and put them on board the boat and carried them to New bern." Consequently, the boys' mothers whose "husbands are in the army" had no one "to help them cut & lay wood & to [perform errands] for them."[12]

For whites, apprenticing African American children promised one solution to their labor problem. African American children represented a valuable source of labor to North Carolina's economy. In slavery, children provided important services to their masters. Although they lacked the strength and endurance of their parents and adult siblings, children as young as four years old worked around the plantation and in the household. Some children performed personal duties. For example, Sarah Debro lived "at de big house to wait on Mis' Polly, to tote her basket of keys an' such as dat." Charlie Barbour, of Smithfield, did housework such as polishing silver, and Joe High "fanned flies off the table."

John Coggin toted water on his head for hands in the fields; he was "too young to do anything else." And Sarah Louise Augustus remembers that "just as soon as I wus able to work any at all I wus put to milking cows."[13]

As slave children grew older they performed slightly more complicated duties. Some served as body servants. Others tended cattle and chickens. Some performed light field work such as harvesting corn. Lily Perry performed general chores around the house. "De fust things dat I can remember wus bein' a house gal, pickin' up chip, mindin' de table an' feedin' de hogs. De slop buckets wus heavy an' I had a heap of wuck dat wus hard to do." Catherine Williams remembered how she graduated to new chores as she grew older. "The first work I done was nursing the children in the home, next I waited on the table, then general housework." Lindsey Faucette worked as a "cow-tender." "I would have to hold de calf up to de mother cow 'til de milk would come down," she explained, "an' den I would have to hold it away 'til somebody done de milkin'." Other duties reserved for children included planting seeds, pulling weeds, and "'mindin' the crows out of de field."[14]

Teenagers proved to be productive workers. They split wood, tended horses, and mastered domestic chores such as spinning and weaving. Many teenagers worked as field hands, chopping cotton and plowing the "softer lands." Betty Cofer stated that as a young woman she "wove the cotton an' linen for sheets an' pillow-slips an' table covers." These were the chores that readied slave teenagers for the kind of work they would perform as adults.[15]

Both parents and masters highly valued children and their work. Indeed, an anxious struggle between slave parents and planters to control slave children foreshadowed the conflicts over apprenticeship during Reconstruction. Marie Jenkins Schwartz argues that an intense competition for children's affection and loyalty brewed in the paternalistic milieu of the plantation. Both parents and masters claimed children's labor and drew comfort from their affection. To secure children's loyalty and cooperation as future laborers, slaveholders cultivated a paternalistic relationship with children. Some slaveholders assumed the role of benevolent master and distributed treats or encouraged visits to the big house in order to sway children's affections. Schwartz argues that the ideology of paternalism required masters to treat children with some benevolence and kindness, and slaves held their masters to that standard. "Slave parents," she argues, "pushed slaveholders to act paternalistically because manifestations of paternalism helped children survive and a people persist." As a result, parents faced a delicate balance: to maintain control of their children without overturning the paternalistic system and thus jeopardizing their children's safety. Given this dilemma, many parents protected their role as disciplinarians, which enabled them to teach children proper behavior before owners and their guests so that the children would not be ill-treated or sold.[16]

With the destruction of slavery any pretense of paternalism vanished. Parents claimed exclusive control of their children. In Reconstruction, children were as important an economic resource as they had been in slavery, but now it was for the benefit of their parents, not planters. Dilly Yellady remembered working in the fields; indeed, labor dominated Dilly Yellady's memories of childhood. She and her brothers and sisters helped their parents with field labor. "Couldn't go to school 'cept when it wus too wet to work," Yellady said. "Work, work, work, thirty acres in cotton an cawn; cawn plowed till de 15th of August, plow, plow, plow, plow hard ground. Nine girls an' one boy workin' from sun to sun." Sometimes parents hired their children out to local planters; in these situations, children lived with their parents and brought home wages. William Scott, for example, was hired out for wages by his mother, and Sarah Harris earned twenty-five cents a week performing chores for Porter Steadman. Sarah remembered that upon receiving her first wages "I just shouted when I got dat 25 cent, and I just run, I couldn't run fas' a nuff to git to my mother to give dat money to her." When John Smith turned sixteen years old he ran away from home, evading his disciplinarian father, who "cut de blood out of me wid a switch." Smith, however, held deep respect for his father's claims to his son's labor, and when Smith became a "free man" at twenty-one, he returned to his father to repay him for his lost wages. "I went back an' paid father for every day I was away from him from de time I ran away at 16 years old till I was twenty-one," Smith recalled. "I owed him dat 'cause I was his until I was free."[17]

Freedmen and employers routinely signed labor contracts that promised black children's labor. These contracts stipulated that at seven years of age children earned their food and clothing. Upon reaching eight years of age children earned an additional five dollars a year. At age thirteen they earned thirty dollars a year, and by the age of twenty some males commanded one hundred dollars a year. Families with many children found these wages essential for subsistence. One man estimated that some large families earned between "500 and 700$." Sometimes employers expected children to work at the same rate as an adult. Harper Williams, a plantation owner, signed a labor contract with Abner Williams, who pledged the labor of two of his and his wife's own children, as well as the labor of three who belonged to another woman, probably a relative who remained under his care. Harper Williams expected all of the field hands who worked to cultivate eight acres. When Abner and his children failed to meet his employer's standards, Harper Williams refused to pay Abner his wages in kind. Abner Williams, who had received one barrel of corn for the forty-three that his family had produced, brought his case to the attention of Freedmen's Bureau agents in the area.[18]

Some former slaveowners tricked parents into labor contracts that pledged their children's labor. Before the war, Mary A. Smith, a South Carolina slaveholder, owned Jacob McCrory, his wife, and their two daughters, Milly and Christina, a pair of fourteen-year-old conjoined twins whom one Freedmen's Bureau agent described as "similar to the celebrated Siamese Twins." Though the girls' parents lived on Smith's plantation in Anson, North Carolina, Smith kept the children with her in South Carolina. Apparently Smith amassed a fortune by "exhibiting" the girls throughout the United States, Europe, and other countries. In June 1865 Smith approached McCrory, falsely informed him that he was not free, and tricked him into contracting his children to her. The contract entitled Smith to "the entire control and management of the persons of the said Twin Children without any let or hindrance from [their parents] during the period of five years." In return, Smith agreed to pay McCrory "¼ the profits."[19]

A few months later, after McCrory learned of his freedom, two Indiana entrepreneurs, Daniel Ladd and Frederick Cartwright, contacted him about the girls. They proposed a more lucrative plan, one that offered several hundred dollars for security of the contract and furthermore allowed McCrory to choose an adult female companion to accompany his daughters from show to show. McCrory signed the contract with Ladd and Cartwright and informed the Freedmen's Bureau of the first contract, which he claimed was fraudulent. The Freedmen's Bureau agent insisted that Smith produce the children at trial in North Carolina, but Smith refused. Instead, she attempted to bribe Freedmen's Bureau agent Captain John C. Barrett "in a private conversation." Though her first bribery attempt failed, her second attempt apparently achieved success, for in December 1865 agent Clinton Cilley revoked an order to restore the twins to their parents.[20]

African American parents such as Jacob McCrory accepted the practices of hiring out children for extra cash or voluntarily apprenticing children to a friend or relative in order to relieve the financial burdens of raising young children. Some African American men and women did not object to voluntary apprenticeship. After all, the system provided economically strapped parents with an opportunity for employing their children. Others had little choice. By apprenticing children, parents who themselves made very low wages reduced the number of children they had to clothe, feed, and educate. Yet parents lost control of their children's welfare and wages when they sought a court-supervised indenture. Martha Hill, of Lumberton, apprenticed her daughter, Mary, and her sons, Aleck and Jerry, because she could not feed or clothe them or provide them with an education. "Maria" bound out her six children, and "Priscilla" bound out her son, Sammy. "Priscilla" hoped to circumvent the law by contracting an indenture that guaranteed her a weekly income. Sammy's indenture required his master to pay five dollars, or one dollar and "a peck of meal a week and 3 lbs of bacon," on the condition that the indenture expired "when either party becomes dissatisfied." Though Sammy's indenture violated legal regulations of apprenticeship, such as income to parents and expiration at volition, it met "Priscilla's" requirements.[21]

Though some parents consented to their children's apprenticeship, many did not. Amos McCollough and Samuel High Smith complained to Freedmen's Bureau Commissioner O. O. Howard when Duplin and Sampson county courts routinely, and without consent from parents, apprenticed African American children. "The colored are in desperate need," they wrote despairingly. "Justice we do not receive here, our children are taken & bound out to the former Masters whether we are willing or not." McCollough and Smith blamed much of the injustice on the county courts. The authorities "take the color children from the parants and bind them out which at the same time the Parantes are not willing for this to be done, but no way to avoide it . . . therefore it is done."[22]

In 1865 North Carolina law allowed courts to apprentice African American children without parental consent if the children had been born out of wedlock and if the parents were not employed "in some honest, industrious occupation." An 1856 state supreme court case had ruled that courts were not required to obtain children's presence in court during the apprenticeship proceedings. At the time the court had acknowledged that it was "usual to have the apprentice present in Court when he is bound out" but continued that "there is no provision in the Act which requires it." Therefore, children, as well as perhaps many or all of their family members, might not learn of their apprenticeship until authorities arrived to take the child to his or her new master.[23]

Some whites argued that these prewar laws and their former status as slaveholders granted white men and women the right to apprentice the children of their former slaves. Two years after the war ended, Mrs. R. C. Pritchard demanded the return of two of her husband's apprentices, who had been "enticed off" by their relatives, on the grounds that the law protected her claims to the children. Even northern states, she argued in a letter to the Freedmen's Bureau, must recognize her rights. "The 'higher law,' which freed the slave in spite of the constitution, must see the moral right of this claim." Mrs. Pritchard claimed that the three children—Esther, aged thirteen, Ben, nine, and Miranda, six—and "their parents, for several generations, belonged to our family & they have been indulged to a fault." At the war's end, Mrs. Pritchard asserted, "no one claimed them, no one offered to take, or asked for them," and the Pritchards had requested court indentures for the children. Thus, she had earned the right to the children's labor. "The war left me with a paralytic husband, 6 children, the oldest only 15 years of age, & a small tract of land," Mrs. Pritchard stated. "Our only workmen, this apprentice [Ben] & our son; a lad. Their work has barely sufficed to support the invalid & younger & very delicate child." Mrs. Pritchard claimed that her former status as a slaveholder preserved her rights to the labor of her former slaves, labor that she desperately needed in postemancipation North Carolina.[24]

Some white men and women justified their claims to their former slave children's labor by alleging that African American parents were incompetent as parents. Daniel Russell, infuriated when he learned that the Freedmen's Bureau had canceled the indentures of some of his apprentices, criticized the agent who had handed down the ruling. The agent, he argued, should not have voided the apprenticeship, because the parents lacked the character to raise their children. "Some individual sets himself up to be a judge and forthwith orders the apprentice to be given up to some lazy negroe," he bitterly complained, "who will raise them up in dirt and filth, that they may be turned loose upon society to become vagrants." Mrs. Pritchard complained that Ben's uncle, who had enticed the boy to leave her plantation, had no rights to the child. "This boy's uncle," Mrs. Pritchard wrote, "is a lawless, bad man." She said that officials should not only disregard the freedman's claims but also take precautions to prevent other freedpeople from claiming their rights as parents at the expense of whites' needs. She couched her protest in the general terms of the extension of blacks' rights. "If the North gives the negro, all of the rights, I fear that the tragedies of St. Domingo will be enacted here."[25]

Just as Mrs. Pritchard and Russell argued that they were entitled to their former slaves' children, Rebecca F. Mottley, of Littleton, North Carolina, refused to cancel the indenture of a ten-year-old boy named Ned Mottley. Widowed by the Civil War, Rebecca Mottley needed Ned's help to raise her small child. When Ned's father, a man named Weaver, demanded that Rebecca Mottley return his son, she refused, claiming that Weaver was not his parent. She asserted that she "was justly entitled to Ned" because his mother, her slave, had died when the boy was small and "I have had all the trouble of raising up this boy since his birth, and I do think it hard, hard indeed that this boy should be taken from me and that by a man that is no more the father of him than I am his mother." With these words Rebecca Mottley summarily dismissed Weaver's claims as the boy's father and asserted her rights as the child's former mistress.[26]

Rebecca Mottley, Mrs. Pritchard, and Daniel Russell, among other white men and women, refused to acknowledge African American fathers' and mothers' claims to their children. Apprenticeships increased not only because of whites' need for labor but also because of assumptions of African American dependency. Laura Edwards argues in *Gendered Strife and Confusion: The Political Culture of Reconstruction* that North Carolina's apprenticeship law denied African American parents their claims to independence. Other historians, Edwards argues, have shown that "ex-masters had their eyes on the labor" of African American children, but "claims on the labor of black children also rested on the assumption that African-American parents did not have legitimate households or legitimate rights to their children." As far as whites were concerned, most African American children belonged in the households of their former masters.[27]

White women, bereft of servants after emancipation, refused to accept African Americans' independence. For these women, race and class determined African Americans' allegedly innate dependency upon whites. White women argued that the slaves, and consequently the freedpeople, were inherently ignorant and dependent upon whites for subsistence. For Catherine Edmonston, freedom was a "terrible cruelty" for former slaves, who were "at their wits ends." She metaphorically compared her former slaves to a boat without a rudder: "Their old moorings are rudely & suddenly cut loose, & they drift without a rudder into the unknown sea of freedom." Her former slaves, she noted, awaited a cruel disappointment, for they no longer could depend upon the care that their innate "state of dependence" had previously guaranteed them. In fact, she argued, blacks could never truly be free; they were wholly dependent upon white paternalism. "They occupy themselves ceaselessly trying their new chains, seeing how little work they can accomplish & yet be fed and endeavoring to be both slave & free at the same moment—a slave on the food, shelter, & clothing question but free where labour is concerned."[28]

As an elite white plantation wife, Eliza DeRosset embraced the opportunity to care for her young servant in a fashion reminiscent of her role as a slaveholding mistress. In the spring of 1866 DeRosset's servant John offered his ten-year-old daughter's services. According to DeRosset, John had begged her to take his daughter "just as tho' she belonged to me." John probably offered his daughter's labor to increase the low wages the DeRosset family paid him. But DeRosset's words suggest that she interpreted his act to mean that she, as the child's former mistress, had full and complete rights to the child. According to Eliza DeRosset, the child no longer belonged to her father, and DeRosset assumed that she would take control of the child and raise her as her servant.[29]

Mrs. J. D. E. Gregory, of South Mills, North Carolina, also assumed that her former slave lacked parental capabilities. In 1867 Gregory thwarted a mother's attempt to retrieve her daughter, Jane Ferribie. Gregory, who said she had raised the child as "her own" and not as a servant, claimed that she had a right to Jane because she possessed the capability to raise her, whereas her mother did not. "The woman has no home herself and no miserable [*sic*] means of support," she asserted. Gregory argued that Jane's mother lacked the character necessary to be a good mother and was unable to raise a child independent of whites, and she used this argument to further her case with the Freedmen's Bureau. "I think she wants the child to hire to support her in idleness," Gregory asserted. "I can give you positive proof that this mother is a lazy worthless women and without a home."[30]

Despite southern whites' efforts to dissolve African American families, parents such as Jane Ferribie's fought hard to restore family relationships that slavery had destroyed. Prior to the Civil War, slave families had constantly faced the threat of sale and separation by their masters. Children sometimes experienced brutal treatment, abuse, and neglect. Slave auctions forever separated some parents from their children. Next to punishment, family separation was one of the most frequent reasons why slaves ran away from plantations; many escapes occurred immediately after a master had sold a spouse, child, or parent. Upon emancipation and the passage of the Thirteenth Amendment some freedmen and freedwomen worked quickly to reunite their families. The task of reunion was not easy. Some family members had not only lost track of their loved ones but also lacked any knowledge of their physical appearance. One woman in search of a daughter taken from her twenty years earlier, at the age of four, was uncertain whether her daughter had changed her name: "Ellen Cummins; least dat *was* her name, w'en dey dun toted her off to Florida." Nonetheless, freedpeople in search of family members left no stone unturned. Husbands and wives eager to legitimize their relationship and their children's births had their marriages legalized for the first time. Marriage at once protected their relationship and preserved the sanctity of their household. Apprenticeship resurrected new fears among freedpeople about family separations.[31]

Labor scarcity and white assumptions of African Americans' dependence, then, motivated whites to apprentice their former slaves' children. When parents resisted the claims of whites, violence sometimes ensued. Samuel S. Ashley, superintendent of schools for the American Missionary Association, worried that violent kidnappings would lead to the reenslavement of freedpeople. "This is a dark hour for the Freedmen," Ashley gloomily predicted. "There is a determination on the part of the whites, to reduce them to a condition, worse, if possible, than slavery." Ashley described whites' treatment of the freedpeople as "brutal." "In Sampson County," he stated, "600 children, some of them 21 years of age, were bound out by the County Court, and then, by an armed, and mounted police force, were torn from their homes, and carried to a forced, and unnecessary apprenticeship." Parents also reported violent kidnappings. Grace Jenkins reported that her former master, Daniel Skipper, of Brunswick County, arrived at her home in September 1865 and "removed by force" her fifteen-year-old son, Henry. When Henry objected, "Skipper told him that he would have to go 'dead or alive.'"[32]

Other whites simply ignored *in loco parentis* responsibilities and neglected or abused their charges. One such person was Reddick Carney, of Washington County, who, one Freedmen's Bureau agent claimed, was "considered 'a desperate character by both black & white.'" Carney, who had shot two African American men and killed one Freedmen's Bureau agent who was sent to arrest him, abused his young apprentice, the son of Starkey Wiggins. Wiggins's son had endured his apprenticeship without any shoes during the winter of 1865–66, even though he had had to walk three miles to retrieve Carney's mail. When Wiggins's son returned to his father, he was "poorly clad," and he explained "that the clothes he had on which were hardly tolerable were only furnished him since Mr. Carney decided to send him to his father."[33]

Letters written by parents and Freedmen's Bureau agents provide vivid descriptions of abuse and neglect, but only a few descriptions written by apprentices tell of the conditions of their indentures. For a deposition in a case against

B. M. Richardson, Daniel Bagley reported the abusive treatment he had received during his apprenticeship. In 1866 Bagley brought charges against his former master. Bagley had worked for Richardson since 1865, performing field work and hauling wood. In 1865 the twenty-year-old had informed his former master, Richardson, that he wanted to be paid for his labor. Richardson had refused, citing that "no boy under twenty one was allowed to draw wages." Bagley had persisted in his complaint. On what had started as a routine day Bagley, who had finished his field work, locked the mules in the stable. Somehow, the mules escaped and wandered into the rice patch. Bagley stated that when Richardson noticed the mules in the rice, "he halloed out to me, and said if I did not get them out of the patch, he would whip me—I told him I could not help them getting out of the stables, as it was impossible to keep them in." Richardson then proceeded to beat Bagley with a stick. When Bagley threatened to report his employer to the Freedmen's Bureau, Richardson tied him up.

> He crossed my hands and tied them behind my back, and carried me into a room. He pulled off my coat, and he made me sit in a chair, where he whipped me with a hoop pole, and then got a double strap about as wide as my two fingers, and whipped me some considerable time with it, asking me if I was going to stay until I was twenty one and behave myself as I ought, I said I did not know I had misbehaved, when the whipping was repeated.

Later, Bagley reported the case to a Freedmen's Bureau agent, who produced the apprenticeship indenture and read it to the freedman. Bagley claimed to have no knowledge of the apprenticeship, and upon hearing that an apprentice must follow the will of his master, Bagley replied to the agent, "I am not an apprentice boy." With these words Bagley refused to accept his status as a bound servant and thereby asserted his independence as a free man. But Richardson, firmly convinced of his role as undisputed master, had never bothered to notify Bagley of the indenture proceedings. Brevet Lieutenant Colonel William H. H. Beadle declared the indenture fraudulent and ordered Richardson to free Bagley. Later that year, Colonel Eliphalet Whittlesey, Beadle's superior, revoked the order. Whittlesey claimed that the Freedmen's Bureau did not have the authority to settle such matters.[34]

One young apprentice, Lilly Pryor, documented feelings of severe depression and contemplation of suicide. In 1865 Pryor's master, seeking refuge from Sherman's advancing troops, had transported Pryor and fifteen other children to Salisbury, North Carolina, for safekeeping until the war's end. The children's parents remained in Virginia while the children served their master as apprentices in North Carolina. Over the next five years all of the children except Pryor escaped to Norfolk, Virginia; Pryor, eighteen, remained behind to serve as a domestic servant. Pryor and her father, both literate, remained in contact with each other through infrequent oral and written communications. In 1870 Pryor penned a rare letter to her father in which she begged him to rescue her. The Baileys, she complained, expressed little sympathy for her loneliness and had informed her that her contract bound her to them until she turned twenty-one. Her master refused to give her up; only military force, he threatened, could remove her from the plantation. Desperate to leave, Pryor asked that her father "do pray get a troop and come after me." She found little hope for any alternative and contemplated suicide if all efforts to return her to Virginia failed. "The White folks says they are determined I shant go unless the Soldiers comes," she lamented. "I Shall go crazy if I dont get to go home soon, I will kill myself soon if I have to Stay here." She urged her father to act quickly and stated simply, "Father I know you can get Soldiers if you want to." Lilly Pryor's letter suggests that other apprentices also might have experienced feelings of despair.[35]

Few children wrote letters testifying to their apprenticeship experiences. Nearly all the letters that appear in the North Carolina Freedmen's Bureau records were penned by parents. Because Lilly Pryor wrote only this one letter to her father, the details of her kidnapping, her siblings' escapes, and her inability to follow them remain unknown. Perhaps her master maintained a watchful eye on Pryor because she alone remained. It is also likely that he knew that he had violated apprenticeship law by removing Pryor from the county (and state) in which she had been apprenticed. Rather than admitting to his mistake, Bailey made a desperate threat intended to force Lilly Pryor into compliance. He probably did not realize that her own desperation would cause her to risk danger by covertly writing her father a letter informing him of her circumstances and whereabouts.

In the first few months after the war's end state and local politicians ignored the cries of apprentices such as Pryor and Bagley. Instead, groups of white men, largely unconcerned by African American protestations of apprenticeship, struggled to seize the reins of power. The Confederacy's defeat left North Carolina's political system in shambles. In 1865 two nascent parties, each with Civil War roots, slowly emerged. In 1862 certain secessionists and some former Whigs broke from the Democratic Party to form the Conservative Party. The

Conservatives, led by Zebulon B. Vance, who had been elected governor in 1862, defended secession, but they despised the centralized government that characterized Confederate President Jefferson Davis's administration. In 1864 the Conservatives ran a gubernatorial campaign that pitted Vance against William W. Holden, a peace candidate, who attracted the votes of Whig planters in eastern counties and poor white Unionists desperate to end Confederate conscription raids in western counties. Vance was reelected, but Holden had attracted a large following. By early 1865 the state's murky political environment had begun to crystallize as it became clear that Holden wanted to end the war and return the state to the Union. Aware of Holden's wartime political record, President Andrew Johnson appointed him provisional governor in the spring of 1865 and directed him to guide North Carolina through the restoration process. Holden complied by calling for a constitutional convention and a new election for governor. In November 1865 Holden lost the governor's chair to Jonathan Worth, a former Unionist who appealed more to the former Whig constituency and less to Holden's poor white followers.[36]

The election that brought victory to Jonathan Worth produced less desirable results for the state's African American population. African Americans met in Wilmington and again in Raleigh to protest their exclusion from the 1865 constitutional convention. The black convention drew up a petition and sent it to Holden, who passed it along to the white convention meeting just a few blocks away. The petition asked for educational assistance for children and the removal of "all the oppressive laws which make unjust discriminations on account of race or color wiped from the statutes of the State." The freedmen's convention also created the North Carolina Equal Rights League. "We don't ask for social equality," the convention proclaimed, "but merely to be recognized as citizens, and entitled to our *political* rights in common with others." The delegates to the white constitutional convention refused to answer the freedmen's convention but requested that Holden appoint a three-member commission to address the freedpeople's rights and refer its recommendations to the General Assembly. In an 1865 speech that requested the creation of the committee, John Pool explained that North Carolina needed a body of laws to provide for ignorant and defenseless freedpeople. "A large class of the population, ignorant and poor," he explained, "has been released from the stringent restraints of its late social and political position, and from its dependence upon the individual obligations of another class for its support, government and protection." Since freedpeople lacked an understanding of their duties and obligations to society, Pool argued, North Carolina required a body of laws to control them.[37]

In compliance with Pool's request, Holden named a three-person committee and appointed Bartholomew F. Moore, another wartime Unionist and former Whig, as chair. In January 1866 Moore's committee submitted its report, which recommended that the General Assembly pass "An Act concerning Negroes, Indians, and persons of color and mixed blood," nine bills that came to be known as North Carolina's Freedmen's Code, or Black Codes. This document included a section on apprenticeship and eight other provisions, which included laws that prohibited blacks from owning or carrying weapons, forbade interracial marriages, and limited blacks' testimony in court. The Black Codes transferred to the state all authority once held by masters over enslaved black men and women. Freedpeople's status as members of civil society was grounded in laws, such as marriage requirements and vagrancy acts, that, first, brought them (like whites) under the eyes of the state and, second, defined them as a second-class citizenry. Moore, who wanted to restore antebellum social hierarchies by placing African Americans on the margins of society and outside state institutions, reiterated Pool's perceptions of African Americans. For example, Moore feared that African American testimonies in courtrooms were unreliable, untruthful, and therefore placed North Carolina whites at great danger. He believed that dishonesty, depravity, and licentiousness proliferated among the state's former slaves. Demagogic whites and blacks would prey upon North Carolina's population of freedpeople. "Already the wicked white man and corrupt dependent negro have banded together in lawless thefts and frauds on industrious and peaceful citizens." Moore demanded that blacks' testimonies be excluded from the courtroom because, he claimed, African Americans' dependent nature made them susceptible to "wicked" men's demands.[38]

The new apprenticeship bill, initially proposed by William A. Jenkins, a planter from Warren County, restricted African American parents' claims to their children. Jenkins hoped to redraw the old antebellum apprenticeship code—a series of statutes for a system once intended to control children of poor widows, single women, and free blacks—to strengthen planters' ability to apprentice the freedpeople's children. The new provision gave former slaveholders preference when courts apprenticed their former slaves. "When they shall be regarded as suitable persons by the court," the bill stated, former masters "shall be entitled to have such apprentices bound to them in preference to other persons." Other sections contained antebellum statutes that the General Assembly had revised slightly to meet the postwar order. One provision required courts to bind out white girls until they turned eighteen, though black girls remained apprenticed until age twenty-one. Another provided that county courts bind out African American children "when the parents with whom such children may live do not habitually employ their time in some honest, industrious occupation." A third carried over the law that required courts to apprentice "free base born children of color." As if to disguise the racial distinctions in the code, legislators added a rather oblique phrase that required courts to bind out black children in the same manner as whites. Jenkins applauded these laws. He argued that "this was a white man's government"; furthermore, he "was unwilling to sanction the inauguration of any new system of legislation which would appease the radical majority of the North." The new modifications of the apprenticeship law simply secured whites' place at the top of the postwar racial hierarchy.[39]

The apprenticeship bill and the other eight provisions passed in the General Assembly, but not without some dispute. In 1865 allegiance to political parties was still fluid, yet distinct interests separated eastern aristocratic planters from whites in the west. Numerous legislators from the state's western counties, which contained significant antebellum nonslaveholder populations, wartime Unionists, and only small minorities of African Americans, voted against both the apprenticeship provision and the Freedmen's Code as a whole. In the Senate, one representative from a western county moved to strike the apprenticeship provision that gave preference to former masters in apprenticing former slave children. The proposed amendment was defeated, twenty-five to fifteen. But the vote breakdown clearly indicates regional division. Seven senators from Piedmont counties, six from western counties, and two from the east voted in favor of repealing the provision. Of those senators who voted against repealing the provision, all but six represented eastern counties, and none came from western counties.[40]

Later, the General Assembly added new acts to the Freedmen's Code. One law imposed harsh penalties upon parents who endeavored to retrieve their children. An April 1866 law for "enticing servants" allowed planters to bring civil action against parents or relatives who removed a contracted laborer from their employ. The law for "enticing servants" also applied to wage laborers. However, the law applied to apprentices as well, and increasing masters' control over apprentices likely offered the legislature another incentive to pass the act. Any man, the law read, who "persuades and encourages another to be faithless to his word" is as "vicious a member of society" as one who willfully violates a contract. One year later, in 1867, the General Assembly added stiff criminal penalties to the "enticing servants act." By 1867 courts could find any parent who removed a child from a master's land guilty of misdemeanor and liable to a maximum fine of one hundred dollars and six months' imprisonment. These laws show that southern whites intended to transform apprenticeship into a system that controlled not only African American children but their parents as well.[41]

The race of apprentices is difficult to discern from postwar records. Antebellum laws had required authorities to record the race of apprentices, but practice grew more muddled in the Reconstruction era as authorities only sporadically documented the racial background of children who were apprenticed. Nonetheless, some counties continued to document race. In addition, jurisdiction requirements help distinguish the numbers of black and white indentures after the war. North Carolina authorities continued to document both black and white apprenticeships, while Freedmen's Bureau agents supervised only black indentures to white masters. Thus it is safe to assume that records from the Freedmen's Bureau indicate black indentures only.

Data drawn from studies by Guion Johnson and Roberta Sue Alexander illustrate that African American apprenticeships increased after the war. In *Ante-Bellum North Carolina* Johnson studied apprenticeship patterns in antebellum Carteret, Pasquotank, Edgecombe, Cumberland, and Orange counties, which she argued were typical of various sections of the state. In these counties Johnson noted the apprenticeships that appeared in county court minutes in three five-year increments, 1801–5, 1831–35, and 1851–55. Years later, Roberta Sue Alexander compared Johnson's antebellum data with postbellum figures compiled by her from the same counties. Alexander noted that four of the five counties registered increases in apprenticeship. Moreover, nearly all apprenticeships in Pasquotank and Edgecombe counties were designated as "negro." Alexander explains that labor availability influenced apprenticeship rates. "The greatest increase in apprenticeships occurred in Edgecombe County where labor was scarce and wages high. In Cumberland, on the other hand, labor was plentiful and wages low, and there the number of apprenticeships decreased."[42]

In 1867 Freedmen's Bureau agents canceled dozens of indentures in several counties to comply with an 1867 court decision, *In the Matter of Harriet Ambrose and Eliza Ambrose.* These cancellations demonstrate the racial inequities of postwar apprenticeship. Some agents canceled all apprenticeships, black and white, that courts and bureau agents had contracted without the parents' consent. For example, in Onslow County agents freed three black children and one white child who had been wrongfully apprenticed in 1865, and they canceled indentures for seventy-one black children and three white children who had been wrongfully apprenticed in 1866. Chowan County agents freed nine "colored" children. Agents in Franklin, Craven, Sampson, Mecklenberg, Duplin, and Carteret counties canceled the apprenticeships of twenty-three children, only one of whom was white.[43]

North Carolina's Freedmen's Bureau records contain only one example of a white parent, a single woman, who sent a letter protesting the illegal apprenticeship of her son. Fanny J. Irving, a Wilkes County woman who had been widowed for thirteen years, complained in August 1866 that "the rebs . . . have took my son from me to Ashe County and bound him out without my lief." Not only had former Confederates kidnapped her son but they had stolen "a hundred worth of property" and destroyed property worth another four hundred dollars. Irving appealed to the Freedmen's Bureau for help, citing her loyalty to the Union forces. In addition, she made a vague reference to a relative who had served in the Union Army. "I want you to no that I am A yankee women and I want you to no that my children is yankee for general Macln is my daughter['s] uncle." Irving claimed that she had secretly provided refuge to "yankee prisoners that got away from the garison." "The rebs is A trying to perish me to death," she pleaded, "and I want my child back from ash county . . . I never had but won lone boy child and it is in ash." Irving's complaint is unique not only because she was a white woman burdened by the illegal apprenticeship of her son but also because she argued that she was a "yankee women" and thus the Freedmen's Bureau should provide her with assistance.[44]

A letter written by Mebrina Wolf, of Bethania, in Forsyth County, suggests that white women more often received charitable support and rarely experienced the forced apprenticeship of their children. In April 1867 Wolf appealed to Governor Jonathan Worth for help with her "sofering Fatherless Children." She claimed that her husband had died in the war and left her "five littel children." Wolf had become desperate. "I have Sold ever thing nearly to by bread for them and I can not by any longer." She even had tried to hire out her children, but "ther is so many olfant [orphaned] children [from the war] that I can not get them put out." She asked Worth for ten bushels of corn to keep her from starving. Rather than suggesting that the county court apprentice her children, Worth complied with her request and sent her ten bushels of corn. Mebrina Wolf's case demonstrates that southern whites, including the governor himself, sought alternatives to apprenticeship for the white children of white women.[45]

Liberal critics strongly criticized the revised apprenticeship laws. The Unionist William W. Holden, who resumed his position as editor of the *Raleigh Standard* after Worth defeated him in the race for governor, complained that the Freedmen's Code "will rather retard than advance the return of the State to the Union." Holden feared that the revised apprenticeship law alone would offend northern states and "keep the State out of the Union." Parents' rights to their children did not concern Holden; rather, he contended that apprenticeship appeared to restore slavery and violate the rights of children. "It is a provision that, in binding out apprentices, the former owner of the Slave shall have the preference." Such a law "may be the better course for the former slave, or it may not; but it will *look* to the Northern mind like a disposition to cling to slavery, by giving the former master an undue advantage; and besides, it deprives the freed colored child of the right of locomotion, and places it in a condition in the eye of the law below the white child."[46]

Freedmen's Bureau agents also protested the Black Codes. Assistant Commissioner Eliphalet Whittlesey, head of North Carolina operations, feared that if the federal government removed its military presence in the state, the General Assembly would enact more laws to reenslave the freedpeople. White North Carolinians, he predicted, would "re-establish slavery just as it was before . . . [or] they would enact laws which would make the blacks virtually slaves." Another agent, Clinton A. Cilley, criticized the code's authors' "wish to impress it thoroughly on the Blacks that they are inferior, and must be so kept by law." Freedmen's Bureau Commissioner O. O. Howard argued that the apprenticeship laws violated the federal government's pending Civil Rights Bill. He pressed his agents in North Carolina to review both the new bill and North Carolina's laws and "to protect these poor people against the iniquitous practice of which you complain."[47]

These protests failed to sway one of North Carolina's most prominent planters. In fact, Thomas P. Devereux, a staunch Conservative and former Democrat, complained that the state's revised apprenticeship code fell far short of its intended purpose. Devereux conjoined whites' fears of labor scarcity and their assumptions of African Americans' inability to raise children independent of whites. In a letter to Governor Jonathan Worth, Devereux questioned the ability of newly freed African American parents to raise their own children. Devereux, a North Carolina planter who claimed the ignominious title of "oldest slaveholder in the State," proposed to his friend a series of reforms to control what he described as the wanton "recklessness" of "the Negro." "The Negro," he argued, lacked the discipline to provide proper nourishment and education necessary to raise African American children, who were the state's future agricultural laborers. Devereux suggested that to head off this problem the state must enact laws requiring parents to provide every child with a stated allowance of food. Those who failed must yield their children to the courts for apprenticeship. "I am within my bounds," the elderly man insisted, "when I say that thousands of negro children, clearly subject to the apprentice laws, are kept by their relatives or pretended friends in a state worse than bondage — they are the 'servants of servants,' and are deprived of that nurture and instruction which a beneficent law has provided for them." It seemed inconceivable to Devereux in 1866 that African Americans could fulfill any duties outside of their roles as "laborers" or "servants." The august responsibility of "parent," he argued, had eluded African Americans, who were naturally dependent upon whites for support. Devereux worried that African American children, unable to receive proper training and sustenance from their parents, wasted their labors as "servants of servants" instead of servants of white men.[48]

Devereux proposed that the state government further expand its power over apprenticeship to ensure government control of the freedpeople. Devereux claimed to be a paternalistic friend to the freedmen. "It is my duty," he proclaimed, "to aid in establishing a system which should advance the material and moral well being of the race, and thereby promote the prosperity of the country." He argued that nature had suited African American men and women to serve the country as laborers. Without this established labor force, "it will take millions of money and years of privation to obtain another race as equal to their performance as the negro." But in order to maintain such a fine work force, southern white men were compelled to establish laws to "protect" blacks, who Devereux believed were unable to care for themselves. "To one who knows him," argued Devereux, "the negro is but an overgrown child, and, like all other children, is extremely sensitive to injustice." Above all, Devereux added, the laws should teach blacks to respect their superiors.[49]

Devereux's plan provided for African Americans' education and training as laborers and for heavy taxes to keep African Americans in their place. But, he argued, nothing served the state as well as apprenticeship. By further revising the law, the state would guarantee a secure and relatively efficient agricultural labor force. His reforms included a law that raised the age limit for indentures to twenty-five and regulated wages according to age. The actions of some county court officials seemed to reflect Devereux's sentiments. Many times officials of

Sampson County had apprenticed children of freedpeople whom they considered incapable of parenting. In March 1866 the court bound out two boys "because their mothers have deserted them and are now living disrespectable [*sic*] lives." The next month the court apprenticed Cherry Jarmon's eight children when a local white testified that she was "incapable of managing or taking care of her children." Days later, officials apprenticed six children aged three to eleven "because their mother is an imbecile and incapable of caring for them."[50]

In an address to the 1866–67 session of North Carolina's General Assembly, Governor Jonathan Worth, who had supported the Freedmen's Code and approved of apprenticeship, applauded Devereux's plan. But unlike Devereux, Worth was a pragmatist. He feared that the discriminatory provisions of the Freedmen's Code violated the Civil Rights Bill and would prevent the state's reentry into the Union. The Civil Rights Bill, proposed in 1865 by the U.S. Congress, required that southern states remove all racial distinctions from the civil code. Worth encouraged the General Assembly to reform the apprenticeship code so as to comply with Congress's demands. He attested that the state should take a more active role in regulating not only black but also white children's lives. "Great numbers of children are growing up without proper training in the habits of steady industry essential to make them moral and useful citizens." Worth identified three areas in which the General Assembly might improve the existing law. The first two provisions permitted greater state control over apprenticeship procedures. First, Worth demanded that the state require systematic procedures for "selecting the masters to whom the tutelage of such children is committed." Second, Worth proposed that the state pass a law requiring each county's grand jury to present to the court a list of names of all orphans and "all children whom you may declare fit subjects of apprenticeship." The third provision addressed Congress's Reconstruction requirements directly. Worth noted that the present version of the Freedmen's Code violated Congress' Civil Rights Bill because the code distinguished between the rights of whites and those of blacks. Therefore, Worth proposed that the General Assembly abolish such distinctions by applying provisions equally to both blacks and whites. The state, he implied, should increase its control not only of African American indentures but of poor white indentures as well.[51]

Worth's message, though it appeared to lift discriminatory practices from the code, nonetheless assumed that certain racial legal distinctions would continue to exist. In his closing remarks to the General Assembly, Worth applauded the authorities' placement of African American children with their former masters.

He noted that the Freedmen's Bureau had claimed jurisdiction over apprenticeship and that Assistant Commissioner Eliphalet Whittlesey wrongly had ordered agents to bind only those children under fourteen whose parents consented to the indenture. Whittlesey's order had undermined southern whites' control over the freedpeople, and Worth renounced it. County courts, he claimed, had reason to apprentice children of former slave parents who lacked the qualifications of parenthood, regardless of the parents' own views on the matter. Such children, he asserted, were better off with their former masters. This expansion of state power, Worth concluded, would impress President Andrew Johnson and General O. O. Howard and would allow North Carolina county courts to remove the Freedmen's Bureau's "arbitrary tribunals" and reestablish authority at the county level. Despite Worth's rhetorical flourishes about civil rights, his apprenticeship plan nonetheless intended to restore former masters' control over the freedpeople's children.[52]

The General Assembly seized upon the governor's mandate to reform apprenticeship in accordance with the Civil Rights Bill. On November 21, 1866, House of Commons member Godwin Cotton Moore, a former Democrat from Hertford County, suggested that the General Assembly form a joint select committee "as relates to the African race and Apprenticeships." The next day, the Senate agreed to the plan, and both houses appointed members (five house representatives and three senators) to the Joint Select Committee on Apprentices and the African Race. The legislature appointed Moore chair of the committee. The committee met for two months, and on January 26, 1867, it presented to the legislature a bill entitled "An Act to Amend the 5th Chapter of the Revised Code, Entitled 'Apprentices.'" In theory this bill removed all racial distinctions from the apprenticeship code and reimposed gender distinctions that required the apprenticeship of North Carolina's children born by poor, single women, both black and white. The bill proposed that the General Assembly replace the wording "also the children of free negroes where the parents, with whom such children may live, do not habitually employ their time in some honest, industrious occupation, and all free base born children of color" after "mother" in the fourteenth line with the wording "and all base born children whose mothers may not have the means or ability to support them" and that the second section of said chapter be amended by striking out the words "if white, but if colored, till twenty-one" after the phrase "eighteen years" in the fourth line.[53]

The revised statute carefully preserved apprenticeship by removing all racial distinctions. But some legislators were not satisfied with the effort to reform the code. H. M. Waugh, a House member from Surry, a county in North Carolina's western Piedmont, complained that the new bill failed to reform actual apprenticeship practices. Waugh proposed an amendment that would require county attorneys to supervise every indenture and according to which "no indenture shall be valid unless attested by [them]." He feared that without proper oversight county courts simply would continue abusive and unfair methods, such as kidnapping, when binding out children. However, Waugh's amendment received little support and failed to pass. The Committee's recommendations seemed to suffice, at least in the eyes of the majority, and no other significant reform measures were proposed.[54]

"An Act to Amend the 5th Chapter of the Revised Code, Entitled 'Apprentices'" thus represented only limited efforts at reform. Apprenticeship continued to remain a threat to unwed and poor widowed mothers. The General Assembly did not vote on the bill until the spring, nor did it endeavor to slow the pace of apprenticeships among the African American population. It would take months of active resistance by both parents and the Freedmen's Bureau and, finally, a North Carolina Supreme Court ruling to alter both law and practice and bring North Carolina statutes into compliance with the federal Civil Rights Act.[55]

Though slavery ended with the Civil War, apprenticeship practices resumed. Southern whites reshaped apprenticeship in an attempt to restore lost labor and to maintain a system that potentially denied African American parents' claims to their children. Former slaveholders drew help from politicians who supported efforts to redefine apprenticeship in terms of race. Though some legislators in western counties disapproved, the apprenticeship provisions in the Freedmen's Code transformed the institution into a system for controlling the freedpeople. The General Assembly proposed statutory changes only under the threat of Congress's passage of the Civil Rights Bill, but the reform efforts were only half-complete. Former slaveholders such as Devereux, who desired an inexpensive work force, fought the changes by perpetuating a view that white southern planters, not African American parents, possessed the independence necessary to raise former slaves' children. Yet southern whites' efforts did not go unchallenged, for African American parents enlisted Freedmen's Bureau agents, men beset by their own ideologies of race and labor, to help them retrieve their children.

CHAPTER THREE

FREE-LABOR IDEOLOGY, APPRENTICESHIP, AND THE FREEDMEN'S BUREAU

Discontinuities in Law and Practice

In the first months after the end of the Civil War southern whites resurrected apprenticeship to reestablish control over freedmen and freedwomen. But southern whites and freedpeople were not the only actors involved with the apprenticeship system during Reconstruction. The struggle between southern whites and African Americans was complicated by the presence of third parties, the Freedmen's Bureau and its agents, who usually administered apprenticeship contracts and disputes between whites and blacks. Freedmen's Bureau agents often perceived the apprenticeship system as distasteful because it violated their principles of free-labor ideology. The resulting tripartite conflict between African American expectations, southern whites' assumptions about race, and the Freedmen's Bureau's ideas about labor organization created overwhelming confusion about apprenticeship law and practice.[1]

Eliphalet Whittlesey's deep faith in free-labor ideology led him to mandate policies that eventually undermined apprenticeship. To him the institution resembled slavery but served as a necessary evil that provided for children whose fathers had failed them. Whittlesey was "very suspicious" of apprenticeship because it "fosters the old ideas of compulsory labor and dependence." Yet he approved it as a "temporary expedient" for certain children as the state endured the transition from slave to wage labor. "By means of the apprenticeship system," he conceded, "comfortable homes have been provided for a large number of orphans and other destitute children." Though Whittlesey distrusted apprenticeship, he approved its use in cases where it appeared that African American parents had failed to provide for their children. Whittlesey's preconceptions about African American parents, especially of fathers, shaped his sentiments. In 1865–66 Whittlesey and other Freedmen's Bureau agents found themselves engaged in an awkward struggle with African American fathers to define black men's roles in the postwar order.[2]

Not long after Whittlesey arrived in North Carolina in the spring of 1865, African American men began asserting their rights as both citizens and fathers. At a New Bern freedmen's convention in September 1865 the former slave Abram H. Galloway demanded his rights as a man and publicly objected to the term *freedmen.* "It is not right," he declared, "we are free men now and should be called 'Freeman.'" Galloway demanded access to education, the vote, and the right to testify against whites in court. Days later, black delegates throughout North Carolina met in Raleigh to protest their exclusion from the state constitutional convention. African American men who convened there demanded not only citizenship but also the right to raise their families free from white interference. The delegates requested education for their children and removal of "oppressive laws which make unjust discrimination on account of race or color." Above all, they demanded their rights as fathers. "We invoke your protection for the sanctity of our family relations," the freedmen resolved. They further requested that the state make "some provision" for the "great number of orphan children and the helpless and the infirm" who otherwise lacked parental protection.[3]

African American men persistently opposed apprenticeship as a violation of their parental rights. In May 1866 Amos McCollough and Samuel High Smith informed O. O. Howard that freedmen in Duplin and Sampson counties suffered from the apprenticeship of their children. "Justice we do not receive here," McCollough and Smith argued, "our children are taken & bound out to the former masters whether we are willing or not . . . take the color children from the parants and bind them out which at the same time the Parantes are not willing for this to be done, but no way to avoide it therefore it is done." W. M. Coleman called apprenticeship "unmanly and ungenerous in the extreme, to say nothing of its injustice." In 1866 delegates to a freedmen's convention defined apprenticeship as an institution in which "our children, the dearest ties of which bind us to domestic life, and which makes the time of home endearing, are ruthlessly taken from us, and bound out without our consent." For these men, preserving African American family life was a prerequisite of freedom.[4]

African American men's family ideals originated in the very rich and complex historical experiences of African American families. In the nineteenth century, African American family patterns were multifarious. No single family model prevailed in slave communities. According to Ann Patton Malone, "The real strength of the slave community was its multiplicity of forms, its tolerance for a variety of families and households, its adaptability, and its acceptance of all types of families and households as functional and contributing." The dominant household type was the simple family, a unit including a "conjugal link" between husband and wife or between parent and child. Married couples without children, married couples with offspring, or single persons with offspring constitute examples of simple families. Other family relationships included brothers and/or sisters living in nonnuclear family households and female-headed households, known as matrifocal families. Even antebellum free blacks faced numerous obstacles to forming cohesive family units. State laws, including apprenticeship, an 1830 prohibition on marriage between free blacks and slaves, and prohibitions on marriage between whites and free blacks created obstacles for families. Patriarchal families, in which men possessed full control over wives and children, represented the norm among whites more often than it did among African Americans. These experiences were behind African American men's demands for control of their children in Reconstruction.[5]

African American men who attended the Raleigh convention in 1865 most likely recognized that freedom alone had not solved the problems of black families. The near-chaotic conditions of early Reconstruction placed additional strains on African American families. Households, at least by southern white standards, did not exist in the refugee camps. The Union army established makeshift and crowded refugee camps to accommodate thousands of slaves who fled the plantations for Union lines. By the war's end the Reverend Horace James, superintendent of negro affairs in North Carolina, had established two main camps that accommodated more than eight thousand refugees on confiscated and abandoned lands around New Bern. The busy and rather crowded nature of these refugee camps forged a way of living that upset conventional gender roles. Few African American men could supervise and support a household of dependents. Most men lived in the camps only until they signed a labor contract that took them into the countryside. Others served as laborers or soldiers for the Union army. Generally, men received wages ample enough to sustain themselves but not their families.[6]

White men's model for the household — a private space where an independent man supervised a household of dependents — never existed in the refugee camps. The camps' residents included mostly women and children who relied upon government rations, not men's wages, for support. The number of women dependent upon government assistance was ten times the number of men who received aid. Freedmen's Bureau agents who encouraged apprenticeships probably did so to reduce the number of children dependent upon the federal government for support. Furthermore, life in the refugee camps discouraged the physical formation of households. Few conventional houses existed in the camps; most shelter was temporary. In New Bern, refugees found shelter in abandoned outhouses, kitchens, and "poorer classes of dwellings." Horace James constructed a thousand "cheap" houses for former slaves, though at least three thousand African Americans lived in "worn and condemned tents." Elsewhere, refugees lived in barracks that housed a hundred people each.[7]

Even those who lived in conventional housing found that the public and private blurred. Military officials patrolled the streets. Their presence was a constant reminder that the Union army controlled residents' lives. For example, inhabitants endured weekly inspections from Freedmen's Bureau agents and sanitation officials. Disease created enormous problems in the camps. Crowded and dirty, camps bred diseases that threatened to wipe out whole populations. When smallpox appeared in New Bern, officials required vaccinations for the refugees. In early 1866 Freedmen's Bureau agents all but panicked at reports that several people had died of cholera in New York. Immediately, Assistant Commissioner Eliphalet Whittlesey issued orders requiring weekly sanitation inspections in homes. He instructed inspectors that all dwelling houses were to be well ventilated, whitewashed, neat, and clean. Unused articles of clothing or bedding were to be burned. Concerned that the refugees might store dirty linens that harbored disease, Whittlesey warned that "nothing should be tolerated about the premises not in-use or useful." Nothing escaped inspectors' attention. Officials searched for vegetable refuse, examined food, and scrutinized outhouses for proper care and cleaning. Even the most private possession, the body, failed to escape inspection. Whittlesey advised that "the people should be strictly cautioned to keep the surface of the body clean by a free use of soap and water, and a frequent change of under clothing." Apparently, the inspectors performed their roles well, for the head surgeon remarked in late October that not one case of cholera had been reported.[8]

Constant surveillance, impermanent housing, and dependency upon the federal government created an environment in the camps that contrasted sharply with patriarchal ideals concerning household relations. The camps, though temporary shelters, were public domains where women interacted daily with employers, military officials, sanitation inspectors, and Freedmen's Bureau agents. Women's dependence upon husbands offered no security in the camps. Women refugees worked as domestics in New Bern during the day and endured the reprovals of sanitation officials at night. These conditions, in conjunction with the threat of apprenticeship, severely curtailed African American men's control over their wives and children.[9]

Another factor that restricted African American men's power over wives and children was changing gender roles. Women engaged both in the workplace and in politics in the black communities of Reconstruction. Approximately one-third of the freedpeople who opened accounts with New Bern's Freedman's Savings and Trust Company were female. Women's deposits consisted mostly of wages and military pensions of deceased husbands and sons. At least 407 African American women opened accounts between 1866 and 1873 in New Bern. Nineteen percent of the women worked as cooks, 17 percent found employment as laundresses, and an additional 15 percent claimed that they were "farming for self." Other women worked as seamstresses, domestics, nurses, hotel and dining-room waiters, and laborers. African American women influenced politics as well as economics. Women attended parades, rallies, and conventions and occasionally voiced their opinions from the crowd. Women demanded their civil rights by lodging complaints in court. Some women actively raised funds for political purposes. A few days before African American men assembled for a freedmen's convention in Raleigh, a crowd of women and "young boys" gathered to discuss fund-raising efforts to defray local delegates' travel expenses to the capital city. Those assembled that night set a goal of eighty dollars. They likely voiced their political opinions as well.[10]

African American male political leaders sometimes welcomed women's public participation and acknowledged women's public activities. In September 1865 black men gathered at a convention in Raleigh and drafted a constitution for the North Carolina Equal Rights League, an organization that encouraged women to join as members. Delegates created the league "to secure, by political and moral means, as far as may be, the repeal of all laws and parts of laws, State and National, that make distinctions on account of color." With headquarters in Raleigh and branches throughout the state, the league accepted as members any person, man or woman, who wanted to join. It further encouraged women's participation by recognizing auxiliary associations in churches, charitable organizations, and schools. At least one black man supported women's voting rights. Abram Galloway, the African American legislator and former slave from New Hanover County who had demanded that he be called a "Freeman," twice proposed legislative bills that would enfranchise women. In 1869 and 1870 he introduced two separate bills to North Carolina's Senate to grant women suffrage. In addition, he pushed for legislation to secure women's rights to property and fight domestic abuse. Galloway's efforts to pursue gender equality were extremely rare among North Carolina legislators. It is possible that his efforts to expand women's public roles reflected a cultural trait rooted in African Americans' diverse family experiences.[11]

African American men who asserted their rights at the Raleigh convention faced multiple challenges to the continuity of their families. Apprenticeship was not the only threat. Refugee camps, Freedmen's Bureau agents' intervention in daily family affairs, and women's assertions of independence all posed challenges to African American men's role as autonomous patriarchs. Yet African American men at the Raleigh convention did not voice their opposition to the camps, the agents, or changing gender roles. Their silence on these matters suggests that they had not come to discuss these issues. They had come to discuss another problem, namely, apprenticeship. The threat of southern whites' kidnapping their children revived their most terrible fears of slavery. It was apprenticeship they must fight.

Despite African American men's claims to parenthood and independence, many people, including prominent Republicans and Freedmen's Bureau agents who claimed to be friends of the freedmen, failed to acknowledge African American men's demands. Instead, they idealized free-labor principles. Albion Tourgée, a northern Republican who served as a judge in Guilford County, concocted a "Plan for the South" based on the premise that African Americans possessed few of the characteristics necessary for independence. Tourgée proposed that the federal government sponsor an organization composed of former soldiers of "the Army of the Cumberland" and "practical Farmers and Mechanics who were willing to move South." Tourgée expected his organization to purchase tracts of land and employ freedmen to work there under the supervision of the members. After one or two years the "most industrious and capable employees" would be able to purchase land at a low interest rate and continue to work under the supervision of the white members. Tourgée's plan included schools and financial institutions designed to teach the freedpeople good business principles.[12]

Though the plan appears benevolent, it nevertheless reflected Tourgée's assumptions about African Americans. Tourgée's plan mimicked a massive apprenticing scheme designed to subordinate freedmen and women of all ages. To be sure, the plan provided freedmen with land and enabled them to "become independent landowners." But it also placed freedmen under the "guardianship" of "earnest practical northern men." Indeed, Tourgée's organization of northern white men represented the archetype of American citizenship. Who would serve as better guardians for the freedpeople, Tourgée reasoned, than "practical" men who fit the Jeffersonian ideal of independence and had defended the Union? Furthermore, Tourgée had designed the plan to teach the freedpeople "the duties and responsibilities of the Citizen." But while Tourgée defined citizenship for northern white men in terms of lofty values, he defined it differently for freedpeople. For freedpeople, *citizenship* meant a lifetime spent laboring for "practical" white men. Not surprisingly, freedmen and women failed to support the plan, and General Howard dismissed it.[13]

Some Freedmen's Bureau agents, including Eliphalet Whittlesey, harbored paternalistic notions about their relations with the freedpeople, and they assumed that slavery had denied African Americans the experience necessary to live independent lives. Whittlesey, a former Connecticut minister, argued that the freedpeople required discipline, education, and lessons in forbearance to match whites. Whittlesey had joined the army in 1862 as a chaplain. Later he had transferred to General Howard's staff, and the two had become confidants. In 1865 Howard assigned Whittlesey the command of the North Carolina bureau headquarters. In addition to his Bureau post, Whittlesey assumed command of a regiment of African American troops. Whittlesey embarked upon his new career with energy and determination. He was committed to the idea that the freedpeople could advance, but only through proper instruction in "civilization" and by overcoming "hardship." Whittlesey argued that inferior freedpeople would overcome suffering and become "the equal of the Anglo-Saxon" through education and hard work.[14]

Whittlesey's preconceived view of African American inferiority prevented him from opposing all apprenticeships. He mandated that under certain circumstances bureau agents could forcibly remove children from their parents. Howard had granted his agents the power to transact and void apprenticeships while the South remained under military occupation. Many county courts often ignored the bureau's authority over apprenticeship matters and indentured children. When agents began to report apprenticeships in the summer of 1865 Whittlesey took immediate action. Unschooled in North Carolina law, which allowed involuntary indentures in certain circumstances, Whittlesey instructed agents not to apprentice children without first obtaining the parents' consent. Whittlesey halfheartedly believed that this was the best policy. "In law parents have a right to their children," Whittlesey conceded. However, he did not believe that this policy should necessarily be followed in every case. "The principle [to defend parents' rights] is an important one, though in exceptional cases, its application may work badly." Unwilling to uphold parents' unilateral claims to their children, Whittlesey for a short time approved of apprenticeship in certain circumstances. In November 1865 he directed the superintendent of the Western District of North Carolina to "bind out children without the mother's consent, if she is clearly unable to support them." Apprenticeship sufficed where children had no parents at all. Orphaned children, he instructed, "who have no parents may be bound out (for the present) with the consent of an officer of the Bureau."[15]

Yet Whittlesey soon began to question his own policy as it contradicted his free-labor principles. At first he firmly upheld freedpeople's rights to free labor and worried that apprenticeship resembled the old slave codes. In January 1866 Whittlesey spoke approvingly of apprenticeship, saying that it provided "comfortable homes . . . for a large number of orphans and other destitute children." In February of that year he issued Circular #1, a document that was more in line with his free-labor principles. Circular #1 prohibited bureau agents from apprenticing any children except orphans and children of parents who had given their consent. "Families should not be deprived of the services of their children," Whittlesey instructed in the document. Above all, agents should prohibit apprenticeships of children aged fourteen or older. Orphans of that age "are capable . . . of supporting themselves as hired laborers," and "if not orphans, they may assist in the support of their parents." Again, Whittlesey cited black children's rights to free labor: "Until some provision is made by county or municipal authorities for the destitute, it does not seem to me right or just that they should assume control over any class who are capable of self support." Despite Whittlesey's efforts to curb the practice, county courts violated federal law that had granted the bureau exclusive jurisdiction over apprenticeship. "The apprenticing of children," he argued, "has given rise to many abuses and hardships. In some instances the Civil Authorities have undertaken to execute articles of Indenture." Unaffected by African American parents' rights, Whittlesey criticized apprenticeship because it violated African American children's rights to their own labor.[16]

The shifting nature of Whittlesey's directives created great consternation and confusion. Circular #1 challenged North Carolina's operative apprenticeship laws. By issuing this circular to his agents, Whittlesey almost completely destroyed the age-old practice of apprenticeship in one fell swoop. Rather than preserve apprenticeship and apply North Carolina's existing laws evenly to whites and blacks as Congress had intended by the Civil Rights Act of 1866, Whittlesey had decided to strike at the heart of the institution. Circular #1 frustrated local agents and infuriated many North Carolina whites. Some agents accepted Whittlesey's command, while others followed legally sanctioned custom and practice. The most revolutionary characteristic of Circular #1 was that it condoned African American resistance to established apprenticeship laws by prohibiting agents from apprenticing children without their parent's consent.[17]

Committed to his labor ideology, Whittlesey criticized apprenticeship and set out to prove to southern whites that employers could teach the freedpeople to work productively as wage laborers. Like other bureau agents throughout the South, Whittlesey encouraged plantation owners and freedpeople to sign labor contracts. Before long he realized that many freedpeople were "distrustful of the honesty of their late masters" and that planters doubted the "willingness of their recently liberated slaves to labor faithfully for wages." It appeared to Whittlesey that "idleness, pauperism, and destitution were universal throughout the State." Thus, he developed a plan that eschewed apprenticeship and would ease the transition into a free-labor economy.[18]

Whittlesey set out to build his own plantation, one that would demonstrate to both whites and blacks that wage labor would succeed. He received encouragement from Howard, who publicly encouraged agents to serve as good business examples within the South. "I encouraged the setting all idlers at work," Howard later explained. "The people cried 'the negroes will not work' therefore I urged the renting and running of plantations to afford practical examples; to encourage joint companies." Within months of his arrival Whittlesey acted on Howard's advice. He established a partnership with two northern friends, Winthrop Tappan and the Reverend Horace James, a bureau agent assigned to the Eastern District of North Carolina. Whittlesey explained to Tappan that he had two reasons for embarking upon the scheme. First, the farms promised profits, and second, Whittlesey hoped to establish a model farm. Tappan explained that this motivation, on which Whittlesey and James "both laid great stress was the example which would thus be set to the Southern planters who were distrustful of their ability to manage free labor and to cultivate their farms under the new order of things." In 1866 the three men leased two plantations, Avon and Yankee Hall, in Pitt County, North Carolina, from a local landowner named William Grimes. Grimes did not pursue a wage-labor operation because he did not believe that he "could command the labor." According to Grimes, few plantation owners had begun preparations for cultivation in 1865, and several landowners he knew had also leased land to "northern men."[19]

Combining their efforts, the three men embarked upon their experiment. While Whittlesey attended to his bureau duties in Raleigh James ran the plantations. James established his residence at Avon and proceeded to hire "colored people — men, women, and boys and girls," who worked under the supervision of whites. The farms employed 150 hands and provided housing for 150 additional children and elderly people. James hired each hand based upon a verbal contract. He arranged for payment on a monthly basis: five dollars to children, seven dollars to women, and twelve to thirteen dollars to men. James provided rations of five pounds of "good solid mess pork per week & a peck of meal for each man and each woman." Children received slightly less pork than their parents. Families could buy additional goods at a company store, which sold calico, butter, cheese, factory-made clothing, tobacco, and snuff but no liquor. Each family received living accommodations, a "sufficient garden for vegetables," livestock pens, and "church privileges"; in addition there were free schools, with students required to pay only for textbooks. Freedpeople who wished to farm on additional plots rented one to four acres, "which they may cultivate for themselves, evenings, nights, and holidays, in corn." James explained that "we have let them have that land in such instances for a rent of one third of what they produce, but the gardens and all the other things are entirely free."[20]

Operations ran smoothly until March 25, 1866, when someone discovered the body of one of the laborers, Alsbury Keel, on the edge of the Tar River downstream from Yankee Hall. Alarmed, two friends of President Andrew Johnson's, Generals John Steedman and James Scott Fullerton, sensed an opportunity to uncover corruption and thereby discredit the Freedmen's Bureau. When Whittlesey failed to pursue the case, Steedman and Fullerton launched an investigation. Keel allegedly had stolen eight pairs of shoes and forty pairs of pants from the company store. As punishment, James had ordered him to dig ditches on one of the plantations. On the first night of his assignment Keel escaped and was later shot. Whittlesey, James, and nine other bureau officials were arrested for crimes related to Keel's murder. As a result, Howard removed Whittlesey from his post and replaced him with General Thomas Ruger, the district military commander. A court-martial that summer found Whittlesey guilty of "conduct to the prejudice of good order and military discipline" and failing "to secure and protect the welfare of the freedmen of N.C." The court ordered that

Whittlesey "be reprimanded by his Commanding Officer," Commissioner Howard. Censured but not discharged, Whittlesey left North Carolina and continued to work for Howard until 1872.[21]

Whittlesey's light punishment reflected the admiration not only of Howard but also of other bureau agents and military officers. In the official court-martial report to the secretary of war, authorities praised Whittlesey's attempts to establish free-labor operations in North Carolina. The report explained that Whittlesey had engaged in the business "to set an example and offer encouragement to the people of the State in the cultivation of their lands, and thus to open an outlet to the flood of pauperizm [*sic*] which was rapidly setting towards the larger towns." Court authorities also approved of Whittlesey's presumptions that the freedpeople required instruction in free-labor ideology in order to rid themselves of their inferiority. "Gen. Whittlesey's efforts," the report explained, "have been attended with success, and it is the unanimous testimony of all these witnesses that the feeling of dependency which had been universal through the State have given place, through the exertions and example of the Accused, to one of confidence in the practicability of free labor both in the cotton and rice plantations of North Carolina." Rather than examine his motivations for wrongdoing by exploring the court's verdicts, the report heralded Whittlesey's attempts to destroy involuntary forms of labor and establish free labor in North Carolina.[22]

Whittlesey's plantation experiment and his orders restricting apprenticeship reflected his faith in free labor and his view that African Americans were inferior. While he was developing his model farm, other bureau agents struggled to make sense of his orders on apprenticeship. For example, Circular #1 required apprenticeship only of orphans and destitute children. The circular defied North Carolina's 1854 apprenticeship statute, which provided for the apprenticeship of illegitimate children and the children of free blacks who were not "honest" or "industrious." The legal contradictions in Whittlesey's apprenticeship policies prompted agents to create new customs that departed from North Carolina's established law.[23]

These differences confused many local agents, who began to interpret the law according to their own beliefs. Some agents decided that the apprenticeship system solved many of the bureau's problems with labor shortages and orphaned and fatherless children, and they eagerly issued apprenticeships. In November 1865 Clinton Cilley informed Whittlesey that "this system of Indentures is an excellent one." Apparently, Cilley had bound out several children who had mothers but no fathers. According to Cilley, this relieved "mother & grand-mother of a vast number of children whom they cannot support." Cilley argued that without responsibilities for their children, women could pursue work out-side of the home. Apprenticeship gave "the children good homes — a trade — & a sum of money to start them in life — & at the same time — let the moth-ers & grandmothers, unencumbered, have freedom to go & find work for them-selves." Cilley neglected to mention that the mothers and grandmothers who gained time to work also ceded all rights as their children's guardians and parents.[24]

Some agents ignored Whittlesey's orders and made up their own rules. One aspect that varied widely was the amount bureau agents required for a security bond. State law set the bond at one thousand dollars, which the master or mis-tress paid as a pledge to keep the child within the county where he or she was bound. Some agents changed the bond requirements to five hundred dollars, others eliminated it altogether, and still others probably pocketed it. In February 1866 William A. Jenkins, a state legislator from Warren County, com-plained that the agent in his county charged as much as $11.50 for indentures, while those in other counties charged only a $1.00. Some agents charged only 50¢, so that even a poor man could afford to indenture a child.[25]

Other incongruities were more substantive. In 1866 the General Assembly amended the law to read that regardless of race, all male apprentices were bound until the age of twenty-one and all female apprentices were bound until age eighteen. Even so, agents bound children for shorter durations, so that the in-denture ended before the child came of age. Some agents bound girls until age twenty-one. In Hertford, Gates, and Bertie counties agents bound out males and females until age twenty-five. Other agents dissolved indentures made before the war. Sometime in late 1865 Whittlesey ordered the release of an apprentice who had been bound as a free black before the war. Joseph S. Cannon, aide-de-camp to Governor Jonathan Worth, immediately wrote a rebuke to the superinten-dent. The indenture was valid, Cannon argued, and Whittlesey had no author-ity over the matter. The governor, Camp asserted, "thinks you have no more power to rescind the Indentures of colored persons born free bound before the war than you have to release a white bound boy from his Indenture."[26]

Despite the governor's objections, some agents interpreted state apprentice-ship law in favor of parents' rights. In September 1866 Richard Mills, a freed-man from Brunswick County, complained to Freedmen's Bureau agent Allan Rutherford that the Brunswick County Court had illegally bound out his son,

Abel, to William Drew. Mills was one of many African American men who sought help from bureau agents such as Rutherford. By reporting apprenticeships, African American men not only asserted their paternal rights but also pressed whites to recognize them as independent citizens. For Mills, the Freedmen's Bureau represented an opportunity to claim rights that North Carolina society previously had reserved for white men. Rutherford recommended that the bureau cancel the indenture. "The Freedman Mills," Rutherford explained, "is a very respectable man who is fully able to support his family and he had no knowledge whatever that the Court was going to take his child from him." Mills appeared to meet the requirements of parenthood. Yet it is not certain that Rutherford would have displayed the same regard for Mills's parental rights had the freedman not proved to be "industrious" and "honest," as North Carolina law required of black fathers.[27]

Nonetheless, Freedmen's Bureau agents apprenticed hundreds of children, and county courts did the same. In March 1866 Samuel S. Ashley, who later became superintendent for North Carolina's public schools, reported that the Sampson County Court had apprenticed "600 children, some of them, 21 years of age" and requested that the Freedmen's Bureau extend its operations there before the situation got worse. It is uncertain whether abuses diminished where the bureau assumed jurisdiction over apprenticeship, for the numbers of indentures remained high. From September to December 1865 agents apprenticed 393 "orphans." By March 1866 they had apprenticed 130 more, and in June Whittlesey informed Howard that the bureau had bound out an additional 165 children.[28]

Some local agents simply defied Circular #1 and apprenticed children without their parents' consent. As with Whittlesey, preconceptions of dependency affected agents' attitudes toward black mothers and fathers. Some agents claimed that black fathers possessed no greater right to their children than black mothers. In fact, the circumstances of slavery led some whites to uphold black mothers' rights more often than those of black fathers. Freedmen's Bureau agent William Fowler argued that during slavery women bore the primary responsibilities for rearing children. "When husband and wife lived on separate plantations and were owned by separate masters," Fowler asserted, "the children went with the mother, who had the entire care and support of them, and the father cannot be regarded as having borne any of the responsibilities or having assumed any of the duties of a parent." Mothers, he concluded, were entitled to their children's labor and their son's military pensions. Fathers, however, had failed to earn these privileges of parenthood. Agent Fowler's assumptions about slavery shaped his belief that former slave mothers, not former slave fathers, deserved custody of their children.[29]

This legacy of slavery haunted black fathers and prevented them from regaining their children. One Greensboro planter was supporting three "nearly helpless women" and their twelve children. The planter applied for apprenticeship of the oldest child, a nineteen-year-old boy, but the boy's father, who lived elsewhere, claimed the boy and desired to "hire him out." Twice the father "inticed" the boy away from home, and twice the local Freedmen's Bureau agent returned him to the plantation. Finally, agent Asa Teal resolved to solve the matter in a letter to his superiors. The planter, he reported, desired to have the boy bound to him until he turned twenty-one. "Now who is the proper person to control this boy," Teal inquired, "the Planter who has raised and supported him or the Father who is barely able to maintain himself?" Whittlesey provided Teal with few clear answers. Though critical of apprenticeship, Whittlesey sometimes found himself unable to escape the quicksand of assumptions that prescribed African American's dependence, and he could not transcend the paradox in which society celebrated paternal rights yet denied those rights to African American men.[30]

Despite the confusion generated by Circular #1, Whittlesey had unintentionally opened a window of opportunity for African American men who otherwise were unable to claim their children under North Carolina apprenticeship law. Freedmen interpreted the new policies to mean that African American fathers possessed full rights to their children. Nat Parker and several other freedmen in Hertford, Gates, and Bertie counties criticized Freedmen's Bureau agent Lieutenant George Hawley for violating bureau regulations and disregarding black men's rights to their children. Parker accused Hawley and another agent, one Mr. Waters, for wrongfully binding out their children. The agents bound some children to their old masters, Parker complained, and "if we talk of going to take them a Way they the masters say that they Will Shote us & if we go to Mr. Harley [*sic*] he Will Not Talk With us But Will Leave us & go to stand with the [secessionists]." Parker appealed to the commissioners to reverse Agent Hawley's wrongs. "Sir We No No outher way to be than to Write to you & we Beleve that you Would Send & see us have our children Back & our Wages that We & them Been at Worke for Ever sence the War closes." He further requested that Howard send other agents to handle the freedmen's cases, "for if We have to stand Jest as We are & no one to Look after us But mr. Harley some of us Will Be Worse of than When We Was Slaves." In fact, Nat Parker remarked bitterly, black men in Hertford, Bertie, and Gates counties had obtained few freedoms and little assistance from the bureau. "We Best Be Slave a Gain," Parker observed. "We freedmen has a Dogs Life."[31]

When Whittlesey asked Hawley to recount his version of events, Hawley claimed that he had only once apprenticed children who had a father. "In *but one* case did I bind out children who had a father & in that case the father is no better than a fool, as I learned from repeatedly seeing the man, & from the statements of all who knew him & the mother an imbecile in very poor health." Hawley argued that the man's children required apprenticeship because although they were not "orphans," they were indeed "destitute." "The four little children," he stated, "were fed & clothed by the lady who formerly owned them." His statement, a sharp contrast to Nat Parker's accusations, at once reveals the extreme tensions that existed between bureau agents and freedmen and demonstrates agents' desire to use involuntary apprenticeship as a transition to free labor.[32]

Hawley readily admitted that he routinely apprenticed children of single women. To him, a planter's interests almost always prevailed over the claims of black mothers. He refused to acknowledge single women's ability to raise children on their own. In the spring of 1866 Hawley questioned several mothers of small children about their means of support, and he reported that most replied "that they thought the 'could get along some way.'" Most of these women, Hawley reported, sought to rent farmland. When Hawley discovered that few owned a horse or a mule, he conjectured that these women "had formed very few plans for the future." Therefore, he apprenticed the children "with a view to the future of these children." The children's education, he argued, would "be better than if they remain with their ignorant mothers, whose principal object appears to be to hire them out for their own profit to avoid laboring themselves."[33]

Though Hawley denied Nat Parker's accusations, Parker nonetheless had lucidly summarized African American men's anxieties about the Freedmen's Bureau. In Parker's view, the agents' purpose, "to Look after us," was clear. By wrongfully apprenticing children, Hawley had failed that goal. Hawley had nullified black men's role as fathers by giving the military control over their children and wives. Parker continued to sharply criticize the military for failing to secure African American fathers' consent to apprentice children. He demanded that Howard send soldiers "to go in Every house & in every village to have our mothers & children set at Liberty." Of course, Howard sent no soldiers to liberate the freedpeople from agent Hawley. To the bureau's credit, Whittlesey's investigation resulted in at least one apprenticeship cancellation. But it was from cases like this one that African Americans such as Nat Parker learned that the Freedmen's Bureau's role in regulating apprenticeship was severely limited by the preconceptions of its agents.[34]

The Freedmen's Bureau's free-labor ideology thus further complicated apprenticeship in the Reconstruction era. Free-labor ideology often shaped agents' knowledge, understanding, and approach to apprenticeship cases. Their sometimes ad hoc treatment of apprenticeship also bewildered African Americans, who faced many odds in their struggle to preserve their families. Yet Freedmen's Bureau officials such as Eliphalet Whittlesey had struck at the heart of apprenticeship by declaring that in most cases children should not be apprenticed without their parents' consent. As a result, the Freedmen's Bureau had opened the door to African American challenges to the institution. In 1867 mothers and fathers, recognizing the bureau's power and its willingness to defend free labor, enlisted its agents as their legal counsel to retrieve their children.

CHAPTER FOUR

RECONSTRUCTING "FREE WOMAN"

African American Mothers and Apprenticeship

A harvest moon revealed two shadows creeping along the road in front of the small frame house. Lucy Ross and her brother, William James, lived there. Both had moved to Rock Spring with Lucy's two children shortly after the fall of Wilmington in 1865. As the gunboats chased Confederate rebels from the parapets of Fort Fisher, the family fled slavery, leaving behind their master, Daniel Russell, in neighboring Brunswick County. More than a year after the war's close, William James and his sister had designed their own meaning of freedom near Wilmington. They were preparing for their first harvest, not a small measure of their independence.[1]

But the two figures on the road that September night meant to threaten the very essence of freedom that brother and sister had produced. They crept to the entrance of William James's home and forced the door. Lucy Ross woke to find two white men brandishing pistols and abducting her daughters, Maria, aged sixteen, and Delia, twelve. Her brother exchanged angry words with the perpetrators, but the men ignored him. One of the two men was the local constable, who arrested James for misconduct. The two men drove off in a wagon with James and the girls, who, still dressed in nightclothes, shrieked for their mother. Lucy Ross, now alone, was struck by a fear that mingled with memories of her enslavement. The man with the constable she recognized as the overseer on her former master's plantation.[2]

The next morning Lucy Ross headed to Wilmington to learn what had become of her daughters. The girls were in jail with several other children who had experienced similar traumas at the hands of Russell's henchmen. James had been released, but the girls remained in jail until word came from the county court that the magistrate had apprenticed them, along with the other children, to their former master. At once angry and horrified, Lucy Ross watched Russell cart away her children, who would now labor in his fields and work in his household. Later that month Lucy Ross reported the crime to the local office of the Bureau of Refugees, Freedmen and Abandoned Lands. Her complaint, registered on September 24, 1866, eventually reached the North Carolina Supreme Court in an influential case, *In the Matter of Harriet Ambrose and Eliza Ambrose.*[3]

Lucy Ross's case reflects some North Carolina African American parents' experiences with apprenticeship during Reconstruction. In 1865 state law had granted former masters preference in the apprenticeship of former slaves' children. Although mothers and fathers both endured the hardships of these losses, women's experiences diverged significantly from men's. North Carolina law presumed that the mother possessed less authority over her children than the father. Freedwomen, suffering from the double burden of race and gender presumptions, occupied a unique legal place in Reconstruction apprenticeship law. Their dual role as women and as former slaves placed them outside the purview of legal institutions such as marriage, bastardy, and apprenticeship laws and created for them an uncertain legal status from 1865 to 1867. Freedwomen fought that status by claiming unlimited rights to their children. Apprenticeship legal cases from 1865 to 1867 reveal that black women challenged two dominant ideologies, one that defined womanhood in terms of white female domesticity and one that reserved the status of independence for white men. Sometimes successfully and sometimes not, they manipulated social custom and legal doctrine to reconstruct the meaning of the phrase *free woman*, defining black women as both women and free and independent citizens. But in rewriting the laws, the Republicans never fully acknowledged mothers' rights to their children. The 1867 *Ambrose* decision (written by a Republican chief justice) and the apprenticeship legislation that followed (passed by a Republican-controlled General Assembly) came to more clearly define the place of black and indeed *all* women. In fact, the legal decision arising from *Ambrose* resulted in a dramatic restructuring of apprenticeship requirements that reflected lawmakers' renewed emphasis on gender, not racial, distinctions.

The uncertainty of former slave women's status rested on the question of womanhood, a term white society reserved for white women. Freedwomen lived in a legal limbo, an ambiguity outside the defined place of free white women. Furthermore, freedwomen found themselves excluded from the dialogue on citizenship in which black men engaged white men. Few North Carolinians consciously considered the ambiguity concealed in the word *freedwoman*, whose racial and class connotations made it very different from *free woman*.

Prior to the Civil War the latter term applied to women born unfettered by involuntary servitude. The term most aptly described the status of white women, who, if married, by law could not own property and remained dependent upon their husbands. The law identified free married women as *feme covert* because their husbands' identities "covered" their own. The term *free woman* also applied to single white women, or *feme sole*, who might own property but could not lawfully maintain custody of children born out of wedlock. Law and custom decreed that free women lacked the rights that came with the status of citizenship conferred upon white men. Hence, white free women were forever dependent upon either male relatives or the county court system, and the proper role for free women was a domestic one. County officials regarded with suspicion free women who strayed from a man's household or did not belong to one.[4]

Despite its connotations of dependency, the status "free woman" offered women limited protections under North Carolina law. Though free married women could not own property, North Carolina law protected a widow's rights to dower, a legal provision that secured a woman's rights to one-third of her deceased husband's property in the form of a life estate. Apprenticeship law prevented free single women from obtaining full custody rights to their children, but bastardy laws enabled women to obtain support from their children's father as long as the mother revealed his name in a sworn deposition. By naming the father, women could obtain financial support and thus avoid apprenticeship as long as the child did not require support from the county. These laws provided free women with some protections while at the same time assuring women's dependency upon men.[5]

The status of freedwoman did not have the same legal implications as the status of free woman. Whereas the term *free woman* implied a romanticized ideal of white women and domesticity, *freedwoman* was a reminder of black women's previous condition of servitude, one that identified them with field labor and menial domestic work. During slavery, race and class defined African American women's roles. Menial domestic work and field labor separated black women from plantation mistresses, who jealously guarded their white supremacist definition of womanhood. Having excluded black women from the definition of womanhood, white society constructed stereotypes, such as the images of Jezebel and Mammy, to explain black women's place in the household. These images associated black women with the notions of sexuality and labor, two concepts that contrasted sharply with whites' notions of womanhood and romanticized domesticity.[6]

North Carolina's Reconstruction elite attributed to the term *freedwoman* similar meanings of domestic work and field labor. Freedwomen in North Carolina lacked many of the protections enjoyed by women born free. Laws of marriage and property had not touched the women while they were slaves. As a result, emancipation brought mixed blessings. The few protections that marriage provided women remained inaccessible to women who were forbidden legal marriage as slaves. In 1865 slave women gained their freedom, which was at once accompanied by propertylessness and the burdens of caring for children who, by the white community's standards, had been born out of wedlock. Though many freedmen and freedwomen married after the war, some women lost contact with their children's fathers, who had been sold away long before. Certain property and bastardy laws, not to mention U.S. Army pension rights, remained out of reach for some freedwomen. White society's laws associated the term *free woman* with notions of womanhood and domesticity; by law the rights and obligations of *free woman* did not apply to freedwomen.[7]

A freedwoman's status most closely resembled the position to which antebellum North Carolina society had once relegated free black women. North Carolina law denied free black women full legal rights as "free women." For example, bastardy law prevented free black women from testifying against white men. In 1849 the North Carolina Supreme Court ruled in *State v. Long* that women "of color within the fourth degree" could not testify against white men in bastardy proceedings. Apprenticeship laws also prevented black women from obtaining full rights as "free women." By 1854 state law had removed the danger of involuntary apprenticeship from women who bore white children, but it nonetheless required courts to indenture "all free base born children of color." Other statutes, such as miscegenation laws, outlawed black women's marriages to white men. And though the state recognized common-law marriages between white men and white women, such voluntary relations between free black women and white men were defined by law as "fornication." These laws effectively prevented free black women who cohabited with white men from claiming dower and inheritance rights upon their partners' death.[8]

Freedwomen thus inherited a unique legal status upon emancipation. Women who had borne children in slavery lacked the few protections bestowed by marriage. The law considered these children illegitimate but then refused them rights under the bastardy laws. Eliza Cook, a freedwoman, realized this when her former master resolved to remove her from his plantation. In slavery Eliza Cook's master, Dr. James H. Cook, had seduced her at the age of sixteen. By 1866 she had borne seven children by him, and her family lived in a shack on his plantation. Sometime after the war Cook married a white woman, who seethed from humiliation at the constant presence of Eliza Cook and her children. In July 1866 Mrs. Cook demanded that Dr. Cook eject Eliza Cook and her family from the plantation. Cook asked the Freedmen's Bureau to supervise the family's eviction. Eliza Cook, he claimed, had paid nothing to occupy his house and had become "insulting and abusive" toward his family. At first Freedmen's Bureau agent A. G. Brady expressed a willingness to comply with Cook, but after hearing Eliza Cook's version of events he reversed his position and ordered Cook to care for his family.[9]

Eliza Cook, apparently hoping to avoid apprenticeship laws and the loss of her children's services, claimed that Cook should support her and all of her children in accordance with North Carolina's bastardy laws. Eliza Cook claimed her rights as a free woman and told Mrs. Cook that "if I had my justice I had as much right here as she had." North Carolina's bastardy laws required every unmarried woman who bore a child to name its father within three years of the child's birth. In order to prevent the child from becoming a county charge, the laws required fathers to support their illegitimate children or face imprisonment. However, the statute of limitations had passed for six of Eliza Cook's seven children. Enslaved during their infancy, Eliza Cook had not testified to their parentage at the time. In short, North Carolina's laws failed to provide for Eliza Cook's case.[10]

Therefore, Eliza Cook claimed that the Civil Rights Act of 1866, which provided that North Carolina's laws applied to all women, regardless of race, entitled her to a free woman's rights under the bastardy laws. Eliza Cook claimed that the Civil Rights Act required the state to provide protection for women who had borne "bastard" children in slavery. She implied that the state must create a new law to provide for her unique situation as a "free woman." Cook offered a compromise. He agreed to support the youngest child, an infant of eighteen months, because Eliza Cook had sworn his parentage within the three-year window provided under the normal laws of bastardy. In return, he required Eliza Cook and her family to leave the plantation. Eliza Cook refused the compromise and, with help from Freedmen's Bureau agents, submitted her case for consideration by the U.S. District Court. However, the court refused to hear the case. It argued that the Civil Rights Act did not apply in Eliza Cook's situation and therefore the case did not fall under the jurisdiction of the U.S. District Court. Cook evicted Eliza Cook and her children, and the family became dependent upon the Freedmen's Bureau for food and shelter.[11]

This case is particularly instructive because it reveals how Eliza Cook attempted to use the language of the federal government to gain her rights as a free woman. North Carolina law had not provided for freedwomen who had borne children by their masters in slavery. Therefore, she reasoned, the Civil Rights Act transferred jurisdiction of her case to the U.S. government. The federal government, however, applied a different interpretation to the act. Judge George Washington Brooks, a federal district court judge for North Carolina, argued that the Civil Rights Act was intended to apply existing state legislation evenly to blacks and whites. Congress had created the Civil Rights Act to ensure that black men and women enjoyed full protection of state laws written for free men and women. In other words, Eliza Cook lost because the court argued that the Civil Rights Act applied only to existing laws established to protect the rights of free women. It was not intended to create new laws that remedied the injustices inflicted upon African American women during slavery.[12]

Because North Carolina authorities did not apply bastardy laws to freedpeople, the law treated children who were former slaves as illegitimate and eligible for apprenticeship. In slavery the law treated African American men, women, and children as property. Marriage laws and the duties and rights that followed did not apply to slaves. Even if it was understood by whites and blacks that a man and woman in slavery lived as "husband and wife," no state law after the war protected parents' claims to their children. In 1866 the North Carolina General Assembly enacted a marriage law as part of the Black Codes to require slave husbands and wives to marry, but even this law did not guarantee the rights of parents who had borne children in slavery. Thus, the threat of apprenticeship loomed over every child that had once been enslaved.[13]

In *Gendered Strife and Confusion: The Political Culture of Reconstruction* Laura Edwards explains that African American men and women hotly contested the apprenticeship of their children. Edwards argues that African American men invoked their rights as household heads before courts and lawmakers. Men who attended an 1866 freedmen's convention argued that apprenticeship was an institution in which "our children, the dearest ties of which bind us to domestic life, and which makes the tie of home endearing, are ruthlessly taken from us, and bound out without our consent." Women also demanded fair treatment. Yet women who defended their rights in court used a political language that differed from that used by men. While men demanded their rights as household heads, women felt entitled to protection from men or the state. Edwards explains that the legal system prevented black and poor women from challenging men's role as household heads. Thus, "poor African American and common white women made their claims to state protection on the basis of their rights as dependent wives and daughters." Edwards reasons that women who invoked their claims to protection "also implicitly accepted the basic outlines of a system that located them within households headed by men."[14]

Yet apprenticeship records indicate that some black women demanded their rights as autonomous single mothers and not as dependent wives. Single freedwomen, who were most vulnerable to losing their children to court-ordered indentures, firmly resisted apprenticeship. These women's claims to their children hinged upon an obscure but significant regulation in apprenticeship law. It was customary, though not required, for courts to provide notice to parents of a child's impending indenture. African American women insistently interpreted this to mean that the law required a mother's consent to indentures. Many women demanded full custody of their children, whose fathers were slaves sold away or former masters who denied paternity. Therefore, women objected to apprenticeship whenever the indenture occurred without their consent. The Freedmen's Bureau records are replete with letters from freedwomen demanding the return of children who had been bound out, they contended, "without my consent." Grace Jenkins witnessed Daniel Skipper dragging her son, Henry, out of the fields where he worked. Indeed, the indenture was unjust because it was made without parental notification. Grace Jenkins, however, did not use that argument for redress. Instead she claimed that she had never given her consent. Other freedwomen reported similar offenses. Elsy Baker objected to the indenture of her six-year-old son, Frank Williams, who was kidnapped in December 1866, and Betsey Jones claimed that Mrs. E. Jones held both her daughter, Hester, and her son, Sam, without her consent.[15]

In protesting children's apprenticeships, African American mothers constructed a definition of womanhood that diverged from the standards held by white society. In redefining womanhood, African American women drew upon the historical experiences of women in slavery. In slavery women had constructed a definition of womanhood that contrasted sharply with white men's and women's definition of womanhood in terms of whiteness and domesticity. For southern whites, domestic work, and not work outside the home, characterized white women's status as "ladies." Therefore, female slaves' work in the fields was characterized as unladylike. Black women's response was to forge a unique form of womanhood in slavery, a matrifocal one in which bearing and rearing children were highly valued activities.[16]

Historians have shown that after the Civil War black women continued to provide new meanings for womanhood. Black women not only challenged ideologies attributing femaleness to white women but also rejected assumptions within their own communities that enabled black men to represent the family in the public sphere and thereby relegated black women to the domestic arena. In the face of white planter resistance, freedwomen in Reconstruction South Carolina defended their own meanings of freedom. Women contracted their own labor, contributed to low-country labor conflicts, and struggled against white employers who attempted to control them as domestic servants. Likewise, freedwomen in Richmond shaped a political culture that incorporated black womanhood in public forums. African American women participated in the political process by attending parades, rallies, mass meetings, and political conventions. Their participation signaled that they envisioned a political worldview built upon the collective autonomy of men and women, and not the "possessive individualism" of liberal democracy.[17]

During slavery and Reconstruction, then, African American women actively critiqued southern white women's narrow definition of womanhood, one bound by the cult of domesticity and whiteness, and crafted a more inclusive definition. As field laborers and domestic workers, black women broadened the meaning of womanhood to include not only white women who adhered to the cult of domesticity but also black women who labored in the fields and at domestic work in other people's homes. This new definition of womanhood encouraged some measure of political participation as well. Thus, African American women created a form of womanhood that embraced their own work and political culture. Apprenticeship and bastardy cases also indicate that black women demanded the legal protections granted to white women. Eliza Cook demanded her rights under the bastardy law, and Elsy Baker, Lucy Ross, and other women challenged court indentures of their children. Their petitions implied that the state must apply the rights of motherhood, however limited, equally to black and white women.

Apprenticeship records suggest that black women also challenged the very foundation of white men's political philosophy of republicanism. Betsey Newsom, a North Carolina freedwoman, used the court system to assert her independence as an African American woman. Newsom, a single woman and former slave who lived in Davidson County, protested her son's indenture because it occurred without her consent. Bureau agent Colonel C. A. Cilley had contracted the apprenticeship of then fourteen-year-old Levi Newsom to his former master. At the time, Betsey and Levi Newsom, who had contracted to work for shares on the plantation of another white man, T. H. Daniel, were completely unaware of the indenture. They learned of it only when Allen Newsom's sons arrived at Betsey Newsom's door, drew their pistols, and forced Levi to leave with them. Allen G. Newsom argued that Levi's father, who lived elsewhere, had consented to the indenture and that therefore the indenture was legal. In early 1867 Betsey Newsom petitioned the Freedmen's Bureau for the release of her son. Freedmen's Bureau agents upheld Betsey Newsom's claim to her child on the grounds that she had not given her consent and that Levi, who was illegitimate, by law had no father. The father, argued agent Jacob F. Chur, "has no consent to give or right to confer."[18]

The notion of consent is steeped in meaning that ties apprenticeship to the larger political ideals of the nineteenth century. According to prominent feminist political theorists, the term *consent* served as the cornerstone of nineteenth-century republican political philosophy. In a republic, free, independent, and intelligent men gave their consent (at the ballot box) to be governed. This consent was a rational one, and only independent citizens possessed the rational capability of providing thoughtful consent. All others, who lacked this rational capability, were denied the right to vote and relegated to the household as dependents.[19]

A freedwoman who rejected the legality of indentures that a court issued without first seeking her consent made a political statement about her ability to think rationally as a citizen. In her complaint to the Freedmen's Bureau, Betsey Newsom claimed that "as a freewoman of the United State & the State of North Carolina" she possessed the common right to the control and service of her own children unless that right was forfeited by some act of her own. Not only had Betsey Newsom cast off the term *freedwoman* in favor of the term *free woman* but she had fundamentally challenged the republican political ideology of the nineteenth century, an ideology that had denied her rights as a parent.[20]

The depositions of Newsom and others provide the historian with a fundamental problem. Like the Works Progress Administration slave narratives and other sources from slavery and Reconstruction, the depositions collected by the Freedmen's Bureau are flawed to the degree that they were written down by someone other than the subject at hand. Historians often have to search for the meaning buried beneath these sources. But ultimately, the central meaning of Betsey Newsom's deposition is valid. Regardless of the text written by the agent who took her deposition, Betsey Newsom refused to submit to political conventions that denied her right as an independent woman and parent. By appearing before the Freedmen's Bureau to contest her child's indenture, she demanded her right to consent in a political system that otherwise denied her this right.

Lucy Ross protested the apprenticeship of her daughters to her former master, Daniel Lindsay Russell Sr. When Ross appeared in the Freedmen's Bureau office, she must have exhibited uncommon courage in challenging one of the most powerful men in Brunswick County. In 1860 Russell owned more than twenty-five thousand acres of land, two hundred slaves, and the second largest turpentine farm in the Cape Fear region. Russell had served as justice of the peace and chairman of the Brunswick County Court of Pleas and Quarter Sessions, holding the latter post for twenty years. As justice of the peace Russell had regularly approved apprenticeships of orphans and of the children of free blacks and single women. Apprenticeship, though it did not replace the wage labor of adults, at least augmented adult labor by providing a cheap and steady source of young workers for planters' fields and turpentine farms. As court-appointed guardians, planters became the children's "masters." The court required masters to feed, clothe, and provide shelter to the children. Many planters requested apprenticeships through Russell's courtroom. In 1866 Russell had apprenticed more than fifty Brunswick County children to local planters, artisans, and farmers. For local planters, apprenticeship offered an opportunity to resolve labor shortages in the Cape Fear region.[21]

Perhaps Russell's experience as justice of the peace had persuaded him that he was above the law. Without regard for the regulations governing apprenticeship, Russell traversed three counties, Robeson, Brunswick, and New Hanover, kidnapping his former slaves' children. Parents who left Brunswick County after the war to escape Russell's probing tentacles learned of the apprenticeships only when Russell and his plantation manager, Mr. Taylor, arrived on their doorstep and demanded their children. Russell incarcerated the children in the local jail until the legal transactions were complete. Then he carried the children to his plantation in Brunswick County. The New Hanover County Court apprenticed five children to Russell. The Robeson County Court apprenticed fourteen children, and a colleague appointed Russell the guardian of a young girl in Brunswick County. In all, county courts apprenticed twenty children to Russell in 1866.[22]

Like many southern whites in 1865, Russell did not endorse African Americans' rights as parents or their claims to independence. In Russell's view, African American men and women would remain forever dependent upon whites. By apprenticing former slaves' children, whites relieved black parents of the burden of caring for their children. When the Freedmen's Bureau challenged Russell's apprenticeships in September 1866, Russell invoked his loyalist background as justification for his actions. "I was as much opposed to Secession as any man living or dead," he declared. It was the Freedmen's Bureau, Russell argued, and not Russell himself, who had acted irrationally in the situation. The Freedmen's Bureau lacked the authority and experience to decide apprenticeship matters. By signing indentures, Russell pledged to care and provide for his apprentices. He bristled over the reality that the Freedmen's Bureau agents possessed the power that he had once claimed as justice of the peace to contract, regulate, and annul indentures. "Humbugery it is that agents of the freedmans Bureau should pretend to apprentice orphan children," Russell fumed, "some individual sets himself up to be a judge and forthwith orders the apprentice to be given up to some lazy negroe who will raise them up in dirt and filth, that they may be turned loose upon society to become vagrants."[23]

Apprenticeship seemed only natural to Russell, who linked apprenticeship issues to larger nineteenth-century notions of citizenship. North Carolina law allowed only "citizens" to apprentice children. Citizenship determined who possessed the qualities of independence. "Dependent" individuals lacked the powers that the state conferred on citizens. Only individuals who were independent—a status that usually reflected property ownership and suffrage—possessed the ability to make rational decisions free from the influence of others. Nineteenth-century North Carolina society reserved independence for white men. Thus, only white men received full citizenship privileges, which included the right to vote and the right to control one's dependents. County courts could not violate the sanctity of white men's household relations, but courts did have the power to take children from the homes of dependent groups—freedmen, freedwomen, and white women.[24]

Parents disagreed, and they challenged the indentures. African Americans argued that both fathers and mothers possessed the independence necessary to raise their children. In doing so, freedmen and freedwomen not only questioned apprenticeship law but also attacked the very foundation of nineteenth-century citizenship ideals. In September 1866 Lucy Ross vigorously protested when Russell kidnapped her daughters, Maria and Delia, and had them apprenticed to him. Ross argued that Russell had treated her children like slaves by throwing them into jail. These were respectable young women who "can earn good wages for themselves." Ross asserted her own claims to independence and demanded that the court release the children immediately. "I am able and willing to support my children," she argued. Ross declared that the courts had granted the indentures unfairly, and she pleaded with the Freedmen's Bureau for assistance. "I pray you," she pleaded, "to assist me to get my children as I have no other hope as Mr. Russell is Chareman of the Court and no justice can be had here."[25]

Male family members and friends bolstered Ross's claims to her children by testifying in her behalf. In a deposition to the Freedmen's Bureau, William James stated that his sister "was fully able to support and provide" for her children. James argued that the children were his sister's responsibility and not his. He therefore absolved himself of any obligations as the head of the household. Another brother, James Ross, seconded William James's declaration. Finally, Charles Aubriden, a neighbor who lived three miles from James and the Ross family, also testified. Ross, Aubriden stated, "is freely able to support her children, having made a good crop during the past season." All three men acknowledged that the Ross indentures were unjust, and they supported Lucy Ross's claims to her children. Here, African American men acknowledged women's abilities to head a family.[26]

James Ross, William James, and Charles Aubriden thus accepted women's relative independence. While southern white men sharply restricted women's rights to property, children, and participation in public, some African American men strongly encouraged a relative measure of independence for women. These three men clearly agreed that Lucy Ross deserved the right to retain custody of her children.

The Freedmen's Bureau also decided to support Lucy Ross. The Freedmen's Bureau agent Allan Rutherford agreed that Russell had violated Ross's rights to her children, and he launched an investigation. Rutherford referred the case to Assistant Commissioner John C. Robinson, who in late 1866 had succeeded General Thomas Ruger and Eliphalet Whittlesey. Unlike Whittlesey, who had distrusted apprenticeship because of its resemblance to slave labor, Robinson detested the practice because it violated the sanctity of family relations. When Robinson arrived on the scene in the fall of 1866, he pledged to eradicate apprenticeship: "The worst feature of slavery was the forcible separation of families, and by Gods help I will prevent its reestablishment within the limits of my command." When Commissioner O. O. Howard instructed Robinson to supervise and regulate apprenticeships according to the pending Civil Rights Bill, Robinson sought to comply. The courts, Howard warned him, "must make no distinction on account of race or color."[27]

Fortunately for Ross and other African American parents, the political climate in North Carolina began a slow shift toward Howard's convictions. The Republican Party had made its debut in the state. In 1867 former governor William W. Holden joined forces with Unionists, northern Republicans, some of whom were Freedmen's Bureau agents, and leaders from North Carolina's African American population, forming a potent adversary for North Carolina's Conservative Party. In March 1867 the Republican Party held its first convention in North Carolina. With Holden at the helm, the state Republican Party pledged to uphold Congress's Reconstruction Acts of 1867, a series of laws that divided the South into five military districts and outlined a strict process for each state's readmission to the Union. The Reconstruction Acts required that each state hold a constitutional convention, guarantee African American men the right to vote, and ratify the Fourteenth Amendment. Once voters had accepted the new state constitution, the state government could apply to Congress for readmission to the Union. The Republican Party's presence in North Carolina created an environment in which parents such as Lucy Ross could seek justice and regain custody of their children.[28]

Freedmen's Bureau agents, intent upon erasing racial distinctions in apprenticeship law and practice, cited the Civil Rights Act in letters and petitions drawn up in parents' behalf. Agent John C. Robinson referred to the Civil Rights Act when he instructed Agent Rutherford to void the Ross indentures. To justify this action, Robinson mentioned an unwritten North Carolina custom that courts could not bind white children who had reached the age of fourteen without their parents' consent "for the reason that having arrived at that age they can help support their parents, or if orphans can labor for their own support." The Civil Rights Act, he rationalized, applied this custom to indentures of children of both races. "No child whose parents are able and willing to support it can be bound without the consent of the parents." In one fell swoop Robinson struck at the heart of apprenticeship law and endorsed Lucy Ross's claims as a parent. Rutherford followed Robinson's orders and canceled the indentures, but Russell refused to return the children. He argued that the Freedmen's Bureau had no authority in the matter.[29]

Lucy Ross and Robinson persisted. With the federal government's assistance, Ross and other aggrieved parents took the case to the Robeson County

Court. Lawyers representing the parents and the Freedmen's Bureau carefully examined the case for a strategy. Robinson hoped that a court victory at the local level would not only void the Ross indentures but annul all apprenticeships that Russell had obtained. But the Ross case presented a problem that fundamentally undermined the bureau's case. Ross was an unmarried woman, and regardless of testimony in her behalf, the bureau realized that it could not present her case to the courts and expect to win. State law allowed county courts to apprentice the children of single mothers, black or white, without contest. According to white legislators, a woman who lived without a male provider lacked the independence necessary to head a household. The 1854 North Carolina Revised Code had outlined several specific instances when courts could apprentice children of single women. Apprenticeship applied to children "not living with fathers," children without fathers who stood to inherit property from their mothers, and all free black children born out of wedlock. Lucy Ross's case fell into this last category. The bureau decided against challenging this aspect of the North Carolina Code on apprenticeship. Even though Lucy Ross had found three male family members and friends to testify in her behalf, her case remained weak.[30]

Instead, bureau lawyers challenged another provision in the code. Antebellum law had allowed courts to apprentice legitimate children from free black households in which the parents were "not industrious." In Reconstruction, apprenticeship violated not only unmarried women's rights as parents but also claims made by African American men. Freedmen's Bureau lawyers were afraid to pin their hopes on an unmarried African American woman, but they thought that a case centered around the civil rights of an African American man might succeed. Thus, they chose to focus the case upon the plight of Wiley Ambrose. By choosing Ambrose as the plaintiff, Freedmen's Bureau lawyers challenged a law that prohibited African American men from claiming their rights as citizens and parents. They left in place a law that relegated women to the status of dependents.[31]

Wiley Ambrose and his wife, Hepsey Saunders, had fought Russell's attempts to apprentice their three children since mid-1865. Hepsey Saunders had borne the three children in slavery by different fathers, and the family had served Russell as slaves. Upon emancipation, Hepsey had married Wiley Ambrose, who assumed responsibilities as the children's stepfather. In December 1865 Russell obtained apprenticeships of the three children, Harriet, Eliza, and John Allen. In June 1866 Saunders entered Russell's premises by order of the Freedmen's

Bureau and retrieved her children. But Russell persisted. In September 1866 he had the court apprentice the children again. In December 1866 Saunders again returned to the plantation, this time without an order to retrieve the children, and removed them from the premises. Russell, who claimed legal guardianship, threatened to have both Wiley Ambrose and Hepsey Saunders imprisoned for harboring their own children.[32]

Freedmen's Bureau Commissioner Howard encouraged agents in North Carolina to pursue justice in accordance with the Civil Rights Act. The federal government, he claimed, would not endorse such overt acts of discrimination. Howard informed Robinson that apprenticing freedchildren without the parents' consent violated the Civil Rights Act, and he encouraged Robinson to pursue the case. Howard showed no patience with Conservatives, who claimed that the written law did not discriminate against African Americans. "Even if the state law makes no distinction on account of race or color," he declared, "the practice or custom does." Howard hoped that a victory over involuntary apprenticeship laws would set the standards of justice and promise relief for freedpeople in other civil-rights matters. "Get the best legal advice you can in the country," he suggested. "You will be sustained in securing justice."[33]

Whereas Howard supported the parents, the state supported Russell. Governor Jonathan Worth denied that this case represented a gross example of discrimination against African American parents. He conceded that Russell may have acted with "cruel oppression" but said that such action "does not prove that the laws are unjust or discriminating against freedmen." Worth assured Robinson that the General Assembly intended to address racial discrimination in the Freedmen's Code, legislation which the Freedmen's Bureau later attacked for violating the freedpeople's civil rights. He inquired whether the Freedmen's Bureau meant to use this case as an example to challenge all state apprenticeship laws. "If this be your design," he asserted, "then I respectfully request to know what is to become of destitute orphans—illegitimate children and those abandoned by their parents, or whose parents do not habitually employ their children in some honest, industrious occupation?" Worth concurred with Russell's opinion that freedmen and freedwomen, such as Wiley Ambrose and Lucy Ross, lacked the unquestioned claims as independent parents that white male citizens possessed. Judge Gilliam, of Robeson County, apparently agreed. In the fall of 1866 he refused to decide the Ambrose case, "giving as his reason for not deciding the case," one agent reported, "his not having time to examine the laws Passed by Congress in regard to Freedmen and persons of color." Russell, certain that the Supreme Court would rule his way, dared the bureau to take the matter to a higher level.[34]

In January 1867 the case *In the Matter of Harriet Ambrose and Eliza Ambrose* appeared before the North Carolina Supreme Court. The Freedmen's Bureau lawyers, "Mr. Person" and "Mr. French," argued that the court should void the indentures on two grounds. First, the court had no power to apprentice children from legitimate households. The Ambrose children, born in slavery, were not "free base-born children of color," the lawyers argued. Antebellum North Carolina law had defined slaves as property, not as bastards. "Great 'inconvenience' would arise," the bureau lawyers argued, "from holding that the Ordinance of Emancipation . . . has the effect of turning these persons into free base-born children of color." Strictly speaking, neither antebellum nor postbellum law had classified the Ambrose children as illegitimate. As slaves the Ambrose children had fallen outside the purview of laws restricting the rights of bastard children. As freedpeople the children fell under the protection of their stepfather, Wiley Ambrose. But the lawyers diluted Ambrose's own claims to independence by avoiding a firm commitment to African American men's rights. Instead, they stated that to violate his rights would create great "inconvenience."[35]

While the first argument focused on the question of the children's legitimacy, the second focused on their rights as citizens. The courts, the lawyers claimed, had failed to notify the parents and the children of the apprenticeship proceedings. Though apprenticeship law did not require courts to notify parties of the proceedings, Person and French pointed to certain rules, such as *habeas corpus*, that applied universally to proceedings of a judicial nature. They argued that *habeas corpus* privileges (a protection in article 1, section 9, of the U.S. Constitution) required that the children be brought to court and notified of the proceedings against them. "It is a clear dictate of justice," they argued, "that no man shall be deprived of his rights of person or property, without the privilege of being heard." The lawyers thus argued that the law required courts to acknowledge citizens' "universal" rights by providing notice to the parents and children. By contrast, Freedmen's Bureau agents Rutherford and Robinson demanded that courts first obtain the parents' consent. Such conflicting interpretations of the law later had significant consequences in the wake of *Ambrose*.[36]

The attorneys submitted these arguments in briefs that landed square in the lap of Chief Justice Edwin Godwin Reade. At first glance Reade's political résumé suggests that he was a man likely to protect African American parents' rights. However, Reade joined the Republican Party in 1867 not in defense of

African American rights but as a former Unionist who had once lived near the bottom rung of North Carolina's social ladder. Reade was born and raised in a yeoman farmer's household in the North Carolina Piedmont. He acquired an education at home, read law on his own, and was admitted to the bar in 1835. By 1860 he had joined the ranks of North Carolina's elite by managing not only a successful practice but a small plantation as well. His property and his nineteen slaves were valued at fifty thousand dollars on the eve of the Civil War. During the war Reade gained a reputation as a strong Unionist and supported Abraham Lincoln, a man who also had yeoman beginnings. After North Carolina seceded, Governor Zebulon Vance appointed Reade to serve the remaining months of a Confederate senator's term. Reade agreed and spent his several months in the Senate safeguarding North Carolina against what he considered to be Confederate encroachments. In 1865 Reade presided over the state's first constitutional convention. Later that year he was elected to the state supreme court, and by 1867 he had proclaimed himself a Republican.[37]

Justice Reade agreed with the attorneys' second argument, and the supreme court canceled the indentures. In the court's written opinion Reade ignored the parents' claims and argued instead that the law entitled the children to certain rights. "It is well settled," he argued, "that judgment without service of process is void." The law entitled individuals, regardless of race, to notification of proceedings. "It is a clear dictate of justice," Reade asserted, "that no man shall be deprived of his rights of person or property, without the privilege of being heard." Reade asserted that the court retained the power to intercede in freedmen's and freedwomen's domestic relations and to ensure that children obtained proper oversight from their parents and friends. The war had had many casualties, he claimed, and the responsibilities and duties of the county courts must increase in proportion. Therefore, delicate matters such as apprenticeship required that all parties appear before the court. After a full presentation of the "facts," justices could make informed decisions.[38]

According to Laura F. Edwards, Reade avoided the argument that recognized fathers' rights. Perhaps Reade harbored an unequivocal view of African American men's claims to citizenship, but he did not voice his opinion in *Ambrose*. Ambrose's attorneys had argued that "children of slaves, under our former laws, were not 'bastards.'" The Marriage Act of 1866 had retroactively legalized the children's parents' union in slavery and secured men's rights as fathers. Furthermore, the "ordinance of emancipation," they argued, "only made them *free*, not free-base-born." In other words, the *Ambrose* lawyers had argued that Wiley

Ambrose's parental rights were inviolate. But Reade argued that any question regarding the parents' status was irrelevant. "It is not necessary," Reade concluded, "and therefore it would be improper, for us to enter into the consideration of these questions, because whether they belong to one class or another, they were entitled to notice before they could be bound out, and as they had no notice and were not present, the binding was void, and therefore they are entitled to their discharge and to go whithersoever they will." Reade, avoiding the issue of Ambrose's rights, argued that the children were entitled to notice and should be present at the indentures. The court had failed to notify the children, and that error alone annulled the indentures.[39]

Nonetheless, Reade had voided the apprenticeships, and his actions had unintended consequences. Freedmen's Bureau agents perceived the case as a major victory in their efforts to secure the freedpeople's rights. In a letter to Allen Rutherford, F. D. Sewell predicted that the case would void all indentures made without the parents' consent. It "will have the effect," he remarked, "to annul all of the indentures of apprenticeship in this State where colored children have been bound out contrary to the will of their parents." Sewell was right. Though Reade's opinion only voided indentures made without proper notice, Freedmen's Bureau agents across the state interpreted the opinion to mean that courts could not apprentice without the parents' consent. Two weeks after the state supreme court released its decision, Acting Assistant Commissioner J. V. Bomford issued Circular #5, which instructed Freedmen's Bureau agents to cancel indentures made without proper notice to the parents. Bomford anticipated that the court's decision would effectively end the practice of involuntary apprenticeship. "The decision," he declared, "will operate to annul all cases of apprenticeship in the State, where the children have been bound out, against the will of their parents."[40]

In the Cape Fear region, some agents followed the directive of Circular #5 and interpreted Reade's decision in the broadest sense possible. Agents canceled indentures not only in cases where courts had failed to notify parents but also in many cases where parents had refused to consent to the indentures. In July 1867 Second Lieutenant John M. Foote reported that he had attended and reviewed Tyrrell County Court proceedings to be sure that apprenticing practices complied with the decision in "Ambrose vs. Russell." According to Foote, courts had proved their conformity to the law by securing the parents' consent. Sometimes agents' interpretations of the law remained ambiguous. Agents released nearly six dozen children from apprenticeships in Onslow County "in accordance with the recent decision of the Supreme Court of North Carolina in the Case of Ambrose v. Russel." Nonetheless, it is clear that by the spring of 1867 General O. O. Howard's distaste for the practice had effectively trickled down into the thinking of some local agents in North Carolina.[41]

Not all agents interpreted the case in such favorable ways. Contrasting legal interpretations created conflict among African American parents, county courts, and Freedmen's Bureau agents. In June 1867 African American Unionists discussed apprenticeship at a meeting in Randolph County. Agent W. R. Frazer had apprenticed many children in the county. Black Unionists protested vigorously by signing a petition to express their "greate dissatisfaction." They said that Frazer had bound the children "unlawfully as we think and without our consent," and the men assembled demanded that Assistant Commissioner General Nelson A. Miles void the indentures. Thirty-eight men signed the petition, which had some effect: not long after the men submitted the petition, Frazer resigned.[42]

As a direct result of *Ambrose* the General Assembly enacted legislative alterations—changes of vast gendered significance—to apprenticeship law. Not long after Reade delivered his opinion, Freedmen's Bureau agent F. D. Sewell recommended to Governor Jonathan Worth that the General Assembly amend the apprenticeship chapter in the Revised Code to reflect the mood of the Civil Rights Act. The General Assembly had proposed such a bill in the fall of 1866 and enacted it after Reade rendered his decision. In 1867 the General Assembly removed racial distinctions from the apprenticeship code. The law, proposed in 1866 by the Joint Select Committee on Apprentices and the African Race, no longer allowed courts to apprentice the children of "free negroes" or African American children born out of wedlock. Instead, there was a new provision, one that allowed courts to apprentice all children born out of wedlock, whether white or black, "whose mothers may not have the means or ability to support them."[43]

The reformed law no longer examined the parents' racial characteristics. Instead, it tested parents' gendered status. White male legislators had extended "household head" privileges to African American men. By imposing white male standards of household relations upon African American families, the new law denied African American women full rights to their children. The new law recognized African American men as household providers. Households headed by African American men achieved what other households headed by women of any race could not: full parental rights to their children. The written code no longer threatened households headed by African American men; however, households headed by women of both races remained under surveillance.

These reforms came under the fire of African American Republicans at the 1868 constitutional convention. As white and black men debated suffrage, the question of apprenticeship's constitutionality surfaced briefly. A Bertie County Republican representative, Parker David Robbins, unilaterally opposed apprenticeship. Robbins, regarded in Bertie County as a free black man before the war, claimed ancestry of both Chowan Indians and African Americans. Before the Civil War Robbins had acquired a 102-acre farm with income he earned as a carpenter and a mechanic. During the war Robbins had attained the rank of sergeant major in the Second U.S. Colored Cavalry and was elected to the 1868 constitutional convention. Opposed to apprenticeship on constitutional grounds, Robbins proposed that the convention abolish all coercive forms of apprenticeship. It was the convention's responsibility, he claimed, to make these laws "nul & void upon the adoption of this Constitution; unless be affirmed by the parent or parents of next of kin of such minors before the proper Court having the jurisdiction there of." Robbins's proposal suggested that all men and women, regardless of their marital condition, deserved full rights and responsibilities of parenthood. Such a revolutionary move by the convention promised to elevate women's status as parents to that of men.[44]

However, influential Republican delegates quickly quashed Robbins's proposal. In fact, Robbins's attempt to eradicate apprenticeship and restore both fathers' and mothers' full rights as parents died in committee. Judicial Committee Chairman William B. Rodman, who had served the Confederate army during the Civil War but had joined the Republican Party because he foresaw it as the nation's dominant party, opposed Robbins's proposal and recommended that it "be discharged from further consideration." Rodman explained that the law of 1867 sufficed, and he saw "no reason for any other change in the law on the subject of apprentices" except for any jurisdictional and technical modifications that the convention intended for the state's judicial organization. Though the delegation had briefly considered granting women the same rights that men had to their children, it quickly abandoned the idea and resumed its plan to create a government that at once relegated women to secondary status both as citizens and as parents.[45]

By preserving the apprenticeship system, William B. Rodman validated Daniel L. Russell Sr. 's ongoing effort to secure custody of Lucy Ross's children. Undaunted by the state supreme court's ruling, Russell reinstated the apprenticeships that the court had voided only weeks earlier. Within a week he applied for apprenticeships at the Robeson County Courthouse. On February 9, 1867, the Robeson County sheriff served notice on Lucy Ross. On February 25 Russell had several children bound to him, including Maria Ross, Lucy's oldest daughter. Later records indicate that Russell also secured guardianship of Ross's younger daughter, Delia. Russell also served notice on William French, a local freedman, and successfully engineered the apprenticeships of his children, Candace and William. Ross, French, and another freedwoman, Elsie Scott, filed multiple complaints with the Robeson and New Hanover county courts to retrieve their children. The fate of the French and Scott children is unclear, but Russell maintained control of the Ross children throughout the year. Records indicate that Lucy Ross filed a complaint with the Freedmen's Bureau as late as October 21, 1867. The bureau instructed the sheriff of Robeson County to serve Russell with a writ of *habeas corpus,* but no records indicate whether Lucy Ross ever regained rights to her children.[46]

Daniel Russell Sr. 's actions in the wake of the *Ambrose* case suggest that he disregarded Justice Reade's ruling and the General Assembly's new legislation protecting African American men's claims to their children. Russell was unable to accept Lucy Ross's claims to her family's constitutional rights of *habeas corpus.* He had even pursued the apprenticeship of William French's children despite the new laws protecting French's claims to his children. Apparently William French triumphed in court, for the only subsequent complaints against Russell came from Lucy Ross. Despite the recent rulings against him, Russell continued to flaunt the law and ignore the claims of African American families. He endorsed a racial order of hierarchy and refused to acknowledge African American men's political and social gains during the late 1860s. Though Republicans had reinterpreted apprenticeship as a system to control women, Russell held firm to the notion that apprenticeship was a system that allowed whites to control blacks.

The experiences of Lucy Ross and other freedwomen add a new dimension to the changes in apprenticeship custom and law during Reconstruction. To be sure, African American mothers and fathers both endured the inconveniences and hardships of coerced apprenticeships, but African American mothers' experiences were unique because state law failed to recognize their transition from slavery to freedom. As a result, laws of marriage, bastardy, and apprenticeship affected black women in ways that white women never knew. Nonetheless, African American women protested their situations, and North Carolina

Republicans responded with laws that only partially addressed African American concerns. The new state law, bereft of racial distinctions, imposed apprenticeship on mothers who "may not have the means or ability to support" their children. Such vague language provided courts with the power to inspect—and dissolve—all homes headed by women regardless of race or class. Women, both white and black, continued to challenge apprenticeship for decades. Their energies, together with other social forces, led to the institution's demise in 1919.

CHAPTER FIVE

PARENTS' RIGHTS OR CHILDREN'S BEST INTERESTS?

The Role of Judicial Discretion in Apprenticeship and Child Custody

Throughout most of the nineteenth century, issues regarding apprenticeship usually involved the rights of the master or the parents. Judges decided apprenticeship cases, such as *Midgett v. McBryde* and *In the Matter of Harriet Ambrose and Eliza Ambrose* upon hearing the arguments of masters and parents; each party defended his or her personal rights to the children in question. Records suggest that judges rarely considered the child's welfare. Chief Justice Reade briefly considered the Ambrose daughters' rights to *habeas corpus* before issuing his decision, but for most of the individuals involved the debate centered upon the rights of Wiley Ambrose, the parent, and Daniel Russell, the master. By the 1890s the question of rights began to take a new turn. Judges, legislators, reformers, and ordinary people began to speak more about the welfare of the child than about the rights of the parent or master. By the nature of apprenticeship, mothers' rights were irrelevant. Yet as courts heard more child-custody cases between fathers and mothers, lawmakers grew more willing to reconsider mothers' rights to their children. Involuntary apprenticeship would not survive once judges recognized mothers as legitimate sole guardians, for one of the purposes of apprenticeship was to deprive mothers of their children. Thus, changing attitudes toward mothers' rights, toward mothers' and fathers' roles as parents, and toward children's welfare and child custody had vast consequences for the institution of apprenticeship.

A redefinition of womanhood accompanied this shift in emphasis from parental rights to the child's best interests. To be sure, postbellum law, like antebellum law, restricted mothers' rights to their children, but the degree of scrutiny changed. With few exceptions, antebellum laws required courts to apprentice children of poor widows, single women, and free blacks. But after 1867, legal authorities created new tests that scrutinized the character of individual mothers and measured their conformity to white notions of womanhood. By the 1880s state law and county officials had become increasingly concerned with the welfare of the child; mothers who failed to meet court standards of womanhood saw their children apprenticed. The character test was applied to child-custody disputes as well. Though the laws governing child custody differed from those governing apprenticeship, they were similar in their treatment of women. In assessing a mother's custody petition, judges first ascertained her conformity to their notions of motherhood.

The court's new measure of scrutiny depended upon contemporary views of womanhood. Late nineteenth-century connotations of womanhood drew from the antebellum stereotypes of the genteel southern lady. Reserved to describe white women of affluence, the term *lady* described a woman, usually of wealth, who was weak, fragile, vulnerable, and in need of protection by white men. The term did not apply to poor and African American women, though women in these groups actively worked to broaden its meaning to include themselves. During the late nineteenth century, white men's greatest fear resided in the stereotypical "black brute" and the alleged threat of rape. They took it upon themselves to protect their ladies from the influences of black men. The stereotype "lady," then, perpetuated not only images of feminine weakness but also racist stereotypes that buttressed white supremacy.[1]

While the term *lady* connoted feminine weakness, it also implied feminine strength. After the Civil War many white women demanded and experienced increasing independence in public spaces. Urban areas flourished as whites moved from rural areas into towns and cities. Some women moved about on city streets with relative freedom. By 1900 thousands of single women were laboring in cotton mills, and others had assumed posts as teachers throughout the state. By the late nineteenth century, middle-class women had embraced both images of the southern lady. On the one hand, women actively became involved in campaigns for temperance and educational reforms. Women justified the public role of organizations such as the Women's Christian Temperance Union and the Women's Association for the Betterment of Public School Houses by emphasizing the public's need for the positive influence of women's innate moral goodness. North Carolina Supreme Court Chief Justice Walter J. Clark, who frequently decided issues of apprenticeship and child custody, supported women's public involvement by publicly endorsing women's suffrage in 1912. On the other hand, women upheld the stereotype of their innate weaknesses by seeking men's protection. Often women's activities were restricted by their own almost universal acceptance of the southern lady's need of men's protection. Women's organizations such as the United Daughters of the Confederacy upheld this stereotype by preserving the memory of their dead male kin. By embracing white supremacy as a means to protect the weaker sex from black men, southern ladies perpetuated the duality of feminine strength and feminine weakness.[2]

Eventually this public role of womanhood would influence women's challenges in the court to established custody doctrines. Paternal custody, which lay at the heart of beliefs about guardianship and apprenticeship, had proved resilient throughout most of the nineteenth century. Custody, a doctrine that involved the right of a parent or guardian to control a minor, could be awarded in matters involving divorce, separation, or *habeas corpus.* Before the 1870s judges and other legal authorities had assumed that the economic stability provided by a patriarchal household best served a child's needs. In theory, patriarchs and dependents—including children, wives, and slaves—maintained a reciprocal relationship. In return for protection and support, dependents pledged submission and obedience to the master. This doctrine, universally accepted among many whites in the South, upheld the father's claim to his children as their natural guardian. Among southern whites, paternal rights generally reigned supreme in custody cases. No similar doctrine protected women's rights to their children.[3]

After the *Ambrose* case in 1867, authorities increasingly granted these same privileges to black fathers. Ostensibly, African American men had earned the same rights to control their dependents as white men had possessed for generations. In 1868 the state constitution granted African American men full rights as citizens. Subsequently, Freedmen's Bureau agent Richard Dillon demanded that the Moore County planter Archibald B. Currie return Ananias and Judson Allen to their father, James Allen, in Randolph County. Ananias had informed Dillon that both boys preferred working for their master, Currie, to working for their father, but Dillon insisted that the boys demonstrate at least nominal respect for their father. "I advised him as he will not work for his Father," reported Dillon, "to give him part of his wages, as it was his *duty* to assist his Parents" (emphasis added). In arguing that James Allen controlled his sons' labor and their wages, Dillon acknowledged Allen's claims as master of his dependents.[4]

Fathers' paramount rights usurped mothers' claims to their children. Mothers found it increasingly difficult to regain rights to their children. Freedmen's

Bureau agents no longer recognized women's claims as parents or their nurturing capacities as mothers. Instead they focused upon men's claims as masters of the household. In March 1868 Helen Lomax complained that her child, Jerry Kirk, was being "badly treated" by the "present wife" of his father, Charles Kirk. Lomax informed the bureau that her son had been born out of wedlock and said that Charles Kirk thus had no right to him. Then she demanded that the bureau restore her son to her custody. Agent Richard Dillon refused. Upon investigating the case he found "no cause for the removal of the boy from his father." Jerry's father, Dillon argued, possessed all the traits of manliness and responsibility. He was "industrious" and "well behaved." The boy, Dillon found, was "well clad, fed," and "kept regularly at school." Dillon upheld Charles Kirk's claims as father even though he possessed no legal right as father because the child had been born out of wedlock. Nonetheless, in the eyes of the bureau Kirk's status as father took precedence over Lomax's rights as mother.[5]

After 1868, guardianship laws favored not just fathers but also male relatives over mothers. Women who remarried forfeited their rights to children of prior marriages, especially if the children had inherited property that a stepfather might squander. In 1876 the North Carolina Supreme Court decreed that married women possessed no rights to children of previous marriages. In *J. F. G. Spears and wife v. R. L. Snell*, Margaret Spears had petitioned for the return of her son, Cyrus Snell, who possessed a small estate. Upon the death of her husband (the boy's father) Spears had remarried and left the boy with his uncle and grandfather. In 1875 Margaret Spears requested that the court restore Cyrus Snell to her custody. A Cabarrus County judge complied and transferred custody of thirteen-year-old Cyrus A. Snell from his uncle, R. L. Snell, to his mother, Margaret Spears, and stepfather, J. F. G. Spears. The superior court judge argued that Margaret Spears possessed a *primary right* to her child.[6]

But the state supreme court found error in the lower court's decision. Justice Richmond Pearson argued that the lower court judge had wrongly assumed that this case pitted the mother's rights against the uncle's rights. According to Pearson, the case did not involve the rights of the mother, for she had forfeited her rights to the child when she married Spears; Rather, the case represented a contest between the stepfather and the uncle. Margaret Spears had submitted herself to her new husband, who was under no legal obligation to support her son. Spears "had separated from the child and subjected herself to the control of a second husband, thus putting it out of her power to support the child without subjecting him to the control of a step-father." Furthermore, Pearson argued, in any apprenticeship or custody matter a minor "at the age of 13 . . . has a right to have his wishes and feelings taken into consideration." The boy had already informed the court that he wished to stay with his uncle. Upon these premises, Pearson overturned the lower court's ruling and restored Cyrus Snell to his uncle's custody.[7]

Pearson's ruling was based upon precedents courts had established in antebellum guardianship and apprentice law. By the 1880s the General Assembly had revised the law to allow mothers to raise children who had inherited property. Though the North Carolina Supreme Court had denied women these privileges in *Spears v. Snell*, legislators chose to reverse the longstanding practice. The first substantive change came in the early 1880s, when the legislature recognized women's ability to manage their children's property. The General Assembly eliminated a statute in the 1883 code that allowed courts to apprentice children who had inherited property from their fathers, stating that "the court, in its discretion, thinks it improper to permit such children to remain with the mother." The antebellum rationale for this law had been that if a woman remarried, she could not prevent her new husband from squandering her child's inheritance. This presumption had driven Pearson's decision in the 1876 case *Spears v. Snell*. By removing this provision from the apprenticeship code, the General Assembly indirectly acknowledged women's ability to manage their children's estates.[8]

Though judges clung to patriarchal custody practices when deciding cases that involved married women, they began to look more favorably upon the idea that single women could retain custody. Judges might find that a woman had met accepted standards of parenthood, but only if no father was present *and* the mother exhibited "good character." In 1872 Marina Mitchell sued Miles Mitchell, her former master, for custody of her children, three boys and one girl. The children had been born slaves of Miles Mitchell, who had petitioned the Hertford County Court for their apprenticeship at the war's end. "After the emancipation of the slaves," the court had granted apprenticeship to Miles Mitchell but was forced to cancel the indentures when it failed to properly notify the family of the proceedings. Mitchell initiated apprenticeship again, but Marina Mitchell and her children, though properly notified, failed to attend the hearing due to inclement weather. The court apprenticed the children to Miles Mitchell. Marina Mitchell filed a petition to annul the indentures, arguing that she was "industrious and frugal, and takes as good care of her children, as colored mothers generally do." To secure her family's subsistence, Marina Mitchell had hired out her eldest son to work for sixty dollars that year, boarded her daughter with a "respectable gentleman," and cultivated a farm with her two middle sons. Together they lived on rented land, delivered one-half the crop to the landlord, and paid for provisions with the remainder.[9]

Associate Justice Edwin Reade dissolved the indentures, thereby granting Marina Mitchell custody of her children. In his decision Reade addressed both procedural and substantive issues. First, Reade admonished the Hertford County judge for improper procedure. The court, Reade declared, should not have apprenticed the children without their presence before him. Then he took a swipe at the apprenticeship laws that required the indenture of all fatherless children. Single mothers, Reade advised, should retain rights to their children provided that they met certain standards of conduct. Courts resorted to apprenticeship, Reade argued, only when orphans did not possess an estate that reaped a profit for their education and maintenance. "Since the wreck of fortunes by the war," Reade asserted, "it is a rare case where a fatherless child can be educated and maintained out of the profits of its estate alone." But by Reade's estimation, the "industrious and frugal" Marina Mitchell had successfully provided for her children by her industry and economy. It would be a "great injustice to the mother and great hardship upon the children" if Miles Mitchell were to attain their labor, worth $150 or more, for free. Therefore, Reade did not see it necessary to "break up these relations" unless the children became dependent upon the county for support "or unless their moral or physical condition requires a change." This decision represented a most unusual departure for North Carolina Supreme Court justices. Even Reade, arguably one of the most liberal justices on the bench, had expressed a much more ambivalent opinion about single mothers' rights to their children in *Ambrose*. In the earlier case Reade had adhered to the North Carolina law requiring apprenticeship of all children born out of wedlock but had nullified the indentures based on a technicality. In *Miles Mitchell v. Marina Mitchell and her children* Reade established a new precedent, one that allowed single women to keep their children, though only under certain circumstances. Nonetheless, his decision was premised on the fact that no father was present and thus no paternal custody rights were at stake.[10]

Marina Mitchell had escaped the unfortunate fate of Margaret Spears because her case did not place into question the thorny issue of paternal obligations. On the one hand, Spears had rescinded her individual rights and submitted herself to the power and control of a man who possessed no paternal obligation or responsibility to her thirteen-year-old son. Therefore, Spears lacked the parental ability to protect her son, who the court argued would find better care elsewhere. On the other hand, Marina Mitchell, whose children were fatherless, had submitted herself to no one and therefore possessed the capacity to care for her children provided that she maintained a reputable standing. By upholding Marina Mitchell's parental rights, Edwin Reade chipped away at the foundation of patriarchal privilege. Reade had declared that a single African American woman could possess the capacity of parenthood. It was only a matter of time before the same argument was used to describe the capacity of a married woman.

In courtrooms throughout America judges increasingly awarded custody rights to mothers, both married and unmarried. The trend had begun in the 1830s, though most southern states did not begin to see a dramatic shift until the 1860s and 1870s. Those judges who awarded custody to mothers did not necessarily do so out of a desire to elevate maternal rights; rather, their decisions reflected a move toward expanded judicial discretion in familial issues. Courts had begun to replace the old patriarchal structure of state and family government with a newer paternalistic notion that viewed parenthood as a trusteeship. According to this view, parents no longer held proprietary right to the children; and judges developed new standards to measure the best interests of the child. "Although biological rights remained important," Peter Bardaglio argues, "parental supremacy was no longer unchallengeable." Thus, fathers could no longer be certain that judges would protect their exclusive natural guardianship rights.[11]

The uncertainties of judicial discretion in custody matters gave mothers an advantage, particularly in cases involving very young children. American judges increasingly favored the "tender years" doctrine, which rested on the belief that until a child reached a certain age, the child's best interests were met by the mother's innate nurturing abilities. Once the child had reached an age at which a mother's influence was no longer crucial, judges returned to the doctrine that established the fathers' paramount rights. Great uncertainty prevailed because no standard age of demarcation existed. Some judges argued that a child could thrive without its mother as soon as it was weaned. Others argued that children required their mother's care until they were nine or ten years old. North Carolina judges recognized twelve years as the age of discretion but acknowledged that this limit was an arbitrary one.[12]

Consequently, the child's age hardly seemed to matter since some judges used more abstract terms to determine custody decisions. In 1879 North Carolina Supreme Court Justice Thomas S. Ashe confirmed a Rutherford County judge's decision to split custody of four siblings in the divorce case of Mary

Scoggins and William Scoggins. The court awarded the three youngest children, all girls, to Mary Scoggins because they were "small and needed her care." The oldest child, a thirteen-year-old boy, was returned to his father despite substantial evidence that William Scoggins frequently became drunk and violently abusive. On more than one occasion he had brandished pistols and threatened to kill his wife. In this case judges affirmed maternal custody rights, but only temporarily. The judges implied but did not explicitly state that the father could retrieve the children at a later age. Even in light of evidence that William Scoggins treated his family cruelly, the judges refused to go against patriarchal beliefs concerning child custody.[13]

Mary Scoggins's victory, though a limited one, represented a recognition by society of women's increasingly public role. The courts may have developed rather ambiguous standards regarding mothers' rights, but the North Carolina legislature was more forthcoming about granting women some of the rights that patriarchs had long enjoyed. In 1883 lawmakers passed a measure that granted natural guardianship rights to a mother if the father had died. The statute specified that henceforth widows would possess the same guardianship rights "to the same extent and in the same manner, plight and condition as the father would be if living; and the mother in such case shall have all the powers, rights, and privileges, and be subject to all the duties and obligations of a natural guardian." In a single legislative session lawmakers formally granted widows full guardianship rights to their children and the power to manage their children's inheritance. It seemed a radical and dramatic transformation in women's rights.[14]

But the new provision was not without some limitations. Women, whom judges viewed as innately domestic and nurturing, could retain their children provided that they used their specifically feminine virtues to create an environment that met their children's best interests. Judges might reject a mother's custody petition if she did not appear to meet certain standards as determined by the court. The 1883 law that recognized widows as natural guardians included an explicit reference to the supervisory and paternalistic powers of the courts. This law, the statute cautioned, "shall not be construed as abridging the powers of the courts over minors and their estates and to the appointment of guardians." In this particular provision the General Assembly made an obligatory bow to judicial authority even as it moved one step further from common-law doctrines that protected the unique and exclusive power of patriarchy. Six years later, lawmakers passed a statute that provided courts with more specific guidelines for deciding custody and apprenticeship cases involving women.

This 1889 amendment to the apprenticeship code prescribed a strict standard of womanhood for single and widowed mothers. It prohibited county courts from apprenticing children whose mothers exhibited "good character," a stipulation that referred to both propertied women and women who conformed to white middle-class norms associated with domesticity and child-rearing. The statute required courts to apprentice children who had "no father and the mother is of bad character, or suffers her children to grow up in habits of idleness, without any means of obtaining an honest livelihood." Presumably, women who conformed to acceptable notions of womanhood would maintain full parental rights to their children regardless of their marital status.[15]

Of course, the *Revised Code* failed to specify the precise meaning of "good character." But in 1890 Chaney Calhoun Ashby, a white woman from Stokes County, put the law to the test. In two state supreme court cases that involved Ashby and her daughter, Mary Etta Margaret Calhoun, judges defined a woman of "good character" as a woman who exhibited certain virtues of womanhood and the financial ability to raise her children. Sometime in 1878 Chaney Ashby, who was then unmarried and known as Chaney Calhoun, gave birth to Mary out of wedlock. Chaney swore to court authorities that Mary's father was a local man named L. Berry Page. When Mary turned two years old, Chaney, apparently unable to raise her daughter on her own, entered into a contract with Page that allowed him the "right to put her [Mary] at any place that he thinks propper for her to stay at untill she becomes a free woman." Page, also unable to care for Mary, requested that his brother, James H. Page, take the child. James Page refused, and L. Berry Page placed his daughter with his parents. About 1883 Mary's father and the grandmother with whom she lived passed away. At that time Chaney asked James Page to take Mary in. For seven years Mary lived with her father's brother, James H. Page, and his wife.[16]

Chaney Calhoun could not support her child alone. However, Calhoun married James Ashby about 1888, and Ashby agreed to support his wife's child. The surest way for Chaney Ashby to retain custody of her daughter was to have Mary apprenticed to her husband James. In the spring of 1889 Chaney Ashby asked the Stokes County Superior Court to apprentice Mary to James Ashby. When James H. Page learned of the impending apprenticeship, he feared the Ashbys would take Mary from him. Immediately he filed an application to have Mary apprenticed to him. Upon investigating each applicant, the court apprenticed Mary to James Page and denied application to Chaney and James Ashby. Chaney Ashby requested that the court rescind the indenture, but Stokes

County Judge Gilmer found in Page's favor and allowed the apprenticeship to stand. Chaney appealed her case to the North Carolina Supreme Court, which ruled that Mary Calhoun had been improperly bound. Page, the court declared, had not provided evidence of Chaney Ashby's inability to care for the child. "If the mother be a suitable person," decreed Justice Davis, "she is entitled to its custody, even though some other may be 'more suitable.'" Thus the state supreme court in 1890 upheld Chaney Ashby's right to keep Mary because Page had failed to show that she was an unsuitable parent.[17]

However, Page learned from the 1890 decision that in order to claim Mary he had to prove that Chaney Ashby was an unsuitable parent. Though the state supreme court had rendered a decision that favored Chaney Ashby, Page refused to give Mary to her. When Chaney Ashby filed for a writ of *habeas corpus*, Page answered by claiming that "he had the care and custody of said infant for the last several years and thinks he is entitled to hold her by reason of such care and custody." Chaney again appealed to the Stokes County Superior Court. The new trial, held in 1890, differed markedly from the first. In the first trial Page and the Ashbys had been the primary witnesses, and neither the defendant nor the plaintiff had introduced character witnesses. Having learned from his mistake, in the second trial Page introduced several witnesses who testified against Chaney Ashby. In turn, Ashby subpoenaed several witnesses who testified to the bad character of James Page. The trial became a public spectacle.[18]

Several witnesses testified to Chaney Ashby's "bad" character. Many were neighbors of the Ashbys. "Chaney is bad and has been all her life," said B. F. King, "bad for virtue, lying, high temper, cursing, swearing," and "she plays cards on Sundays." Other neighbors attested that Chaney had borne other illegitimate children. James Bennett Jr. and James Bennett Sr. both testified that Chaney "treated the child brutally before the Pages took it." James Bennett Jr. added that when Mary was two years old, Chaney "beat [her] brutally, cursed [her], and wished [her] dead & in hell." John Calhoun, Chaney's brother, stated that his sister "is a woman of violent high temper, curses and swears, and has a bad reputation in the neighborhood." Calhoun observed that Chaney was "vulgar" in front of her children at home. In fact, John Calhoun feared for Mary's safety if she were to live with the Ashbys: "I am satisfied it would greatly endanger the life of Mary to take her from Mr. Page and give her to Chaney. I don't believe she would live long."[19]

Other neighbors attested to James Ashby's inability to care for Mary. B. F. King claimed that Ashby "is not a bright man, but considered to be a half wittied [*sic*] fellow." R. R. Boyles, who lived 1/4 mile from the Pages, concurred: "James Ashby has not much sense, rather foolish, and is under control of his wife." However, Boyles believed that Page had the capacity of an able parent, and he defended Page despite rumors of Page's own infidelities. "The only thing I ever heard against Mr. Page was that 2 or 3 years ago, one [Susan] Webster charged a child to Mr. Page, but nobody in the neighborhood believed it, & I have heard her swear on oath since that she was hired or persuaded to do it, she was then charging one of the Overby boys of being the father of her child." One witness testified that Page had committed adultery and bribery and had had "illicit intercourse with several disreputable women . . . all women of ill fame." Even Page's wife, Edith, was "a high tempered, quarrelsome and a neighborhood tattler" engaged in "immoral conduct" who exhibited only a "pretended love" for Mary.[20]

Several witnesses testified in Chaney Ashby's favor. Neighbors and family argued that Chaney Ashby was "industrious, economical and a good peaceable neighbor." Robert Owensby, who lived "within 1/2 miles of plaintiff and about the same distance from the defendant," claimed to have known Chaney Ashby all her life. In his opinion, "Mrs. Ashby is kind to her children and to her husband and . . . she would care for and furnish a good home for the child." Owensby added that James Ashby was a "hard-working, sober man who provides well for his family and who is a man of good habits and good character."[21]

The defendant and plaintiff also testified. James Page argued that both James and Chaney Ashby were of "bad character." James Ashby was "weak minded," and Chaney had had three illegitimate children before her marriage to James Ashby, "all said to be by different men." The Ashbys, Page claimed, were "very poor & hard run to make a living." Though they had a large family, neither could read or write. They did not send any of their children to school "and have no means to educate them." Page added that they were renters and lived "on the land of other people wherever they can get a home." James Ashby countered by claiming that Page retained Mary only for her labor. He said that the Pages' profession of love and affection for Mary "are the merest pretense." Mary, he argued, "does the cooking and virtually all the household work and for these reasons above the defendant and his wife wish to keep the girl." Chaney Ashby noted that Page, "a man without means," owned no land in his own name.[22]

Both parties brought neighbors and family to court to testify as character witnesses, but neither offered any material evidence, such as court documents, to prove any of the charges. Nonetheless, Judge McCorkle rendered a decision.

McCorkle argued that Mary should remain with the Pages. The character witnesses testifying against Chaney Ashby had appeared to him more persuasive than those testifying against James Page. "The plaintiff," he opined, had borne "three bastard children before her present marriage" and thus "is a woman of bad character for virtue and morality and that she is not a fit person to have the custody of the child." Mary, he concluded, would live with Page, "a man of good moral character" and "a suitable person to have the custody of the child." In 1891 Chaney Ashby appealed to the North Carolina Supreme Court a second time. She argued that the local court had erred by admitting additional evidence into the case. But this time the court affirmed Judge McCorkle's decision. The additional evidence that Page had submitted about Chaney's character was "allowable," the court argued. "It was competent for the Court," Justice Clark argued, "to hear any additional testimony, and it was its duty to find the facts before entering its judgment." The new evidence, the court concluded, had shown that Chaney was of "bad character" and therefore "not a fit person to have the custody of the child."[23]

Thus, courts in the 1890s assessed a mother's character prior to apprenticing her children. The character test measured women's conformity to standards of womanhood. Chaney Ashby's case demonstrates that courts disapproved of mothers who were poor, had borne children out of wedlock, and failed to conform to middle-class notions of domesticity and education. Had Ashby's case materialized in an antebellum court, officials would have removed her child because of her status, but post-*Ambrose* courts assessed the character of mothers, a legal approach that differed markedly from antebellum patterns. In sum, antebellum North Carolina courts had routinely apprenticed poor women's and single women's children. In 1865 courts apprenticed the children of former slave men and women. After 1868 courts apprenticed children of mothers who exhibited "lewd" or "immoral" character. These were women, often poor or single, who failed to conform to court standards of womanhood. The state supreme court's decision in 1890 had allowed Ashby to retain Mary because Page had not offered any evidence that she was not a suitable parent. However, once Page presented evidence that she was an unsuitable mother, the court reversed its decision. To be sure, Chaney Ashby had countered with evidence of Page's unsuitability as a parent, yet Ashby's evidence was viewed as irrelevant. Postbellum law required courts to test women's, but not men's, suitability for parenthood. Although the judge heard negative testimony about Page, it seems that he made his decision based on the bad character of Chaney Ashby.

The Guilford County Court maintained the same standard for womanhood as late as 1914. In separate cases the court apprenticed children of "Mrs. Emma Phillips," "Mrs. John Parrish," and Susan Crisco. In each case the court determined that the mother was of "immoral" or "bad" character. None of the children had a father present, and according to the court, the mothers had compromised the welfare of their children. "The children," the court argued in each case, "are under 16 years of age, who on account of the crime, neglect, drunkeness, lewdness and immoral character of the mother with whom they reside, are in circumstances exposing said infants to lead an idle and dissolute life." Therefore, it was in the children's best interests to be apprenticed to "some suitable and christian person" so that "they may be reared, nurtured and educated [to] become honest and useful citizens of the community."[24]

Nonetheless, mothers who exhibited good character posed a significant new challenge to fathers who claimed their prima facie rights. Increasingly, single mothers' custody petitions forced justices to wrestle with their assumptions about women's limited custody rights. Both *Mitchell v. Mitchell* and the *Ashby* cases, *Chaney Ashby v. James H. Page* (1890, 1891), had introduced reasoning that women could use to circumvent doctrines privileging paternal custody. In *Mitchell v. Mitchell* Justice Edwin Reade had set a new precedent that single women possessed guardianship rights equal to fathers' provided that they exhibited "good character." The *Ashby* cases opened this line of argument to married women. In 1910 Associate Justice William A. Hoke upheld this reasoning to preserve custody rights of a formerly single mother who married and petitioned the court for control of her illegitimate child.

In 1910 Nancy (Nannie) Green, formerly Nannie Jones, filed an appeal for reconsideration of her petition for a writ of *habeas corpus* for her nine-year-old daughter, Mary Jane Jones. Nannie Jones had given birth to her daughter out of wedlock, and with no place to go, she had found herself "helpless and homeless." When the child was three months old Jones's uncle, Prince Jones, found the mother and child on the public road in front of his house. He and his wife invited them into their home, cared for both, and sent Mary Jane to school, where she became "well advanced in her studies for one of her age and condition in life." A few years later Nannie Jones married Simon Green "and went to live with him." Immediately Simon and Nannie Green sought custody of Mary Jane, "from time to time and repeatedly" asking the Joneses to relinquish the child, but with no success. On one occasion the Greens tried to "take the child away from [the Joneses] by force," but the child screamed, which apparently foiled the attempt. Disconcerted by their own attempts to retrieve Mary Jane, the Greens petitioned the Vance County Court, which adjudged that the child's welfare was best served by keeping her with the Joneses, at least until she turned fifteen, at which time she could decide with whom she wished to live.[25]

North Carolina Supreme Court Justice William A. Hoke strongly disagreed with the Vance County judge and awarded custody to the Greens. His reasoning demonstrates the difficulty judges faced when they had to weigh parents' rights and the children's best interests. Though the court must consider the child's best interests, Hoke acknowledged, it must first uphold the principle that "the parents of a child who are living together as lawful man and wife have *prima facie* the right to control and custody of their infant children." Citing *Mitchell v. Mitchell* and *Ashby v. Page,* Hoke argued that this right extended to cases involving illegitimate children, where fathers' prima facie right existed, though "perhaps to a lesser degree, in the mother." Parents who evinced "good character" had a paramount right to children when "they have the capacity and disposition to care for and rear them properly in the walk of life in which they are placed." This right, Hoke explained, grew out of parents' duty to provide for their children, an obligation grounded not only in law but also "in the strongest and most enduring affections of the human heart." By this reasoning, Hoke implied that Nannie Green possessed a natural and legal obligation to care for Mary Jane, a duty that did not apply to her uncle, Prince Jones. The court acknowledged no such obligation of Simon Green, Nannie's new husband. In this case the natural and legal obligation rested with the maternal parent, though the court acknowledged Simon Green's "respectability" and willingness to participate in Mary Jane's upbringing.[26]

Nannie Green's victory in *In Re Habeas Corpus of Mary Jane Jones* contrasts sharply with previous similar cases. The case contained many parallels to *Spears v. Snell.* In the earlier case the widow Margaret Spears and her new husband had sought custody of her child, Cyrus, held by the child's uncle, circumstances very similar to Nannie and Simon Green's. Significant differences included the fact that Spears's child had been born within wedlock, while Green's had not. But both women had subjected themselves to the control of a man who did not possess any legal obligation to care for his wife's child. Justice Pearson had rejected Spears's custody request on this ground, but the new standards requiring judges to assess women's character, introduced in *Mitchell v. Mitchell* and *Ashby v. Page,* led justices of the 1910 court to a different conclusion. By their reasoning, Nannie Green had not completely forsaken her rights and obligations as a mother when she married Simon Green. Nannie Green, Hoke argued, possessed the same prima facie right as a father, though "perhaps to a lesser degree." Thus, she retained a small measure of independence, a fact confirmed by the court's final judgment, which "awarded" Mary Jane to "the mother."[27]

As judges used their judicial discretion to award certain mothers custody rights, some disputed the nature of fathers' rights, once considered absolute. This controversy escalated in 1921, when a father in Beaufort County challenged his late wife's parents for the custody of his fifteen-month-old daughter, Rosa Hamilton. The child, born in 1918, had accompanied her ailing mother to her parents' home. According to the child's maternal grandparents, Hatton Hamilton, the father, had refused to visit his family and sent only "one bottle of Wampole's Cod Liver Oil and a small quantity of fresh meat" to the family. When his wife died of tuberculosis in 1919, he paid only a fraction of the funeral expenses. His neglectful behavior, the grandparents argued, constituted abandonment. In fact, prior to her death the child's mother had stipulated in her last will and testament that her parents should receive custody. The grandparents' arguments depended heavily upon their own assumptions about a mother's innate nurturing capacity for a child of "tender years." "More than any other human being," they argued, "this wife and mother was interested in the welfare and best interests of her child, and it is respectfully insisted that the judgment of a mother as to who best will care for and raise her child when she is taken is or ought to be the most powerful evidence in a case of this character." Clearly, they concluded, the court in its discretion should find in favor of the maternal grandparents, the only relatives who could serve the child's best interests and welfare.[28]

At both the county and state levels judges were divided on Rosa Hamilton's case. On one side were those judges who favored the use of judicial discretion in determining the child's best interests. On the other side were those who privileged the father's paramount rights. George Paul, of the Beaufort County Juvenile Court, initiated the debate when he acknowledged the fathers' right to custody. Others, such as the superior court judge to whom the grandparents appealed, reversed the lower court's decision and found that the child's best interests were served by the maternal grandparents. The state supreme court was also split. W. P. Stacy, who issued the majority opinion in this case, acknowledged the father's prima facie right but argued that "this right is not an absolute one and must yield when the best interests of the child requires it." According to Stacy, the maternal grandparents had adequately proved that Hatton

Hamilton was "not a fit, suitable or proper person" to care for his daughter and provide her with necessary treatment for her "spinal trouble." But Justice Platt D. Walker disagreed. The father deserved custody, he argued, because the evidence submitted against him was not substantial enough to deprive him of his prima facie right. In fact, testimony suggested that the father's failure to visit his wife and child "was not the father's fault, but the fault of those who now seek to retain the custody of the child." Walker acknowledged the importance of the "best interests" doctrine, but he cautioned that the court should "not deprive the father of his right except upon clear and strong evidence, which is not present in this case."[29]

What disturbed Walker most was the court's increasing reliance upon judicial discretion in custody matters. His dissent served as an indictment of that principle, which he viewed as an infringement upon the "precedents" and the "general principles of justice" that had established a man's paramount rights to control his child. Since in this case Hatton Hamilton had done nothing to forfeit those rights, Walker concluded that "there is no room for the exercise even of a sound discretion in favor of the grandparents who have possession of the child." The court should follow historical precedent and not vest itself "with a larger discretion than is given by the law." The only flaw in Walker's reasoning was that the court had already established its judicial discretion in previous cases. New precedent already had subverted the old.[30]

Yet Judge Walker had recognized a heightening conflict between paternal rights, maternal rights, and children's best interests that would agonize the court in subsequent cases in which both parents appeared perfectly able to act as sole custodian. This conflict exploded in 1923 and again in 1924 when justices tried to resolve a bitter and painful custody dispute between Isaac N. Clegg, a Presbyterian minister in Rowland, North Carolina, and his estranged wife, Annie McIntosh Clegg. Although this case focused upon a custody battle and not a dispute over apprenticeship, the outcome of the case marked a significant change in judges' thinking about mothers' custodial rights that fundamentally undermined the very purpose of apprenticeship, to deprive certain married women of their children. This bitter and prolonged dispute reflected the uneasiness that courts generated, not only among their members but also within the larger community, when they purposely recognized women as custodians. The Cleggs had settled in Rowland in about 1916. There Annie Clegg had given birth to her fourth child, Archie. By the time the state supreme court issued its first decision in 1923, Archie was five years old and Margaret,

Ann Monroe, and Newton, his sisters and brother, had turned seven, ten, and twelve, respectively.[31]

The marriage was not a happy one. According to Annie Clegg, her husband's controlling and abusive behavior had forced her to leave the home and seek refuge with her mother in Richmond, Virginia. He had made her life "intolerable" and had never bestowed upon her "any privileges in my home as a mother or house-keeper, he assumed all the responsibilities of the home from the first day I married him." He even purchased all of the items for the home, a responsibility she considered her own. The source of greatest contention between them was the matter of who possessed authority over the children. Annie Clegg cared for them as infants, but later her husband took control. "I had no control over my children," she complained, "my little babies of course, he couldn't do anything with the babies, but after my children got two years old he took them from my control." When Annie Clegg attempted to discipline the children, Isaac Clegg intervened and grew physically abusive toward her. Clegg dismissed his wife's complaints as brazen and inappropriate. For example, when Annie Clegg found Isaac's will pledging all of the property to the children and none to her, she threatened to leave. "[She] is no clinging vine," he argued. "If the court will carefully read her own testimony it will find that [she] is one of the strong minded sisters who believes in running things themselves and who is not willing to turn over that part of the partnership to the management of the husband." By law Isaac Clegg owned all of the property, including that which Annie, whose parents were affluent, had brought into the marriage. It is likely that Annie was angry with her husband for willing her inheritance out of her control.[32]

In 1922, unable to withstand her husband's abuse any longer, Annie took her daughters to Richmond, Virginia. Isaac Clegg refused to allow Archie or Newton to make the trip. At one point Clegg visited his wife "to see if a reconciliation could be effected," and Annie agreed to return to North Carolina temporarily, but only to retrieve Archie. They agreed that Newton, the oldest, would remain with his father.[33] Annie returned, and she planned to leave with Archie one week later. However, the night before her train was to depart, Annie received a threatening visit from the Ku Klux Klan. Annie had locked the doors and proceeded upstairs to undress. She wondered why her husband was walking back and forth into "the front room where it was dark and he didn't turn the light on." Eventually "Mr. Clegg came to my room and said there is somebody downstairs wants to see you." When Annie Clegg asked who it was, Isaac insisted only that she come downstairs "just like you are." As she descended the stairs, she saw standing in the doorway "a line of white figures" that she later described as "great tall men." The men were "all dressed in white, with white over their head and . . . something red on their breast." One of the men waved, and Clegg said "go on down there." "You must be crazy," Annie responded, and she turned and ran back up the stairs, but not before one of the robed men thrust a letter at her through the banister. Annie ignored the letter, ran to her room, and locked the door, despite continued appeals from her husband to return downstairs. Later she found the letter, addressed to "Mrs. I. N. Clegg," under her door, but she continued to ignore it. The next morning Annie accused Isaac of sending his "mason friends" to threaten her. It had not occurred to her that she was visited by anyone else until her son Newton said, "Mother that was the Ku Klux." Immediately, Annie prepared for departure, but her husband forced her to leave Archie behind.[34]

Upon her arrival in Richmond, Annie Clegg was met by Dan McLaurin, a man she had observed "in close conversation" with her husband at the Rowland train station. McLaurin had followed her to Richmond and handed her the letter. At that point she recognized him as one of the robed men from the night before. "I suppose it is the same letter you left at my door last night," she stated indignantly, "now you have handed it to me like a man." The letter, signed "Ku Klux Klan," registered a veiled threat should Annie Clegg remove her children to Richmond. "Dear Lady," it began, "we stand for home, women and children." The letter asked Mrs. Clegg "to consider [the] children and Mr. Clegg's work." If she meant to leave him, it continued, she should go to Richmond but leave the children with their father, "and [the Klan] would see that they were taken care of." Though the letter imparted no direct threat of violence, Annie understood the letter and the means by which it was delivered to indicate that any challenge to her husband's authority over the children would bring negative consequences, possibly including violence. Despite the threat, Annie Clegg filed a petition for *habeas corpus* in Lumberton, North Carolina, on June 15, 1923.[35]

Understandably, Annie Clegg was at once terrified and furious at the Klan's letter and threatening behavior. In 1922 the Ku Klux Klan was initiating a national revival. Millions of Protestant men across the country joined the Klan in reaction to what they presumed to be undesirable changes in immigration, women's independence, and African Americans' migration northward and their consequent literary and political renaissance in places such as Harlem, New York. Though Klansmen usually unleashed extralegal violence on African

Americans, Jews, and Roman Catholics, they also targeted women who appeared to defy the Klan's "traditional" parameters of morality.[36]

Klansmen viewed women as property. White women denoted prestige, and black women could be abused with impunity. Women who exhibited autonomy in work, sexuality, and politics threatened the patriarchal, white supremacist hierarchy that the Klan envisioned for America. Among a Klansman's greatest fear was the "loss" of a white woman to someone of another "race." In fact, much of the violence Klansmen waged was out of fear of interracial intimacy. But divorce and contentious child-custody disputes also challenged men's views of women as property. Since the Civil War the divorce rate had risen 2,000 percent. By the 1920s one in six marriages ended in divorce, and Klansmen anxiously sought to stem the rising tide.[37]

The Ku Klux Klan appeared at Annie Clegg's door only months before the organization held its first national meeting in Asheville, North Carolina, in July 1923. There, Klansmen expressed their justifications for protecting the authority of men such as Isaac Clegg. Klansmen vitiated all groups that appeared to threaten a white supremacist, patriarchal, "Protestant America." African Americans, speakers argued, were an "inferior race." Japanese Americans required careful scrutiny because they remained "subject to the dictates of a foreign power." Likewise, Roman Catholics were not "one hundred percent American" because they "ow[ed] allegiance to a foreigner or foreign institution." People of Jewish faith "refus[ed] to accept the Christian religion." Simultaneously, Klansmen praised the constitutional provision that separated church from state, and they insisted upon a Protestant America. They condoned extralegal violence but pledged law and order. As one speaker put it, "The Klan stands for law and order, freedom of speech, freedom of the press and freedom of conscience, for the free public school, separation of church and state, white supremacy and Protestant Christianity." To the Klan, then, a man such as Isaac Clegg, a Presbyterian minister with four small children, represented the future and heart of America. For Annie Clegg to challenge him in a child-custody dispute threatened the very principles for which the Klan stood.[38]

It mattered also that the custody dispute involved young boys. Though Annie Clegg did not seek guardianship of the older boy, Newton, she did want control of her youngest child, Archie. Fearing that she could not force the older boy to stay with her, Annie Clegg leaned upon the "tender years" doctrine as her custody defense for the other three children. The Klan, however, intended to foil Annie's plans to take Archie to Richmond to meet his grandmother and sisters. By taking her son Annie Clegg would violate another principle of the Klan: that only fathers could properly instill the Protestant, patriarchal, white supremacist principles in their sons. In a paper entitled "Responsibility of the Klankraft to the American Boy" a Klansmen at the Asheville meeting argued that boys represented the future "masters of posterity." The Klan argued that it possessed a sacred duty to provide boys with a "practical safeguard and dependable help" in a "Boys Auxiliary" that would initiate young boys into a "Junior Order of the Ku Klux Klan." Girls needed no auxiliary, it was implied, because they would share in the "the benefits and blessings" of boys' newfound leadership skills. The auxiliary would give boys the special encouragement and discipline they required. "The principal causes of delinquency and degeneracy among the boys," according to the paper, "are, divorce, poverty, and the godless home." Although Annie Clegg was not pursuing divorce proceedings against her husband, in the view of the Klan she would be endangering her son's future by separating him from his father.[39]

But perhaps the most exalted KKK principle that Annie Clegg had violated by taking her children from her husband was one that required women's subordination to men. According to the Klan members that met in Asheville that 1923 summer, wives must submit without question to their husbands. "A noble woman," argued another speaker, "is the embodiment of loyalty and love. She will stand by her husband right and wrong." Like a beloved pet, a woman belonged at her husband's side. Even the power to vote did not grant women any special autonomy. Rather, women were to use the ballot to complement their husbands' votes. The power to vote, he argued, represented a "challenge" to women "to arise and claim their rights and take their places alongside" their men. Klansmen could not envision women's political empowerment separate from their duties and obligations to their husbands. Therefore, when Annie Clegg attempted to leave with her son, she challenged these very fundamental gender assumptions held by the Klansmen who visited her that night.[40]

Judges agonized over this custody dispute. Judge W. A. Devin, of the Robeson County Superior Court, argued that both father and mother were suitable parents. Therefore, he granted custody to Isaac N. Clegg but allowed Annie Clegg control of the children from June until September of each year. Both parents rejected this arrangement, and the case landed on the docket at the North Carolina Supreme Court. In considering the Cleggs' problem, Associate Justice Heriot Clarkson struggled with the often conflicting decisions the court had made in previous decisions. Two earlier cases, *In Re Constance Turner* (151 NC

474) and *A. T. Newsome v. Q. T. Bunch* (144 NC 15), had confirmed from earlier precedent the father's entitlement to his children but recognized that the children's welfare was the "polar star" guiding the courts. *In Re Mary v. Means, Infant* (176 NC 307) also underscored fathers' rights, but when both parents appeared "equally worthy, the mother may be allowed the superior claim when it is shown that the welfare of the child requires it." Thus Clarkson and his associates faced a case that required them to weigh the father's rights, the mother's rights, and the children's best interests. But in this case the judges could rationalize no single answer from North Carolina case precedent. To place the children with one parent clearly violated the rights of the other, and both were unwilling to accept a joint arrangement.[41]

Unable to find an answer in the court's past decisions, the judges turned instead to literary, political, and religious sources that referenced the family and its place in society. Many references, Clarkson said, established the husband's authority. For example, the social contract, the very foundation of republican principles, preserved men's rights to govern not only in public but also in the home. "The home is the rock foundation for the governmental structures," Clarkson asserted. "If the unity of the home is weak, some day the structure may crumble." Clarkson also referenced the apostle Paul's New Testament directions that wives revere their husbands, and he cited Washington Irving, who described a wife as a "vine" who twined her tendrils in support around her husband. "So it is beautifully ordered by Providence," Irving wrote in "The Wife," "that woman, who is the mere dependent and ornament of man in his happier hours, should be his stay and solace when smitten with sudden calamity, winding herself into the rugged recesses of his nature, tenderly supporting the drooping head, and binding up the broken heart."[42]

Paternal authority was well established in these sources, Clarkson intimated, but children nonetheless required their mother's care and affection. Recent emphasis placed upon women's role as mothers and recent precedent establishing women's custody rights at once required Clarkson to consider Annie Clegg's claim to her children. "Let us not forget to consider the equal right of the mother," he intoned. In fact, Clarkson cared less about Annie's rights to her children than he did about her responsibilities as their mother. Therefore, the court upheld the superior court's decision to grant custody to Isaac Clegg but allow Annie Clegg control from June to September each year. The only modification the supreme court made to the superior court's decision was to forbid Annie Clegg from taking the children out of the state. In effect, the court required her to keep the children at her brother's home in Old Fort, North Carolina, rather than at her mother's home in Richmond, Virginia. Either parent could visit the children upon request.[43]

Eventually Annie won custody of her children. Just months after the court reached its decision in 1923, her family's circumstances changed. Isaac was released from most of his ministry obligations in Rowland, and he found work in Fayetteville, some distance from the homestead. He placed the children with his sister, who refused Annie access to them, and became physically violent when she insisted upon visits. The children complained that they rarely saw their father and that "Aunt Marie" forced them to do most of the housework. Annie filed a new petition in the Robeson County Superior Court, and the judge found in her favor. The children's welfare, the court argued, "will be promoted by so awarding them to the custody of their mother, on account of the changed conditions in the home life of [Isaac Clegg] and the changed circumstances in which the children are placed since the respondent abandoned them to the custody of the mother." The superior court had accepted Annie Clegg's argument that Isaac Clegg had in effect shirked his fatherly duties by placing his children in his sister's care. Since they had been "abandoned" by their father, the children's welfare was best met by their only remaining "suitable" parent, Annie Clegg. The court granted Annie Clegg custody of the children and gave Isaac Clegg control of the children from June until September each year, a decision that reversed the original arrangement set by the court in 1923.[44]

Annie Clegg won custody after a prolonged battle not only with her husband but also with the hard-and-fast principle that a father's right to his children was paramount. When justices began to view Isaac Clegg as an unsuitable parent, Annie Clegg was able to make the claim that she alone could meet the best interests of her children. Isaac Clegg's paternal claims to his children, once considered almost inviolate, had eroded significantly by 1924. As middle-class women began to assume a more public role at the turn of the century, concepts of womanhood changed. Women had begun to extend their role as nurturers from the home and into the public by claiming that society required women's innate moral influence in the areas of certain reforms, including education and temperance. Judges at every level of the government infused this new definition of womanhood into child-custody and apprenticeship matters. Court cases such as *Mitchell v. Mitchell, Ashby v. Page, Mary Scoggins v. William Scoggins*, and *Annie McIntosh Clegg v. I. N. Clegg* (1923, 1924) established new legal precedent that allowed mothers control of their children when it was in the children's best interests. Decisions rendered in child-custody cases help us to better understand why apprenticeship declined.

Yet this new trend favoring maternal custody did not necessarily mean that judges had changed their minds about women's rights. Women had in no way usurped men's rights as custodians, but fathers could no longer claim unlimited control of their children. Mothers could only claim primary guardianship if the father appeared unsuitable and the mother met the conditions of good character, an abstract measurement usually determined by a mother's class status and community reputation. Therefore, women's claims to the guardianship of their children developed not in response to their demands for equality but as a by-product of judicial discretion imposed in cases once decided upon established law that favored fathers. In the end, children's best interests, not parental rights, prevailed. Nonetheless, some women benefited from this more favorable climate despite the vociferous protestations of reactionary groups such as the Ku Klux Klan. Ultimately, the new climate would spell the end of apprenticeship.

In the agricultural South, children provided an invaluable labor resource. Photo taken 1920,
Tabitha Marie DeVisconti Papers.
Courtesy of the Special Collections Department, Joyner Library, East Carolina University.

To the Worshipful Justices of the Court of Pleas and Quarter Sessions of Brunswick County

The Petition of Temperance Chavers humbly Sheweth that she has raised two Boys Billy and Elick from their birth to the present time with much difficulty trouble & expence and that just as they are Beginning to remunerate her by plowing & other services She is threatened with their being bound out which She thinks a great hardship but if the law of the State required She humbly beseeches that they may be bound to Gen: Smith in whose justice to raise them properly and have them taught useful trades She can Confide — Your Worships granting this will be an Alleviation to her Distress & She as in duty bound will ever pray &c —

Jan: 27th 1810

Temperance — Chavers
her mark

Witness
Ben B. Smith

The "Petition of Temperance Chavers," dated January 27, 1810, demonstrates the difficulty poor women faced when the state required their children's apprenticeship. Chavers argued that her children's apprenticeship caused her "a great hardship" and requested that the court apprentice her children to someone she knew.

Courtesy of the North Carolina Office of Archives and History, Raleigh, North Carolina.

State of North-Carolina,
Guilford COUNTY.

THIS INDENTURE. made the 21st day of November in the year of our Lord one thousand eight hundred and 20 between Jno Howell Chairman of the county court of Guilford county and state aforesaid, on behalf of the Justices of said county and their successors, of the one part, and Matthew Young of the other part: WITNESSETH, That the said Jno Howell in pursuance to an order of the said county court, made the 21th day of Nov and according to the directions of the Act of Assembly in that case made and provided, doth put, place and bind unto the said Matthew Young an Orphan, named Betsey Pool aged 12 years old last May with the said Matthew Young to live after the manner of an Apprentice and servant, until the said Apprentice shall attain to the age of Eighteen years during all which time, the said Apprentice shall faithfully serve, all lawful commands, every where readily obey: her master shall not at any time absent herself from her said master service without leave, but in all things as a good and faithful servant shall behave towards her said master —And the said Matthew Young doth covenant, promise and agree to and with the said John Howell that he will teach and instruct, or cause to be taught and instructed, the said Betsey Pool to learn Give her One bed & furniture worth $30. One Spinning wheel two suits of Cloth. & Learn her to Read & write the Clothes are as freedom suits and that he will constantly find and provide for the said Apprentice, during the term aforesaid, sufficient diet, washing, lodging and apparel, fitting for an Apprentice; and also all other things necessary, both in sickness and in health.

IN WITNESS WHEREOF, the parties to these presents have interchangeably set their hands and seals, the day and year first above written.

Signed, Sealed, and Delivered,
in the presence of
Jno Hammer &c   John Howell Chairman
                    M Young {Seal}

In 1820, North Carolina law required masters to provide apprentices at least one new suit of clothes, six dollars, and a Bible when they gained their freedom. Guilford County master Matthew Young also promised his apprentice, Betsey Pool, other material objects including furniture and a spinning wheel.

Courtesy of the North Carolina Office of Archives and History, Raleigh, North Carolina.

After the Civil War, freed children continued to perform the work that they had done in slavery. Four-year-old Billy Compton removes cured leaves from a tobacco plant in Carr, North Carolina.

This 1939 photograph, taken by Marion Post Wolcott, FSA, is housed in the Library of Congress.

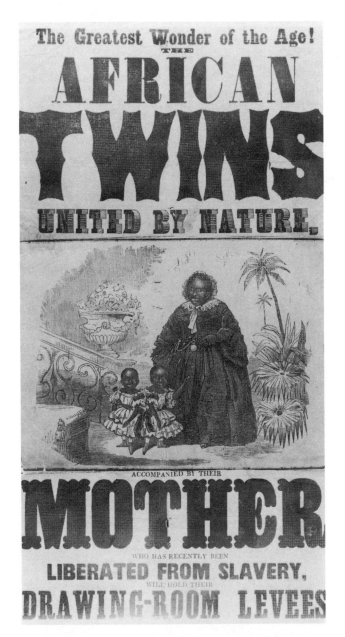

The Greatest Wonder of the Age!

THE

AFRICAN

TWINS

UNITED BY NATURE.

ACCOMPANIED BY THEIR

MOTHER.

WHO HAS RECENTLY BEEN

LIBERATED FROM SLAVERY,

WILL HOLD THEIR

DRAWING-ROOM LEVEES

Freedmen's Bureau agents often facilitated contracts between parents and masters. Strictly speaking, North Carolina apprenticeship law did not govern the contract that determined the fate of conjoined twins Milly and Christina McCrory. But their labor contract serves as an example of the complicated relations between masters, parents, and Freedmen's Bureau agents.

Poster circa 1857, courtesy of the North Carolina Office of Archives and History, Raleigh, North Carolina.

Many Freedmen's Bureau agents routinely apprenticed children to masters, though some agents derided the practice. Agent H. H. Foster signed this indenture that apprenticed four siblings to John Vann in Sampson County, a rural county where missionaries reported that hundreds of children were forcibly and sometimes violently seized from their parents.

Courtesy of the National Archives and Records Administration.

Forced apprenticeship sparked much controversy among agents, and some insisted upon securing parental consent. One agent in Magnolia, a rural town in eastern North Carolina, secured the "free and voluntary consent" of freedwoman Emily for her son's indenture.

Courtesy of the National Archives and Records Administration.

In 1917, the state founded the State Board of Charities and Public Welfare to oversee the twenty-one orphanages, most of them privately sponsored, that existed across North Carolina. This circa 1910 photograph depicts children who are residents of the Nazareth Orphans' Home in Crescent, North Carolina.

Courtesy of the North Carolina Office of Archives and History, Raleigh, North Carolina.

These orphans from the Nazareth Orphans' Home dig up stumps in a field to pay for their keep. Pictured, from left to right, are Robert Carrier, David Miller, Ben Artz, and Will Carrier. Photo dated 1917.

Courtesy of the North Carolina Office of Archives and History, Raleigh, North Carolina.

In 1919 the North Carolina General Assembly replaced the apprenticeship laws with the Child Welfare Act. The new act included child-labor regulations, a juvenile court system, and an act entitled "Control over Indigent Children." This 1908 photograph by Lewis Hine depicts three young textile workers in Gastonia, North Carolina.

Courtesy of the North Carolina Office of Archives and History, Raleigh, North Carolina.

CHAPTER SIX

"THE DAY OF APPRENTICESHIP IS PAST"

The Demise of Apprenticeship and the Triumph of Child Welfare

August in North Carolina is oppressive. Waves of heat rise from any reflective surface, and the air is so thick with humidity that it is difficult to breathe. But in 1909 fifteen-year-old Richard Watson found relief in walking the streets of Charlotte, finding refuge in the shadows as the sun marched across the afternoon sky. The Mecklenburg County courts had recently convicted and sentenced his father, a farm laborer and "confirmed dope fiend," to the county prison, where he would remain for two years. With his father incarcerated, his mother deceased, and his grandmother an inmate at the Mecklenburg County Home, the young Watson had nowhere to go. When a local resident complained to the police about Watson's vagrancy, the justice of the peace demanded the boy's arrest. On August 26, 1909, the sheriff arrested Watson for "loitering and sauntering about the streets of Charlotte" without a home, occupation, or any means of support. Upon his conviction, the court committed him to the Stonewall Jackson Manual Training and Industrial School, a reformatory for white boys that had opened just months before. Little did Richard Watson or his father, Samuel S. Watson, realize that the state would retain Richard well beyond the thirty-day maximum imprisonment for vagrancy. Upon release from prison in 1911, Samuel Watson immediately filed a petition for a writ of *habeas corpus* in behalf of his son. In the older Watson's view, he had earned his freedom and it was time for him to resume his duties as a parent.[1]

Many of the state's most influential authorities did not share Watson's outlook. Reformers, legislators, and the North Carolina courts, including the justices of the state's supreme court, had begun to embrace a belief in more frequent state intervention in families. A new concern for children's rights and children's welfare initiated dramatic realignments in Carolinians' beliefs about gender, class, and race. Early in the twentieth century, reformers and legislators maneuvered the state into a paternalistic role that supervised the training of poor white children, once the province of individual patriarchs. As a result, the apprenticeship institution and the laws and practices that had upheld it for two centuries crumbled. In its place rose a new and complex system of child welfare that marked important shifts in perceptions of childhood. Children, particularly white males, once viewed as a family resource, were suddenly viewed as precious and vulnerable future citizens who required the state's paternalistic supervision and protection from the consequences of juvenile delinquency, as well as from the vagaries of presumably inadequate fathers such as Samuel S. Watson. Apprenticeship, which placed children under the supervision of individual men and not state agencies, could not meet that demand.[2]

Though apprenticeship remained on the books until the Child Welfare Act replaced it in 1919, reformers began an assault on the institution as early as the 1890s. Just as Chaney Ashby's cases came to a close, legislators imposed new laws that restricted masters' almost unlimited power over apprentices. Previous antebellum and Reconstruction apprenticeship laws had required masters to provide shelter, food, clothing, and education to apprentices. Masters who violated these laws had come under public scrutiny, but the most that courts could do was void the indentures. In 1892 the General Assembly changed the law to enable courts to convict neglectful masters of a misdemeanor. Masters had thirty days to amend any problem reported to the court. If they failed, they risked heavy fines or imprisonment.[3]

Apprenticeship also suffered as the state increasingly turned to orphanages as repositories for children. Governor Tod R. Caldwell's message to the General Assembly session of 1873–74 reflects the changing social attitude that favored orphanages over apprenticeship. Apprenticeship, he explained, provided children with no sure means of education as moral citizens. "It is well known that very few bound orphans are ever sent to any school, and that most of them are growing up in ignorance of the laws of God and of the laws of their country. Having lost their natural guides and protectors, and feeling that society has failed to afford them the means of improvement, they naturally sink into vice and degration [*sic*] and become a plague and a burden to the State." But, he continued, orphanages could provide children with necessary support, discipline, and education.[4]

When Caldwell delivered his message in 1873, few orphanages graced the state. That year the Oxford Orphan Asylum, sponsored by the Grand Lodge of the Order of Free Masons, opened its doors to white children. In 1883 several Baptist organizations together opened the Colored Orphanage Asylum of North Carolina, also in Oxford. By 1899 there were ten orphanages in North Carolina, and by 1929 that number had increased to thirty. Few orphanages received any funding from the state of North Carolina. However, both Oxford orphanages received some state funding, though the amount of appropriations to the white institution easily eclipsed the amount given to its African American counterpart. In 1917 the state founded the State Board of Charities and Public Welfare to oversee orphanages and empowered this board to inspect and license orphanages throughout the state. That year, the board supervised twenty-one orphanages, most of them privately funded by churches or voluntary organizations. A few generated income from the sale of products manufactured at the institution. Only one orphanage, the Buncombe County Children's Home, was supported entirely by the county. In 1895 the state's seven orphanages housed approximately 650 children, some of whom were not truly orphans but children from broken homes in which one or both parents were still living. For example, twelve of the seventy-five children at the Colored Orphanage Asylum, had at least one parent still living.[5]

Children who lived in orphanages carried heavy work loads. Though many orphanages provided children with some form of education, all relied upon children's labor to meet the institution's operating costs. Life for a child in an orphanage mimicked a mass-apprenticeship system: children completed chores, learned skills, and performed tasks under the supervision of professional authorities rather than individual masters. Generally, boys learned skills in farming, printing, shoemaking, baking, repairing, and a host of other crafts, including leatherwork and bricklaying. Girls performed domestic duties such as cleaning, cooking, sewing, nursing, and secretarial tasks. Orphanage authorities boasted about the work performed by children, especially in cases where all the institution's needs could be met by the children's labor alone. In 1900 an editorial for the publication *Charity and Children* explained the value of children's work in the orphanages. "The children not only have to work," the writer explained, "but they are taught to look upon all honest work, however humble, not by any means as degrading but on the contrary honorable and ennobling." Orphanage authorities and apprenticeship advocates at once embraced notions about the importance of children's self-supporting labor and believed that children's work should take place in more supervised and regulated environments.[6]

But for a large group of middle-class reformers, society required more than a few orphanages to address children's needs. Southern reformers embraced a paternalistic mission to justify social and political control by the middle class. Class and race relations had grown increasingly volatile during the late nineteenth century, as poor whites and African Americans established coalitions in the Populist and Republican fusion campaigns. Democrats, fearful of losing political control, developed a white supremacist campaign intended to split the poor white and African American coalition. By 1900 the white supremacist campaign had culminated in de jure segregation, disfranchisement, lynching, and one-party rule. As the twentieth century progressed, some middle-class reformers endorsed views that included both a commitment to white supremacy and a belief in the necessity of African American progress and reform. Alexander McKelway, a prominent North Carolina child-labor reformer and a leader in the 1900 disfranchisement campaign, held firmly to the idea that social equality would lead to "the destruction of the white race itself, the loss forever of the Anglo-Saxon strain." Yet he believed in a segregated social order in which whites were obligated to uplift blacks "to the highest possible plane." In his view, blacks should have educational opportunities but not political opportunities available to them. McKelway's opinions came to represent many southern reformers' paternalistic intentions. His views contrasted sharply with those of other North Carolina whites, such as Thomas Dixon, author of *The Clansman*, Senator Furnifold Simmons, and Colonel Alfred Moore Waddell, who had instigated the Wilmington Massacre of 1898. These men and others argued that since emancipation African Americans had retrogressed into bestiality and that only violence, intimidation, or removal to foreign parts would prevent them from despoiling white society.[7]

In addition to harboring these paternalistic assumptions about race, middle-class reformers also viewed the working class and rural whites as a dangerous social element in North Carolina. For example, social reformers feared the power that working-class whites might gain in the chaotic social and extralegal environment that lynching produced. Lynching, though an important part of the fabric of early twentieth-century white supremacy, created unease among some southern white reformers. By encouraging mob rule, lynching opened the doors to lawlessness and social collapse. McKelway, among other reformers, attributed lynching and mob rule to the "backward" and "barbaric" demeanor of lower-class whites. Less concerned with the plight of innocent victims, McKelway emphasized the lawlessness that resulted from lynching, arguing that a "malicious woman with a small amount of intellect and character" possessed the ability to unleash tremendous violence "with a word from her lying tongue." Thus, reformers such as McKelway advocated an elitist and white supremacist paternalism intended to maintain social order and racial peace.[8]

McKelway, a Presbyterian minister from Fayetteville who became a leading advocate for child welfare, argued that this paternalistic social order should be maintained by laws grounded in a new understanding of childhood. Unlike their nineteenth-century counterparts, who viewed children as useful laborers or property, twentieth-century reformers argued that global destiny rested upon the shoulders of children, particularly white children. Therefore, McKelway argued, children should be protected from early toil because it led to a "stunting of the body," a "dwarfing of the mind," and a "spoiling of the spirit." Child labor was inhumane and unchristian, McKelway maintained, and represented the "power of greed" among Americans. A new concept of child nurture, reformers argued, should replace older beliefs that supported child labor. Future social progress necessitated the protection of childhood. These new conceptions of childhood eventually would bring about the end of apprenticeship, a system that in theory if not in practice upheld children's work as an essential element of their development as citizens.[9]

McKelway's views of child labor reflected a larger national pattern of changing attitudes toward childhood and adolescence among reformers. Industrialization, new ideals of "companionate marriage," women's heightening role as nurturers, and the growing influence of social reformers prompted new attitudes about childhood. Children, once valued for their economic productivity, had come to represent an emotional rather than a commercial asset. But the shift was not a painless one. From 1870 to 1930 conflicts raged among working and middle-class parents, reformers, and employers over cultural definitions of childhood. Reformers viewed children as sentimental objects and feared that laboring children, valued more for their economic contributions, were not properly loved. One historian has argued that "the price of a useful wage-earning child was directly counterposed to the moral value of an economically useless but emotionally priceless child." Reformers and scientists also popularized new concepts about teenagers that reflected their ambivalence toward urban society. In 1904 G. Stanley Hall published *Adolescence*, in which he argued that after childhood, young people entered a behavioral stage marked by moodiness, uncertainty, self-absorption, and foolishness. To protect young people and to segregate them from the adult world, reformers encouraged insular activities such as Christian youth organizations and educational experiences such as college.[10]

Racial and class paternalism pervaded McKelway's views of childhood. He was concerned primarily with the destiny of white children, who he believed were the future of society and civilization. Child labor, he argued, threatened "the race in its upward progress" and turned it "towards degeneration and extinction"; by protecting white children, the South would achieve progress. Furthermore, he feared that child labor in southern mills had created a debased class of workers, which ultimately would bring about "racial degeneracy." In 1906 he told a meeting of the National Child Labor Committee that "we are brought face to face with the fact that the depreciation of our racial stock has already begun" with the proliferation of child labor in factories. Child labor produced tremendous social and political instability because child workers were held in ignorance and bondage, lacked maternal "naturalness" and "sensitiveness," and knew only the routines of "work and sleep." Family life was reversed as children became adults "too soon" and lacked respect for authority. These paternalistic assumptions influenced McKelway's and other reformers' implementation of state laws to end child labor.[11]

McKelway's ideas about social order resonated with the King's Daughters, a statewide women's organization committed to uplifting poor and disadvantaged white boys. In 1902 the organization led a campaign for a state reformatory for white boys. At first the General Assembly opposed their proposal, but the King's Daughters persisted. Within two years they had raised a thousand dollars and purchased fifty acres of land. The General Assembly chartered a reformatory but refused to appropriate funds for operating the institution. This only sparked the King's Daughters' resolve, and they enlisted help from the United Daughters of the Confederacy and the North Carolina Federation of Women's Clubs, which eagerly expanded lobbying efforts for a state-run reformatory.[12]

In 1907 the clubwomen renewed their efforts to establish a state-run reformatory for white boys. Women reformers and several allies in the legislature presented a bill aimed at both prison reform and memorializing a beloved southern hero. According to the bill's proponents, the "Stonewall Jackson Training School" would fulfill the twofold "duty of the State to prosecute and punish young criminals," a responsibility that was "inseparable from its obligations of guarding them and giving them a chance to reform." The new law named four women to serve as trustees, and it required the governor to consult the four before naming additional board members. Though apprenticeship remained in the law books, 1907 marked a turning point as women reformers gained unprecedented influence over the fates of disadvantaged and delinquent male children.[13]

Benefactors and school administrators embraced a mission based upon the assumption that the school would admit only white boys who were orphaned or delinquent. The alternative, reformers feared, would require boys' imprisonment alongside African American criminals. In recounting the experiences of one boy who apparently suffered such a fate, the editor of *The Uplift*, the school's weekly publication, emphasized the child's impoverished roots, the death of his illiterate parents, and his conviction for stealing from distant relatives, for which the boy was imprisoned and assigned to a chain gang. In an 1892 letter to a future benefactor the presumed boy, Hubert Smith, described the chain gang as a dangerous place for a God-fearing young boy. "Mr. Cook, this is a hard place," Smith wrote from jail, "it tries a boy. . . . Sometimes the boys cuss and fight." In his letter Smith repented for his sins, begged forgiveness, and asked God to protect his mother (who evidently had not died, contrary to the editor's statement in the weekly magazine). The editor, most likely the school superintendent, Charles E. Boger, omitted most of Smith's narrative and instead decried the boy's place as "the only white person" on the chain gang. "WHY HE WAS CHAINED TO A NEGRO," Boger lamented in *The Uplift*, but Smith had never mentioned the race of the other prisoners; in fact he had not made an issue of race. Fearful of poor white boys' fate in the presence of African American criminals, white reformers hastily raised the funds necessary to open and then expand the school. By memorializing Stonewall Jackson and granting his widow a seat on the board of trustees, the institution's benefactors further reinforced its white supremacist mission.[14]

Emphasizing the self-sufficiency of its students, the Stonewall Jackson Manual Training and Industrial School served as an alternative to apprenticeship. Located on approximately three hundred acres in Concord, just north of Charlotte, the school included cottages that served as the boys' quarters, an administration building, a classroom building, a chapel, a sewerage system, a well, and, by 1920, an electrical connection. Boys worked in a well-stocked barn and learned vocational skills in the Roth Industrial Building. Boys alternated schooling, exercising, and working. While some attended classes, others worked at construction, farming, woodworking, and any number of other jobs, including sewing and laundering their own clothes. The school became well known for its printing office, where boys printed publications, including the school weekly. Each afternoon boys took part in military drills and football or baseball. Each Sunday they assembled in the chapel. According to Boger, most boys behaved while living on the campus and only rarely required constraints such as "ankle bracelets." Weekly reports of boys' activities produced in the printing office assured benefactors and the state that boys worked under the supervision of the superintendent and his staff. It seems that Boger, the school's benefactors, and the state viewed the school as a more carefully controlled environment for poor white children than individual masters' homes.[15]

At the Stonewall Jackson Manual Training and Industrial School state paternalism of poor white children flourished. Richard Watson was a case in point. County courts, which once had utilized apprenticeship to control orphaned children, immediately embraced the school as a place to deposit orphans and delinquents. In 1920 the school housed 241 boys from "through-out the State whom the public schools could not manage, parents could not control and whom society had practically ostracized." Sometimes the boys came to the school without the consent of their parents. For two hundred years single mothers and African American fathers had experienced problems in retaining custody of children. But now, poor white fathers such as Samuel S. Watson also risked losing custody, especially if they had an unsavory history themselves. Watson, released after two years' imprisonment in Mecklenburg County, experienced the state's power when he tried to obtain custody of his son, Richard. Watson argued that the court had restrained his son for two years, an illegal and unconstitutional punishment for vagrancy, which ordinarily carried a maximum sentence of thirty days. In Samuel Watson's view, the state had overreached its jurisdiction over his son.[16]

But the North Carolina Supreme Court disagreed. Drawing upon his belief in the state's paternalistic function, Associate Justice William R. Allen argued that the state, as *parens patriae,* or substitute parent, may detain a child when the parent is "unworthy." Though several witnesses had testified that Samuel S. Watson was "a fit and proper person to have the custody of his son," Judge Allen raised his earlier criminal conviction as evidence of his incapacity as a parent. "When it is remembered," Allen argued, "that if [Samuel Watson] was an unworthy parent when his child was taken charge of by the State, he had abdicated his parental authority, it is not unreasonable to say to him that the interest of the child and society have become paramount, and that these must by considered in passing upon his application for the custody of the child." Allen cast his decision in terms of parental duty and children's best interests. Whereas Samuel Watson had "abdicated" his parental authority by his conviction for a crime, the state possessed the power to serve as Richard Watson's substitute parent until he reached adulthood. Thus, Richard Watson's detention served not as a form of imprisonment but as an opportunity for reform. The State, as *parens patriae*, could retain Watson because it suited his best interests.[17]

Though the Stonewall Jackson Manual Training and Industrial School supervised numerous poor white boys on behalf of the state, it had not replaced apprenticeship, which remained law despite continuous attack by reformers. Increasingly, North Carolina organizers endorsed a child-welfare law in place of apprenticeship. In 1918 the North Carolina Conference for Social Service sponsored an inquiry by the National Child Labor Committee into the question of child welfare in North Carolina. In a volume of essays that resulted from the study, investigators attacked the apprenticeship system. Mabel Ellis Brown denounced apprenticeship as "an obsolete idea" and declared that "it should be abolished in North Carolina as it has been abolished in other states where it once held sway." Brown explained that society had progressed from the "handicraft stage," which necessarily utilized apprenticeship, to an industrialized economy, which required other means of labor and training. Apprenticeship was outmoded, she declared, because society no longer used the system to teach children useful skills. "Indenturing a child," she said, "now means little more than bartering his potential worth as a servant for his support during childhood and it practically takes from him the choice of a vocation." Thus, the system violated national principles. "It is out of accord with modern democracy," Brown exclaimed, "and it must go." W. H. Swift agreed. "The day of apprenticeship is past," he asserted, "the right of the clerk of the court to apprentice children should be abolished." Both investigators called for the General Assembly to adopt child-welfare legislation that included labor laws, state-supervised reformatories, schools, and the creation of county juvenile courts.[18]

More state intervention was consistent with reformers' ideologies of progress. Social reformers endorsed government intervention that centered on scientific and rational methods. By adopting techniques of scientific management, the state would create a socially efficient bureaucracy that would secure uniform laws in education, health, and child welfare throughout the state. The school reformer Charles L. Coon argued that common health problems disappeared when children and parents adopted good sanitation practices. Fearing that ignorance and carelessness prevented some rural southerners from accepting new sanitation practices, reformers demanded laws, as Coon explained, "to force some people to learn who will not learn otherwise that they have no inalienable right to do as they please about anything." In 1914 the North Carolina state superintendent of public instruction ordered all school districts to include sanitary privies in newly constructed schools. The state intervened in other areas of reform as well. In 1915 the General Assembly replaced the system of local school districts with a county system. Four years later state officials wrested control of county school systems' financial matters when the General Assembly enacted statutes to consolidate school finances.[19]

Perhaps North Carolina's most enthusiastic proponent for child-welfare reform was Thomas Walter Bickett, governor of North Carolina from 1917 to 1921. Educated at Wake Forest College and the University of North Carolina, Bickett was admitted to the bar and eventually became senior partner in his own firm, Bickett, White, and Malone. Elected to the state house of representatives in 1907, Bickett secured legislation to improve state facilities for treatment of the mentally challenged. From 1909 to 1917 he served as the state attorney general. As governor, Bickett gained an early reputation for reform by encouraging the inclusion of facilities for teaching agriculture and home economics in rural schools. In response to his entreaties, the General Assembly enacted laws to expand the duties of the state board of health and the board of charities and public welfare. Bickett also pushed a statewide teacher-certification program, increased teachers' salaries, and backed a half-million-dollar bond issue for the construction of new schoolhouses.[20]

Child welfare lay at the heart of Bickett's reform agenda. In his address to the 1919 session of the General Assembly, Bickett implored legislators to improve conditions for North Carolina's children. The Great War, he reminded the General Assembly, had just ended in Europe. To recognize North Carolinian soldiers who had fought in the war, Bickett implored the legislators to create an everlasting memorial worthy of the soldiers' sacrifice. "The finest memorial we can build to our brave," he told them, "is a State that will rank as high over here as they did 'over there.'" Bickett argued that the republican ideals for which soldiers had fought would best be preserved by expanding state power through a series of laws that uplifted North Carolina's children. The first step "in the building of this State," he maintained, "should be the welfare of the children, for 'the child is the father to the man.'" Bickett listed what he perceived as every child's natural rights, rights that the state was obligated to protect. First, the bastardy laws should be reformed because "every child has a right to know who his father is." The courts should identify and locate fathers of illegitimate children and charge them with the maintenance and education of their children as if they had been born in lawful wedlock. Second, every child "has a natural right to a fair start." Courts should not grant marriage licenses to mentally challenged individuals and thus condone their procreation. "The State," Bickett complained, "is a party to an awful crime against childhood when it permits idiots and imbeciles to perpetuate their species." Third, children born with mental or physical defects had the right to have their conditions corrected by medical or surgical means. Fourth, every child had the right to an education for at least six months per year. Finally, every child had the right to protection from child labor.[21]

By proclaiming that children had these five natural rights, Bickett departed significantly from nineteenth-century views of childhood. During the nineteenth century, issues involving children revolved around parents' rights, not children's. Prior to the 1880s few courts put the best interests of the child ahead of the rights of the parent or master. Fathers possessed almost supreme rights to their children. Though mothers possessed fewer rights, courts usually weighed their interests before ruling against them. Chaney Ashby's cases demonstrate a shift in emphasis from parental rights to the child's welfare: the court ruled that Ashby was the wrong sort of mother to care for her child. Nearly thirty years later Thomas Walter Bickett firmly condoned assumptions about children's rights in his address to the General Assembly. Though his sentiments had begun to gain popularity decades earlier, his speech affirmed a new understanding of childhood.

It was as if Bickett had opened the floodgates for discussion. Social workers streamed into Raleigh for the annual session of the North Carolina Conference for Social Service. The meeting began on February 13, 1919, and featured such topics as public and child welfare and public health. The *Raleigh News and Observer* praised attendees' efforts and noted that that the "example of the Social Service workers has been fairly contagious." In his presidential address, entitled "The Child," Dr. Howard E. Rondthaler called for the creation of "a children's Magna Charta, a children's bill of rights, [and] a children's Declaration of independence." Rondthaler emphasized the importance of preserving childhood for future civilization. Social welfare, Rondthaler argued, "is the dictate of common sense because the child is the citizen in the making and upon that making rests the weal or woe of the future, and the dictate of religion because the little child stands in our religion as the symbol of all that is pure and good and sweet." He called upon the state to support institutions for handicapped and orphaned children, the establishment of foster homes in place of apprenticeship, a juvenile-court system, compulsory school attendance, child-labor laws, and reformed bastardy laws.

The state could obtain many of these reforms, he acknowledged, by the creation of a "Children's Code." According to Rondthaler, the children's code would grant the state, through a "central board of children's guardians," powers to supervise children "in or outside their own homes." In addition, the children's code would include a centralized supervisory authority responsible for probation, health, and education. Furthermore, the code would provide for mothers' and widows' pensions "when nothing more serious than poverty interferes," carefully controlled school systems, and revised laws intended to protect children born out of wedlock. After Rondthaler concluded his remarks, Josephus Daniels, a North Carolina native and secretary of the navy, endorsed every child's "right to be well born and well cared for." Daniels also emphasized the state's duty to the child and "made [a] vigorous appeal" for child-labor legislation.[22]

Legislators in session nearby at the General Assembly kept up with the developments at the conference. They surely could not have escaped the lengthy reports of the conference that appeared on the front page of the *Raleigh News and Observer.* As if to appease reformers' vigorous demands, several reform-minded legislators introduced bills related to child welfare at the 1919 General Assembly session. These bills were intended to establish new legal concepts of childhood that reflected the mood of social reform. The state's old bastardy laws were the first to come under fire. A bill introduced by Senator Robert L. Burns, of Carthage, proposed to repeal the bastardy laws and implement new legislation to secure the best interests of the child. Burns disapproved of state laws that prevented children born out of wedlock from seeking paternity (and thus establishing themselves as heirs) and statutes that failed to enforce child support. The new law would require every physician or other birth attendant to report the birth of children born out of wedlock to the superior court, which would proceed to establish paternity, locate fathers, and require them to provide for their children's maintenance and education. Unlike previous laws, the new act threatened negligent fathers with imprisonment. With greater certainty that fathers would provide for their children, mothers were less likely to see their children apprenticed. Though the bill had positive consequences for single mothers, Burns sponsored the bill to improve children's status. As he said of his bill, "It looks to the welfare of the child, who is born into the world in a condition for which it was in no wise responsible and for which it is unjust and unwise to hold it responsible." The bill's easy passage in late February was no measure of its significance in elevating the child's best interests over the rights of the father.[23]

Reformers embarked upon a campaign to save wayward children with the introduction of the juvenile-courts bill. This bill reflected efforts to improve the future of children through proper molding and education. In late January Senator H. E. Stacy, of Robeson County, introduced a bill that would give superior courts primary jurisdiction over all delinquents under eighteen years of age. The bill required that a probation officer in each county look after wayward children or those who were neglected or dependent upon the public for support. Supporters praised the bill. The *Raleigh News and Observer* called the bill "the foundation of child salvation and . . . the very backbone of the measures intended for child welfare in the State." According to the editor, delinquent children could be reformed into good citizens and thus did not belong in ordinary criminal courts. "The object of a juvenile court is to investigate conditions surrounding each case of juvenile delinquency, to find out their causes, to remove them if possible and to so dispose of the case that the child will be saved to itself and to society and good citizenship before he has time to graduate into real crime." A juvenile court should be "educational, directory, and supervisory," and its management should lie in the hands of a skillful, sensitive, and intelligent county probation officer. The bill met with little opposition in the General Assembly, and reformers breathed a sigh of relief that the best interests of even the most delinquent children would be preserved.[24]

More controversial efforts to secure the state's control of indigent and neglected children met with ambivalent responses from legislators. Some reformers argued that the state should claim as public wards those children whose mothers lacked the funds to raise them. This proposal struck at the heart of the apprenticeship system, for the bill also stipulated that once the state declared a child a public ward, county commissioners would issue funds for the mother to raise the child provided that the courts found no instance of neglect. Not unlike the modern system of Aid to Families with Dependent Children, the bill "to declare certain children public wards and to provide for same" provided funds enabling single and widowed mothers to keep their children. With state support, mothers would not have to fear court-ordered apprenticeship of their children. The bill passed the Senate with no modifications and was sent to the Committee on the Judiciary in the House of Representatives, where it met a much different fate than it had on the floor of the Senate. After three days committee members rejected the bill and issued an unfavorable report. The bill died. Another bill, "Control Over Indigent Children," which granted the state the authority of parent or guardian over all children in the state's orphans' and children's homes and over those children deemed dependent, neglected, and indigent, met a better fate and passed. These bills marked reformers' attempts to secure the safety of children in the hands of the state with or without their parents' consent.[25]

Yet the passage of these new laws was not enough for many legislators. Some demanded more radical changes in the form of a child-labor law that would replace the state's apprenticeship code. Perhaps more than any other change, child-labor reform represented the quintessential transformation from the old apprenticeship code to a child welfare act. But the reform did not come about easily. In 1919 the General Assembly engaged in a heated battle over two child-labor-reform bills. The triumph of the manufacturers' bill, known as the Neal Substitute, over the reformers' proposal, known as the Connor-Saunders child-labor bill, demonstrates the limitations of child-labor reform and of children's rights in North Carolina.

Representative William Oscar Saunders, a newspaper editor and politician from Perquimans County, fought to improve children's rights in North Carolina. Saunders, the son of a poor farmer who struggled to provide a modest living for his large family, first became involved in politics as a newspaper editor in Elizabeth City. There, he expressed his political views in a one-page paper, *The Independent,* begun in 1908. Saunders often wrote hard-hitting editorials that spoke out against fundamentalism, anti-Semitism, and racial prejudice. In addition, he championed birth control and educational improvement. In 1919 Saunders won election to the General Assembly, where his efforts earned him a reputation as a radical. While in office, Saunders formed a political partnership with Senator Henry G. Connor and the commissioner of labor and printing, M. L. Shipman. The business community viewed this partnership as a radical alliance. Textile manufacturers reviled Shipman for drafting a child-labor bill that promised to bring North Carolina into line with recently passed federal laws. In fact, manufacturers disliked Shipman so much that one legislator proposed a bill in the 1919 session to abolish Shipman's office. Fortunately for Shipman and other pro-labor groups, the bill died in committee.[26]

The Connor-Saunders Bill, as Shipman's proposal came to be known, attempted to bring North Carolina laws more closely into compliance with Congress's 1916 interstate-commerce law, "An Act to prevent interstate commerce in the products of child labor and for other purposes." The federal law imposed a heavy tax on all industries employing children under fourteen years of age or employing children under sixteen years of age for more than eight hours a day or forty-eight hours a week. Congress granted the Department of Labor the power to enforce the act by allowing rigid inspection of factories. Shipman's bill reflected the federal law and established the Child Labor Commission, made up of the state superintendent of public instruction, the secretary of the state board of health, and the commissioner of labor and printing. Additionally, his bill authorized the commissioner of labor and printing to enforce the bill by inspection, provided for timely prosecution in the state courts, and defined violations as misdemeanors requiring punishment by fines and/or imprisonment. In 1917 Shipman had asked the secretaries of the U.S. Labor and Commerce departments to review his bill. Both had approved it and "practically assured" him that if North Carolina passed his measure, the federal government would leave the duty of inspections to North Carolina's commissioner of labor and printing. In a letter to Governor Bickett, Shipman emphasized the popularity of the idea that North Carolina, not the federal government, would control its own affairs regarding child labor. "We hear a good deal of talk about State's rights," he argued. "Here is an opportunity to show the extent of our convictions upon that question."[27]

Saunders introduced Shipman's bill (House bill 289) on January 29, 1919, and the bill was immediately referred to the Committee on Judiciary. The Connor-Saunders Bill quickly drew ire from manufacturers, particularly William Lunsford Long, who immediately helped other sympathetic legislators draft a substitute. Long was from Northampton County, which coincidentally neighbored Perquimans County, Saunders's birthplace, in northeastern North Carolina. The two men likely never crossed paths, though, because of the enormous differences in their social standings. The Longs were a plantation family known for its Confederate colonels and for descending from a prominent governor, Hutchins G. Burton. As a boy Long studied under private tutors, and he graduated from the University of North Carolina in 1909, one year after Saunders began his controversial one-page newspaper. Within ten years Long belonged to the upper echelons of the business community, serving as the vice president and general counsel of Roanoke Mills and later as president of the Rosemary Manufacturing Company, both located in Roanoke Rapids. In 1916 Long, aged twenty-six, was elected to the House of Representatives, where he probably met the thirty-two-year-old Saunders for the first time. In the legislative session of 1919, by which time Long had been elected a senator, the two young men faced off for the first major legislative battle of their careers.[28]

Long assisted Representative W. W. Neal, a hosiery manufacturer from McDowell County, in proposing a bill, which came to be known as the Neal

Bill, to replace the Connor-Saunders child-labor bill. The Neal Bill contained many of the same provisions as the first bill, but as the *Raleigh News and Observer* remarked in its headline of February 4, "Mr. Neal's Bill Would Take Teeth Out of Child Labor Law." The Neal Bill prohibited children under fourteen from paid work but omitted the significant provisions of both the federal law and the Connor-Saunders Bill that restricted the labor of children under sixteen years of age to eight hours a day or forty-eight hours a week. In addition, the Neal Bill specified no regulations for inspections, nor did it specify procedures for prosecuting violators. Most significantly, the bill eliminated the role of the Commission of Labor and Printing as policeman, with the governor replacing the commissioner of labor and printing on the Child Labor Commission. The *Raleigh News and Observer* facetiously likened the bill's omission of the labor commissioner to a play by Shakespeare without its main character. "It is practically the same bill as that drawn by the Commissioner," the editor mused, "only Hamlet is left out of the play."[29]

On February 21 the Committee on Education reported unfavorably for the Connor-Saunders Bill, spelling the end of Saunders's efforts. Meanwhile, Neal created a substitute for his bill by tacking on an addendum that required six months' compulsory school attendance for all children. Saunders redoubled his efforts to destroy the Neal Substitute. According to Saunders, committee members should reject the Neal Substitute because its authors were manufacturers, a group who "should not be permitted to write child labor law." The manufacturers' position did not represent popular opinion. Saunders claimed that "children should not be worked longer hours than grown ups." If the committee recommended the bill, Saunders warned, "wage earners have their remedy for resenting the affront at the ballot box and are well able to protect themselves." Above all, the people would reject the manufacturers' bill because "the moral sentiment of the state will not stand for working children longer than eight hours a day much longer." The *Raleigh News and Observer* heartily agreed with Saunders. In editorials published in the days prior to the vote on the bill, the paper proclaimed that the Neal Substitute should be rejected because it had trivialized the duty of the Department of Labor and Printing. "Child labor is inextricably wrapped up in the general labor problems . . . labor's interests are in the care of labor departments." But the worst feature of the bill, the paper declared, was that it did not conform to the federal child-labor law. "Why should the manufacturers object to a bill that will be as good a bill as that passed by Congress?" Loss of a few profits should not compare with the overall improvement in health and opportunity to the state's children.[30]

Several public sources joined the *Raleigh News and Observer* in vilifying the Neal Substitute and praising the Connor-Saunders Bill. Dr. J. Y. Joyner, superintendent of public instruction, praised the defeated Connor-Saunders Bill as "wise, just and conservatively progressive." Prior to the bill's demise, Joyner hoped that it would not only pass but "afford needed protection to Childhood and also to all cotton mill owners that are honestly opposed to the exploitation of child labor for private profit." The commissioner of labor and printing, he added, was the proper policeman for the job. Even Governor Bickett, whose office would replace Shipman's on the Child Labor Commission if the Neal Substitute were to pass, registered his praise for the Connor-Saunders Bill. "I utterly fail to see any objection to the Commissioner of Labor and Printing being a member of this commission, and in view of the turn that matters have taken in the General Assembly, I deem it eminently wise and proper for him to be a member of this commission and to be the executive officer of the commission as outlined in the bill."[31]

Organized laborers resoundingly backed the Connor-Saunders Bill. Child labor threatened organized laborers' livelihoods, and they demanded a strong law. They argued that Commissioner Shipman's office was meant to protect wage earners as "the teachers are represented in the Department of Education, the doctors in the Department of Health, farmers in the Department of Agriculture." Representatives of more than eighty thousand organized laborers from skilled trades, such as railroad engineers, firemen, machinists, plumbers, and barbers, expressed "vigorous disapproval" at the intimation that the enforcement of the child-labor law might be placed in the hands of an office other than a department of labor. Workers feared that without a strong child-labor law their workplaces would be subject to federal, rather than state, inspections. Organized southern workingmen despised the possible humiliation of federal inspections. "We confidently assume," their official statement read, "that the members of the General Assembly will have sufficient State pride to obviate the necessity of Federal legislation on this subject, the mental honesty to concede the necessity for the passage of the Connor Saunders Child Labor bill, the political sagacity to 'register off' after a protracted stay at half way house and pass this bill *without emasculation*" (emphasis added). Organized workingmen clearly feared the "emasculation" of federal inspections, though the record is silent on the opinions of unorganized working people, including cotton textile laborers.[32]

The Neal Substitute's progress through the General Assembly is best described as precarious. In early March 1919 the bill was passed in the House without much fanfare, but it met a different fate in the Senate. Early in the day on March 7 the Senate Education Committee rejected the Neal Substitute and resurrected the Connor-Saunders Bill. Representative Saunders waited nervously, but probably with pleasant surprise, as his colleagues defended his bill. However, Long refused to sit idly by and threatened to submit a minority report that would bypass the committee and introduce the Neal Substitute on the floor of the General Assembly. As the committee met in a night session, Long pursued his plan. The Neal bill came to the floor with a new amendment that charged the state welfare commissioner with the duty of factory inspections. Likely less vigorous a policeman than the labor commissioner, the welfare commissioner represented an appealing alternative to manufacturers. Though some senators objected, the Neal bill passed in the night session of March 7 with a vote of 27 to 20. John A. Livingston, writing for the *Raleigh News and Observer*, expressed his disappointment with the new law but nonetheless offered some positive remarks: "In passing this law as a welfare measure the General Assembly was inconsistent in not providing sufficient funds to carry it out and further in failing to put it in the department where it belongs. However, the law on the books is still a step forward and will eventually result in putting North Carolina squarely in line with other progressive States." Yet manufacturers such as Neal and Long could claim a major victory. Not only had they skirted federal laws that the U.S. Supreme Court would eventually declare unconstitutional but they had caused North Carolina to become the only state in the nation with a child-labor law enforced by a welfare commissioner rather than a labor department.[33]

Like the Juvenile Courts Act and the Control over Indigent Children Act, child-labor reformers attempted to redefine childhood in a way that protected children from an exploitative work world. According to reformers, to remove or restrict children from the work force preserved their childhood and prevented them from becoming adults too soon. Legislators such as Saunders and other public officials hoped to reshape North Carolina children's legal status to accomplish this. But not everyone shared the reformers' zeal. Organized laborers, though very much in favor of child-labor reform, appeared to sponsor the measure to protect themselves from the "emasculating" humiliation of federal factory inspections. And of course manufacturers feared reductions in their profit margins if the state or the federal government vigorously enforced child-labor inspection and conviction laws. The debate over the Connor-Saunders Bill and the Neal Substitute clearly demarcated these battle lines. During the seemingly revolutionary passage of child-welfare laws in 1919, manufacturers had successfully limited reformers' efforts to preserve children's rights. Therefore, it is inaccurate to conclude only that as child-welfare measures supplanted the archaic apprenticeship system in 1919, concerns for children's welfare completely replaced the notion of parental rights. Thanks to legislators such as Long and Neal, the new laws were dramatically weakened by manufacturers' efforts to protect their own interests.

Yet it is still important to recognize that the new child-welfare laws replaced the old apprenticeship code, an event that, though limited in force, changed the relationship between the child and the state. Lawmakers combined the Juvenile Courts Act, the Control over Indigent Children Act, and the child-labor law into the Child Welfare Act of 1919. The act defined the state's responsibility in three new areas: child-labor regulations, juvenile courts, and control over indigent children. The new statutory code created a state child-welfare commission that had the power to inspect workplaces and enforce regulations. In one stroke the General Assembly dismantled the state apprenticeship code and replaced it with a juvenile-court system that endowed superior courts with exclusive primary jurisdiction over any case involving a child less than sixteen years of age. Legislators added explicit instructions that the new "Article 2: Juvenile Courts" would take the place of the "Apprentice Law" and the "Juvenile Delinquent Law, 1915." The General Assembly had replaced the antiquated laws that preserved relations between individual masters and apprentices with new legislation that radically expanded the state's jurisdiction over children.[34]

Throughout much of North Carolina's history single mothers, widowed mothers, and African American men faced the threat of their children's apprenticeship. Apprenticeship had never targeted white men, but the language of the Child Welfare Act threatened white fathers' autonomy as well. With the Child Welfare Act the General Assembly granted the state unprecedented powers to intervene in the households of parents who did not raise their children according to middle-class expectations. Lawmakers' objectives for the juvenile courts serve as one example. In specifying the jurisdiction of the juvenile courts, legislators defined the term *delinquent children* so broadly as to include not only children who violated any municipal or state law but also children who were "truant, unruly, wayward, or misdirected." Because the law was so broadly construed, legislators had given the courts exclusive control over children of "neglectful" parents, as well as children who were "dependent upon public support" or children who were "destitute, homeless, or abandoned or whose custody is subject to controversy." For example, the description "whose custody is subject to controversy" could serve as a useful catchall phrase to deprive certain fathers (such as the ex-convict Samuel Watson) custody of their children.[35]

The stiff child-labor regulations and new juvenile-court system further imperiled the autonomy of parents who hired out their children's labor. W. S. Starnes, a millworker at the Albion Manufacturing Company in Mecklenburg County, tried to circumvent these laws by persuading his employer to hire his five children in the mill where he worked. At least two of the children, Fred and Harry, were under twelve years old, but the superintendent, Mr. Downum, employed them anyway. Thomas Mullis, the timecard keeper, later testified that no timecard existed for either child. When he had alerted Downum to the problem, the superintendent instructed him "not to put their name on the sheet at all." Downum explained that apparently the management had received complaints and faced possible indictment for employing children under the age specified in the child-labor law. Unfortunately, one of the two boys was severely injured by a carding machine, and Starnes sued his employer for negligence. The North Carolina Supreme Court found that not only had the Albion Manufacturing Company violated the child-labor law but it was liable for the injury as well. In issuing their decision, the justices affirmed the power of the state not only to enforce labor laws but also to command school attendance. "The right to the labor of the child is not a vested right in the parent, nor is it of any more importance than the right to control its education. Both are subject to the paramount power of the State when it deems it necessary to exercise it for the general good." In other words, the child-labor law mandated by statute that employers refuse to hire children regardless of their parents' wishes.[36]

The statute mandating compulsory school attendance inflicted similar burdens upon poor parents. With the passage of the compulsory-attendance rider to the Neal Substitute, parents who had previously hired out their children's labor or who depended upon their children's work on the farm had no choice but to send their children to school. During the same session that the General Assembly passed the child-labor and compulsory-school-attendance laws, legislators also introduced and passed a bill that detailed how the state was to treat poor families who refused or were unable to send their children to school. This "Compulsory Attendance of Indigent Children" provision allowed for parents to submit an affidavit testifying that for reasons "of necessity to work or labor for the support of itself or the support of the family," their children could not attend school. The law required the juvenile courts to investigate such cases and to provide funding "not to exceed ten dollars per month" to enable the child to continue the compulsory term. If parents refused, the state reserved the right to dispatch a truant officer for further investigation. The truant officer possessed the power to charge the most intransigent parents with a misdemeanor, for which the maximum punishment was thirty days in jail. The Compulsory Attendance of Indigent Children act represented one of the most extreme cases where reformers intervened in the affairs of North Carolina's poorest families. Based upon the idea of protecting children's rights, the Compulsory Attendance of Indigent Children act was evidence of the transformation of nineteenth-century ideals of family to twentieth-century concepts that linked the state to family relationships.[37]

Reformers embraced compulsory school attendance as part of a larger school-reform plan designed to incorporate white middle-class values of professionalism and standardization in a state-supervised school system. White supremacist doctrine was an important part of this bureaucratization of schools. In *Schooling the New South: Pedagogy, Self, and Society in North Carolina, 1880–1920,* James L. Leloudis argues that white middle-class reformers instituted a "new education plan" to preserve the white supremacist environment of segregation and disfranchisement. Few white reformers supported the education of African American children alongside white children. Under the leadership of Governor Charles Brantley Aycock in 1900 North Carolina passed a constitutional amendment known as the "education amendment," which required anyone desiring to vote to pass a literacy test. Though a grandfather clause allowed illiterate whites to register to vote until 1908, the education amendment, adopted in the election of 1900, posed a serious threat to both African American and poor white men. Some Conservative Democrats who supported the new education plan believed that poor white adults were beyond reform, but that hope remained for poor white children. The purpose of the new education plan, then, was to educate poor white children so they could pass the literacy requirement. African American children, however, would not benefit from the new education reform. Instead, some reformers agreed that the most suitable form of learning for African Americans was industrial education, which encouraged "docility, obedience, zeal and fidelity" and served white society's interests.[38]

Despite the white supremacist purpose of school reform, many southern whites were reluctant to comply with the law. In *The Paradox of Southern*

Progressivism, 1880–1930, William A. Link argues that during the 1920s North Carolina failed to enforce the compulsory-school-attendance law because of community pressure and resistance. Compulsory school attendance failed in communities for several reasons. First, local officials sometimes ignored the law, perhaps due to parental pressures. An investigator for the Laura Spellman Rockefeller Memorial reported that communities deep in the western mountains of Cherokee County observed the law "only in sporadic instances." Local officials, the agent continued, were "as interested in finding reasons why the child should be excused from school" as they were in enforcing the law. Second, some parents in remote or rural areas found it impossible for their children to attend faraway schools during poor weather. In a letter to state officials one mother inquired how authorities could expect children to attend school "in all kind of weather Such as rain and snow?" The law, she argued, should not require students to attend school "under unreasonable advantages." Third, poverty prevented some parents from sending children to school. One parent kept one of his three children at home to work. "I have got to have some help," the parent explained to a truant officer, "and I cant hire any . . . that is the Reasun he is not at School." Another farmer reported that he kept his children home to work because the family had "to live by Sweat of our face." Local officials, such as a school superintendent in western North Carolina, encouraged requests to suspend school for "a week or two" in hopes of promoting better attendance later in the year. To the dismay of reformers, Link explains, compulsory school attendance was "one of the most serious failings" of the state's new welfare system.[39]

Some parents wanted their children to attend school but resisted certain requirements, such as vaccination and physical education training, that school administrators demanded of children. Administrators, who possessed few means to force children to comply with these regulations, simply suspended from classes those children who lacked proof of vaccination or whose parents forbade them from participating in physical education. Eventually authorities arrested parents who refused to comply and whose children remained at home. When smallpox cases appeared in an Anson County neighborhood in November 1923, the Anson County Board of Health passed a resolution that required proof of vaccination from all children, black and white. Some parents, such as T. C. Johnson, refused to vaccinate their children, and they were sent home. Johnson argued that many parents in the county opposed vaccination "for the reason that the neighborhoods without the appearance of small pox did not think it necessary and authorized by law."[40]

Johnson, who wanted his children to attend school but refused to vaccinate them, was arrested and charged with violating the compulsory-school-attendance law. In his courtroom defense Johnson argued that the law violated his right to due process rights, as specified in the Fourteenth Amendment of the U.S. Constitution. No state shall deprive any person of life, liberty, or property without due process, he asserted, and the compulsory-attendance law "denies the citizenship of the State the right to control their own children and say when they are needed at home on the farm or elsewhere without the consent of some school teacher that has no way of knowing what the fathers and mothers of the State are in need of their children doing." Eventually the North Carolina Supreme Court dismissed Johnson's case on the grounds that his failure to send his children to school was not a crime but a misdemeanor. In its ruling, however, the court upheld the constitutionality of the compulsory-attendance law. Though Johnson had violated the law by allowing his children to remain out of school, he could not be criminally indicted.[41]

Another parent, M. S. Lewis, of Cabarrus County, also desired that his children attend school but was forced to keep them home when school administrators suspended the children for refusing to participate in physical education exercises. After observing that one child had developed "a knot in her [right] side practically as big as a goose egg and on the left hand side there was a knot about as big as an ordinary hen egg" and hearing complaints from his children, Lewis instructed them not to participate. Over a period of several months school administrators whipped two of Lewis's children for insubordination, sent them home on several occasions, and engaged in fruitless confrontations with Lewis. Finally, school authorities refused to admit the children, and Lewis was arrested. Lewis, who served as his own legal counsel, emphasized his desire to educate his children in the public schools despite the draconian nature of school regulations. This case proceeded to the North Carolina Supreme Court, where justices dismissed it on the same grounds as those on which it dismissed the Johnson case. Justices upheld the compulsory-attendance law but refused to make criminals of parents who kept their children home.[42]

Despite its shortcomings, the compulsory-school-attendance law, in conjunction with the Child Welfare Act of 1919, empowered the state to assume the role of primary guardian for North Carolina's children in theory if not always in practice. In his 1918 report to the North Carolina Conference for Social Services, W. H. Swift celebrated the state's role for the twentieth century. "Every child born in the state is or should be its ward." Swift explained that the state must ensure that every child be given the "fair chance" to grow into the "strongest possible man or woman." Thus, he declared, the state possessed supreme guardianship responsibilities and rights over children. "The rights of the state rise above family rights in the child and there should never be any hesitation about invading the family circle when the best interests of the child demand it." According to Swift, state control promised sanitation and hygiene, the elimination of poverty, and surroundings "clean and healthful, sweet, refining and good." Swift warned, "Ignorance, indifference, and greed have yet to be banished from the earth, and many parents are still under their blighting shadows." Archaic nineteenth-century practices that privileged the individual patriarch's rights to his child or apprentice had no place in Swift's brave new world.[43]

The state's elimination of apprenticeship laws and enactment of child-welfare legislation heralded a new era. North Carolinians had traded one form of social control for another. Individual men no longer possessed unlimited household autonomy. Instead, the state assumed significant power over the domestic arena. The state's new role had evolved from a system that measured poor women's behavior to a series of laws that allowed the state to inspect poor men's behavior as well. The new Child Welfare Act, though somewhat limited in its protection of children's rights in the workplace, imposed stiff restrictions on all households unable to adhere to middle-class standards of domesticity and child-rearing. Judges now issued new standards of womanhood by instituting rules for measuring women's capacity to nurture. But the new Child Welfare Act shows that reformers and legislators also embraced the expansion of state paternalism. White fathers, particularly those with criminal histories and working-class or rural backgrounds, suddenly experienced the possible threat of state intervention in their families. A changing understanding of race was a crucial component of the Child Welfare Act as well. The new laws also were meant to improve the lives of southern white children in preparation for a white supremacist order. Significantly, the new child-welfare legislation not only reshaped but also reinforced southern hierarchies of gender, race, and class. New standards of womanhood, state control over poor men's children, and de jure white supremacy marked North Carolina reformers' visions of the New South.

CONCLUSION

The right of parental control is a natural, but not an inalienable one," stated a Pennsylvania court in 1839; the words reverberated in North Carolina more than seventy years later. Upon these words Associate Justice William R. Allen rested his opinion in the 1911 case *In Re Richard Watson.* Allen fully embraced the Pennsylvania court's interpretation of parents' constitutional rights. Although parents were entrusted with their children's care, the earlier court had argued, no "declaration of rights" protected fathers' and mothers' claims to their children. Indeed, legislatures possessed an "ordinary legislative power" to intervene in families when that intervention promoted the child's best interests. In a clear reaffirmation of the 1839 decision, Allen justified the state's detention of young Richard Watson at the Stonewall Jackson Manual Training and Industrial School. "The principle on which the authority for legislative interference rests," said Allen, "is that the child may be saved, and that society may be protected."[1]

The issue of parental control is a timeless one. Governments have long held the power to remove children from their parents' custody. Apprenticeship was perhaps the earliest institution used by courts to deprive parents, particularly poor mothers and African American men, of their children. Modern cousins of apprenticeship include state juvenile-court systems and departments of social services. Born in the era of progressive reform, these newer institutions have continued the debates among authorities, reformers, and parents about the rights and nature of parenthood. Today, legislatures and courts frequently raise the "best interests of the child" doctrine to defend state intervention. Instances vary widely. Courts have upheld laws favoring state intervention not only in cases of child abuse and neglect but also in custody disputes between parents and grand-parents. In one highly publicized case a New York court in 2002 wielded its power as *parens patriae* to restrict a mother's visitation rights to her child because of the health risks that "second-hand smoke" posed to her thirteen-year-old son. As *parens patriae*, the court argued in the latter case, the state "has broad authority to regulate and control the helpless, infirm, and infants within its ju-risdiction." This modern adaptation of the "best interests" doctrine resonates clearly with Associate Justice Allen's 1911 decision in *In Re Richard Watson*.[2]

Yet the "best interests" doctrine is a modern one. Its popularity among courts and legislatures increased as apprenticeship declined. The victory of child wel-fare over apprenticeship is best explained by the shift of guardianship from the individual master to the state. Where twentieth-century family relations rest upon the state's role as *parens patriae*, eighteenth- and nineteenth-century family matters were governed by the principle *in loco parentis*. When parents, namely, women and African American men, protested their children's indentures, they cast the debate in the terms of parents' and masters' rights to their children's la-bor. Single mothers and black fathers, parents argued, possessed the same pa-rental rights that white men enjoyed. The court, they insisted in case after case, could not bind out their children without seeking parental consent. Eighteenth- and nineteenth-century courts responded by weighing the parents' rights against those of the master. Thus, the courts rarely, if ever, considered the child's best in-terests. Spectators in twentieth-century courtrooms witness an entirely different debate. Though parents demand their custodial rights in much the same fashion as parents of earlier centuries, courts recast the conflict in new terms. Parents no longer find themselves pitted against an individual white master, one who is a lo-cal member of the community and enjoys great legal privileges. Rather, they find themselves embroiled in a conflict with the government, a great, impersonal bu-reaucracy originally established by early twentieth-century progressive impulses.

Thus a study of apprenticeship offers a fascinating opportunity to examine the origins of, and change in, family and state relations. In this history of ap-prenticeship I have tried to illuminate the dynamism of race, class, and gender distinctions within the law. Nineteenth-century apprenticeship was not a static institution but an evolving one. It was shaped not only by legal authorities but also by common people who contributed to the creation of new legal meanings through their resistance to old ones. Race, class, and gender, then, were social categories that became reflected in North Carolina apprenticeship law. As social and legal interpretations of these categories changed, so did apprenticeship law and practice. As power relations shifted, the relationship between race, class, and gender within apprenticeship law also changed. A white paternalistic doctrine in North Carolina perpetuated the racist and gendered apprenticeship system that emerged after the Civil War. In addition, apprenticeship was a tool of the elite to control the indigent and their children, which is why the institution became a means of supplying low-cost servants and workers to white masters rather than a steppingstone for society's future artisans, its more common function elsewhere. Finally, apprenticeship experienced its most fatal blow in 1919, when middle-class men and women rejected it in favor of a child-welfare system based on the "best interests" doctrine.

As this book demonstrates, four period shifts, marked at once by prominent North Carolina Supreme Court cases and legislative reform, illustrate apprenticeship's evolution in North Carolina. The first shift coincides with two North Carolina Supreme Court cases, *Midgett v. McBryde* (1855) and *Frolick v. Schonwald* (1859–60). Authorities, who used apprenticeship primarily to control poor women, intensified efforts to control African Americans as well. The second shift corresponds to the racial conflicts that occurred during Reconstruction. The 1867 case *In the Matter of Harriet Ambrose and Eliza Ambrose* and pursuant North Carolina legislation represented male Republicans' efforts to lift racial restrictions that had prohibited African American men from controlling their children. But gender-based regulations remained, and once again women (both black and white) retained very limited rights to their children. The third shift is marked by two court cases that involved Chaney Ashby's attempts to retrieve her daughter. In these cases, the North Carolina Supreme Court established the "good character" rule, which required women to meet certain requirements of motherhood to keep their children. Thus, in *Ashby v. Page* (1890) and *Ashby v. Page* (1891) justices fully embraced the nascent concept of judicial discretion. However, they had not yet fully articulated their position on the question of the child's "best interests." Lawmakers gained this experience during the next three decades, when they developed a cohesive view of child welfare enshrined in the 1919 watershed legislation, the Child Welfare Act. Middle-class reformers had become increasingly concerned about the "welfare of the child," a concept rarely discussed in early and mid-nineteenth-century courts and legislatures. By this act, reformers codified a juvenile-court system, a compulsory-school-attendance act, and a child-labor act to promote children's welfare.

By 1919 apprenticeship was dead. But its history shows constant flux in the relationship between parents and the state. Apprenticeship and child welfare in

North Carolina were fundamentally affected by gender, race, and class relations. A study of gender relations reveals the source of women's disadvantage. Likewise, an examination of African Americans' conflict with powerful whites helps us to understand their struggles. Finally, a close look at middle-class views of parenthood reveals the problems that impoverished parents faced. By defining the parameters of parenthood, those who controlled the reins of power determined the character and composition of independent households. For many, this independence, marked not only by children's financial contributions but also by their love and affection, remained elusive.

NOTES

INTRODUCTION

1. "The Petition of Harriet Ambrose and Eliza Ambrose," September 24, 1866, *In the Matter of Harriet Ambrose and Eliza Ambrose*, 61 NC 91 (1867), original court transcript 9020, North Carolina Supreme Court Documents (hereinafter referred to as NCSCD), North Carolina State Archives (hereinafter referred to as NCSA), Raleigh.

2. Eric Foner discusses the impact of apprenticeship in Maryland in *Reconstruction: America's Unfinished Revolution, 1863–1877* (New York: Harper and Row, 1988), 40–41. Peter Bardaglio explains the racial and patriarchal character of the southern legal culture, specifically in apprenticeship law, in *Reconstructing the Household: Families, Sex, and the Law in the Nineteenth-Century South* (Chapel Hill: University of North Carolina Press, 1995), 23–36, 103–7. For a discussion of artisan apprenticeship see W. J. Rorabaugh, *The Craft Apprentice: From Franklin to the Machine Age in America* (New York: Oxford University Press, 1986).

3. *Nancy Midgett v. Willoughby McBryde*, 48 NC 21 (1855); *Fanny Frolick v. James T. Schonwald*, 52 NC 427 (1859–60).

4. Key North Carolina Supreme Court cases that demonstrate these changes are *Ambrose*; *Chaney Ashby v. James H. Page*, 106 NC 328 (1890); and *Chaney Ashby v. James H. Page*, 108 NC 6 (1891).

5. The counties under study include, but are not limited to, Brunswick, Duplin, Guilford, Mecklenburg, Robeson, Wake, and Wilkes. The apprenticeship bonds of each are catalogued in the NCSA. Letters and reports of the agents of the Bureau of Refugees, Freedmen and Abandoned Lands are located at the National Archives in Washington, DC, and are available on microfilm. Bureau records that relate to North Carolina can be found in Record Group 105 and microfilm series 843. William S. McFeely discusses Whittlesey, and Robinson, and the relationship each forged with his supervisor, O. O. Howard, in *Yankee Stepfather: General O. O. Howard and the Freedmen* (1968; reprint, New York: Norton, 1994), 249–53, 269, 293.

6. These statistics are compiled from the apprenticeship bonds for Brunswick, Duplin, Guilford, Mecklenburg, Robeson, Wake, and Wilkes counties, 1860–61, NCSA.

7. Informal apprenticeships arranged within the legal community are discussed in Gail Williams O'Brien, *The Legal Fraternity and the Making of a New South Community, 1848–1882* (Athens: University of Georgia Press, 1986), 130.

8. Joan Wallach Scott, "Gender: A Useful Category of Historical Analysis," in *Feminism and History*, ed. Scott (Oxford: Oxford University Press, 1996), 169–75. Kathleen M. Brown employs a similar analysis in *Good Wives, Nasty Wenches, and Anxious Patriarchs: Gender, Race, and Power in Colonial Virginia* (Chapel Hill: University of North Carolina Press, 1996), 4. She argues that class, race, and gender discourses, constantly interpreted and reinterpreted, shaped colonial Virginians' complex identities.

9. Rorabaugh, *Craft Apprentice*, 55–56, 74–74, 97; David Montgomery, *Citizen Worker: The Experience of Workers in the United States with Democracy and the Free Market during the Nineteenth Century* (New York: Cambridge University Press, 1993), 4–12. An as-yet unpublished anthology of essays on apprenticeship promises to address the variety in North American apprenticeship (see Ruth Wallis Herndon and John E. Murray, eds., "Bound to Labor: Varieties of Apprenticeship in Early America," in review).

10. For a definition of white supremacy see George M. Frederickson, *The Black Image in the White Mind: The Debate on Afro-American Character and Destiny 1817–1914* (New York: Harper Torchbooks, 1972), 321; and idem, *White Supremacy: A Comparative Study in American and South African History* (Oxford: Oxford University Press, 1981), xi.

CHAPTER ONE

ORPHANS, BASTARDS, AND FREE BLACK CHILDREN

1. Robert W. Winston, *Andrew Johnson: Plebian and Patriot* (New York: Holt, 1928), 4–14. A more recent biography of Johnson, which unfortunately omits a detailed discussion of his childhood, is Hans Louis Trefousse, *Andrew Johnson: A Biography* (New York: Norton, 1989).

2. Joan Lane, *Apprenticeship in England, 1600–1914* (Boulder, CO: Westview, 1996), 1–3, quotation from p. 2; Robert Francis Seybolt, *Apprenticeship and Apprenticeship Education in Colonial New England and New York* (New York: Arno Press and the New York Times, 1969), 1–21.

3. Seybolt, *Apprenticeship and Apprenticeship Education*, 36–40, quotation from p. 38; Eric Foner, *Tom Paine and Revolutionary America* (New York: Oxford University Press, 1976), 43–44.

4. Edmund S. Morgan, *American Slavery, American Freedom: The Ordeal of Colonial Virginia* (New York: Norton, 1975), 116–28.

5. *Records of the Executive Council, 1755–1775*, ed. Robert J. Cain (Raleigh: North Carolina Department of Cultural Resources, 1994), 8:xxxix–xliii; Marvin L. Michael Kay and Lorin Lee Cary, "A Demographic Analysis of Colonial North Carolina with Special Emphasis upon the Slave and Black Populations," in *Black Americans in North Carolina and the South*, ed. Jeffrey J. Crow and Flora J. Hatley (Chapel Hill: University of North Carolina Press, 1984), 71 (quotation), 104–7, 113.

6. Robert J. Steinfeld, *The Invention of Free Labor: The Employment Relation in English and American Law and Culture, 1350–1870* (Chapel Hill: University of North Carolina Press, 1991), 6–7, 79–80; *Records of the Executive Council 1755–1775*, 8:xxxix–xli.

7. Chief Justice Frederick Nash elucidates this interpretation of apprenticeship in *Harriet Owens v. Jasper Chaplain*, 48 NC 323 (1856). According to Nash, every indenture of apprenticeship

was a contract made between the master and the county for the benefit of the apprentice. A primary objective of apprenticeship was to relieve the county of the child's "maintenance."

8. "Chapter 49: An Act Concerning Orphans," in *The State Records of North Carolina*, ed. Walter Clark (Goldsboro, NC: Nash Brothers, 1904), 23:70—71.

9. Ibid. Alan D. Watson provides a concise overview of colonial orphan laws in "Orphanages in Colonial North Carolina: Edgecombe County as a Case Study," *North Carolina Historical Review* 70 (April 1975): 105—19.

10. This case is drawn from the "Minutes of the Chowan Council," August 3, 1716, in *The Colonial Records of North Carolina, Published under the Supervision of the Trustees of the Public Libraries, By order of the General Assembly*, ed. William L. Saunders (Wilmington, NC: Broadfoot, 1993—94), 2:241.

11. Ibid., 2:56.

12. Ibid., 5:495—97.

13. Ibid.

14. Ibid., 6:20—29; *Records of the Executive Council, 1755—1775*, 9:63—64. See also Watson, "Orphanages in Colonial North Carolina," 106—8.

15. *State Records of North Carolina*, 23:550, 563, 577—83. The crown repealed later versions of all three acts by an order in council on December 14, 1761 (see *Records of the Executive Council, 1755—1775*, 9:389; and Watson, "Orphanages in Colonial North Carolina," 106—8). Hugh T. Lefler and William S. Powell provide a detailed account of the tensions between the North Carolina assembly, the governors, and the crown in *Colonial North Carolina: A History* (New York: Scribner, 1973), 113—28.

16. An Act for the better Care of Orphans, and Security and Management of their Estates, in *State Records of North Carolina*, 23:577—78.

17. Ibid., 23:581; Zedekiah Stone to John Gray Blount, March 24, 1793, *The John Gray Blount Papers* (Raleigh: State Department of Archives and History, 1959), 1:xx—xxiii; ibid., 2:248—49.

18. *State Records of North Carolina*, 23:581; John Hope Franklin, *The Free Negro in North Carolina, 1790—1860* (New York: W. W. Norton, 1943), 35—37.

19. William Blount to John Gray Blount, August 11, 1787, *John Gray Blount Papers*, 1:xx—xxiii, 334—35 (brackets in the original).

20. Michael Grossberg, *Governing the Hearth: Law and the Family in Nineteenth-Century America* (Chapel Hill: University of North Carolina Press, 1985), 254—68; *State Records of North Carolina*, 23:581—83.

21. Peter Bardaglio provides a general description of the court system in *Reconstructing the Household*, xvii—xviii, 7—9; and Gail Williams O'Brien discusses North Carolina's court system in *Legal Fraternity*, 22—26. The courts' responsibilities are also outlined in the state code (see "Chapter 5: Apprentices," *The Revised Statutes of the State of North Carolina, Passed by the General Assembly at the Session of 1836—7* [Raleigh: Turner and Hughes, 1837], 1:67).

22. "Chapter 5: Apprentices," *Revised Statutes*, 1:67; *Cornelius Dowd v. Stephen Davis*, 15 NC 61; *Midgett v. McBryde; William Hooks v. William T. Perkins*, 44 NC 21 (1852).

23. *Prue v. Hight*, 51 NC 265 (1859).

24. Timothy S. Huebner examines Ruffin's opinions in *The Southern Judicial Tradition: State Judges and Sectional Distinctiveness, 1790—1890* (Athens: University of Georgia Press, 1999), 130—37. See also Thomas Ruffin, *The Papers of Thomas Ruffin*, ed. J. G. de Roulhac Hamilton

(Raleigh: North Carolina Historical Commission and Edwards and Broughton, 1920), 4: 269–90.

25. Bardaglio, *Reconstructing the Household*, 26. Victoria E. Bynum provides a lucid interpretation of Ruffin's opinions, as well as the views of several other supreme court justices, in *Unruly Women: The Politics of Social and Sexual Control in the Old South* (Chapel Hill: University of North Carolina Press, 1992), 64–73.

26. Paul D. Escott, *Many Excellent People: Power and Privilege in North Carolina, 1850–1900* (Chapel Hill: University of North Carolina Press, 1985), 116.

27. Ibid., 15–19, 108; Bynum, *Unruly Women*, 19, 68. Bynum discusses the power of the elite in North Carolina courts.

28. Bardaglio, *Reconstructing the Household*, 31. Several North Carolina Supreme Court cases confirm coverture laws (see *Samuel R. Potter v. Sterling B. Everitt & Al.*, 42 NC 152 [1850]; *John G. Hooks and Al. v. Blackman Lee and Al.*, 43 NC 157 [1851]; and *Elizabeth L. Goodrum v. James Goodrum and Al.*, 43 NC 313 [1852]. See also "Chapter 37: Deeds and Conveyances," *Revised Statutes*, 1:224–29, 233–34; and "Chapter 56: Husband and Wife," *The Revised Code of North Carolina, enacted by the General Assembly at the Session of 1854* [Boston: Little, Brown, 1855], 327–28).

29. Married women's right to property conveyed by separate estate is established in *Nancy Harris & Al. v. Herbert Harris & Al.*, 42 NC 111 (1850); "Chapter 37: Deeds and Conveyances," *Revised Statutes*, 1:224–29, 233–34; and "Chapter 56: Husband and Wife," *Revised Code*, 327–28.

30. Michael Grossberg discusses the evolution of nineteenth-century custody rights in *Governing the Hearth*, 234–85. See also Tapping Reeve, *The Law of Baron and Femme, of Parent and Child, Guardian and Ward, Master and Servant, and of the Powers of Courts of Chancery* (Burlington, VT: Chauncey Goodrich, 1846), 319–20; "Chapter 54: Guardian and Ward," *Revised Code*, 316–24; and for state supreme court cases that delineate the county court's power to appoint, *Mills v. McAllister*, 2 NC 303 (1804), and *Grant, an orphan, by his Guardian, v. Whitaker, from Halifax*, 5 NC 231 (1806).

31. Henry Potter et al., eds., *Laws of the State of North Carolina* (Raleigh: J. Gales, 1821), 2:829–30.

32. Ibid., 2:931.

33. The General Assembly retained its exclusive right to grant divorces until 1818, when legislators shifted this power to the superior courts (ibid., 2:1445). Data on men's and women's petitions to the General Assembly are derived from the North Carolina General Assembly Session Records, House and Senate Bills and Petitions, November–December, 1800, NCSA, Raleigh.

34. "Petition of Elizabeth Whitworth," November 1800, and "Petition of Elizabeth Lawwell," November 1800, ibid., Petitions for Divorce, Name Change, etc.

35. "Petition of Rachel Johnston," November 1800, ibid.

36. Potter et al., *Laws of the State of North Carolina*, 2:931.

37. J. G. de Roulhac Hamilton, *Life of Andrew Johnson: Seventeenth President of the United States* (Greeneville: East Tennessee Publishing, 1928), 2; Winston, *Andrew Johnson*, 3–25.

38. "Chapter 5: Apprentices," *Revised Statutes*, 1:67; "petition of Temperance Chavers," January 27, 1810, Apprenticeship Bonds, Brunswick County, NCSA.

39. "Chapter 5: Apprentices," *Revised Statutes*, 1:67.

40. Ibid., 1:67–69; *Prue v. Hight.*

41. "Chapter 5: Apprentices," *Revised Statutes*, 1:67–69; Franklin, *Free Negro in North Carolina*, 129; Apprenticeship Bonds, 1801–60, Guilford County.

42. "Chapter 5: Apprentices," *Revised Code*, 77–78.

43. *Midgett v. McBryde*.

44. *Frolick v. Schonwald*.

45. Barbara Jeanne Fields, *Slavery and Freedom on the Middle Ground: Maryland during the Nineteenth Century* (New Haven: Yale University Press, 1985), 35; Lorenzo J. Greene et al., *Missouri's Black Heritage* (Columbia: University of Missouri Press, 1993), 64; Letitia Woods Brown, *Free Negroes in the District of Columbia, 1790–1846* (New York: Oxford University Press, 1972), 137; William H. Williams, *Slavery and Freedom in Delaware, 1639–1865* (Wilmington, DE: Scholarly Resources, 1996), 157.

46. Apprenticeship Bonds, 1801–60, Guilford County; indentures of Betsey Chavis, February 23, 1844, and John Chavis, February 24, 1844, Apprenticeship Bonds, Wake County; indenture of Bell Ashe, November, third term, 1856, Apprenticeship Bonds, Guilford County.

47. Indenture of Betsey Pool, November 21, 1820, Apprenticeship Bonds, Guilford County; "Chapter 5: Apprentices," *Revised Statutes*, 1:68.

48. Rhoda Pollard to Berry Surls, August 10, 1838, Apprenticeship Bonds, Wake County.

49. Indenture of Jackson Robinson, May 21, 1838, Apprenticeship Bonds, Brunswick County.

50. *James W. Bell v. Caleb L. Walker, et. al.*, 50 NC 43 (1857).

51. *Haywood Musgrove v. Wm. J. Kornegay, et. al.*, 52 NC 71 (1860). Paul Faler and W. J. Rorabaugh argue that voluntary indentures declined severely in northern states during the antebellum years. Faler argues that the decline resulted from a shift to mechanization and unskilled labor. Rorabaugh argues that antebellum markets shifted to cash economies and that as a result young people preferred to work for wages rather than consent to unpaid indentures (see Faler, *Mechanics and Manufacturers in the Early Industrial Revolution: Lynn, Massachusetts, 1780–1860* [Albany: State University of New York Press, 1981], 96–97; and Rorabaugh, *Craft Apprentice*, 57–96).

52. Apprenticeship Bonds, 1801–60, Brunswick, Duplin, Robeson, Guilford, Wake, Mecklenberg, and Wilkes counties. For a more complete definition of security bonds, see the discussion of *Prue v. Hight* on pages 42–43.

53. Apprenticeship Bonds, 1801–60, Brunswick, Duplin, Robeson, Guilford, Wake, Mecklenberg, and Wilkes counties.

54. Ibid.

55. Minutes of the Court of Common Pleas and Quarter Sessions, Mecklenburg County, 1811–20, 1851–60, NCSA. Some data are drawn from this source, transcribed by Herman W. Ferguson in *Mecklenburg County, North Carolina: Minutes of the Court of Common Pleas and Quarter Sessions: Volume IV: 1831–1840* (Rocky Mount, N.C.: Herman W. Ferguson, 2002).

56. Francis Charles Anscombe, *I Have Called You Friends: The Story of Quakerism in North Carolina* (Boston: Christopher, 1959), 160–69.

57. Blackwell P. Robinson and Alexander R. Stoesen, *The History of Guilford County, North Carolina, U.S.A. to 1980, A.D.* (Guilford County: Guilford County Bicentennial Commission, 1971), 58–59; Apprenticeship Bonds, 1801–60, Brunswick, Guilford, and Wake counties; Guion Griffis Johnson, *Ante-Bellum North Carolina: A Social History* (Chapel Hill: University of North Carolina Press, 1937), 707; Anscombe, *I Have Called You Friends*, 69, 264.

58. Apprenticeship Bonds, 1801–60, Brunswick, Guilford, and Wake counties.

59. Franklin, *Free Negro in North Carolina*, 74–78, 102–3.

60. Ibid., 196–97, 211.

61. U.S. Bureau of the Census Manuscript Records, Population and Slave Schedules, Moore County, 1850; Wayne County, 1870; Brunswick County, 1870.

62. Ibid., Currituck County, 1860.

CHAPTER TWO

"JUSTLY ENTITLED" TO APPRENTICES

1. Eliphalet Whittlesey to O. O. Howard, January 15, 1866, Registers and Letters Received by the Commissioner (hereinafter referred to as RLRC), Records of the Bureau of Refugees, Freedmen and Abandoned Lands (hereinafter referred to as FBR), 1865–1872, RG 105, M752, reel 23. For some brief discussion of race and apprenticeship in North Carolina, see Roberta Sue Alexander, *North Carolina Faces the Freedmen: Race Relations during Presidential Reconstruction* (Durham: Duke University Press, 1985), 112–19; and Rebecca Scott, "The Battle over the Child: Child Apprenticeship and the Freedmen's Bureau in North Carolina," *Prologue* 10 (Summer 1978): 101–13.

2. Bernard Bailyn, *Education in the Forming of American Society* (Chapel Hill: University of North Carolina Press, 1960), 29–36, 97–99; Ian M. G. Quimby, *Apprenticeship in Colonial Philadelphia* (New York: Garland, 1985), 140–56; Faler, *Mechanics and Manufacturers in the Early Industrial Revolution,* 96–97; Rorabaugh, *Craft Apprentice,* 55–56, 74–75, 97; Montgomery, *Citizen Worker,* 4–12, 31, 50–51.

3. Apprenticeship Bonds, 1861–64, Brunswick, Duplin, Robeson, Guilford, Wake, Mecklenberg, and Wilkes counties.

4. Emory M. Thomas, *The Confederate Nation, 1861–1865* (New York: Harper and Row, 1979), 152, 260–61; Lindley S. Butler and Alan D. Watson, eds., *The North Carolina Experience: An Interpretive and Documentary History* (Chapel Hill: University of North Carolina Press, 1984), 267.

5. LeAnn Whites, *The Civil War as a Crisis in Gender: Augusta, Georgia, 1860–1890* (Athens: University of Georgia Press, 1995), 77–78; John W. Blassingame, *Black New Orleans, 1860–1880* (Chicago: University of Chicago Press, 1973), 33–39; Benjamin Quarles, *The Negro in the Civil War* (New York: Da Capo, 1989), 57–77. Other scholars who discuss the experiences of free blacks during the Civil War include Clarence Mohr, *On the Threshold of Freedom: Masters and Slaves in Civil War Georgia* (Athens: University of Georgia Press, 1986); Michael Johnson and James Roark, *No Chariot Let Down: Charleston's Free People of Color on the Eve of the Civil War* (Chapel Hill: University of North Carolina Press, 1984); and Bell I. Wiley, *Southern Negroes, 1861–1865* (New York: Rinehart, 1953).

6. Alan D. Watson, *History of New Bern and Craven County* (New Bern: Tryon Palace Commission, 1987), 402; Joe A. Mobley, *James City: A Black Community in North Carolina, 1863–1900* (Raleigh: North Carolina Department of Cultural Resources, 1981), 1–65. William McKee Evans discusses the war's economic impact on Wilmington, North Carolina, in *Ballots and Fence Rails: Reconstruction on the Lower Cape Fear* (New York: Norton, 1966), 176–210. Wayne Durrill examines the war's impact on propertied and unpropertied families in Washington County in *War of Another Kind: A Southern Community in the Great Rebellion* (New York: Oxford University Press, 1990), 219–28. Laura Edwards discusses gendered conflicts in Reconstruction North Carolina in *Gendered Strife and Confusion: The Political Culture of Reconstruction* (Urbana: University of Illinois Press, 1997).

7. Sarah A. Tillinghast to David R. Tillinghast, May 5, 1866, and Eliza B. Tillinghast to William N. Tillinghast, September 7, 1865, Tillinghast Family Papers, Special Collections Library, Duke University, Durham.

8. Major H. H. Beadle to Whittlesey, March 10, 1866, Letters Received by the Assistant Commissioner (hereinafter referred to as LR), Records of the Assistant Commissioner for the State of North Carolina, FBR, 1865–1870, RG 105, M843, reel 7.

9. Bardaglio, *Reconstructing the Household*, 162; Edmund L. Drago, *Black Politicians and Reconstruction in Georgia: A Splendid Failure* (Baton Rouge: Louisiana State University Press, 1982), 117; Paul A. Cimbala, *Under the Guardianship of the Nation: The Freedmen's Bureau and the Reconstruction of Georgia, 1865–1870* (Athens: University of Georgia Press, 1997), 200; William C. Harris, *Presidential Reconstruction in Mississippi* (Baton Rouge: Louisiana State University Press, 1967), 137; Barry A. Crouch, "Seeking Equality: Houston Black Women during Reconstruction," in *Black Dixie: Afro-Texan History and Culture in Houston*, ed. Howard Beeth and Cary D. Wintz (College Station: Texas A&M University Press, 1992), 56–59; Fields, *Slavery and Freedom on the Middle Ground*, 153.

10. Apprenticeship Bonds, 1865–66, Brunswick, Duplin, Guilford, Mecklenburg, Robeson, Wake, and Wilkes counties. For examples of indenture contracts see "Register of Indentures," 1865–1866, FBR, RG 105, M843, reel 35. This microfilm reel also contains county lists of indentures canceled by the Freedmen's Bureau in 1867. See "List of names of White and Black bound as apprentices by the county court of Onslow and canceled in accordance with the recent decisions of the Supreme Court of North Carolina in the case of Ambrose v. Russel," 1867; "Ordered that the indentures of apprenticeship of the following named colored children by this court be and are hereby cancelled," Chowan County, August term 1867; and indentures, Franklin, Craven, Sampson, Mecklenberg, Duplin, and Carteret counties, 1867, all in "Register of Indentures."

11. See Alexander, *North Carolina Faces the Freedmen*, 116; Whittlesey to Howard, April 10, 1866, RLRC, FBR, RG 105, M752, reel 29; and statistics compiled from "Register of Indentures." See also Whittlesey to Howard, March 16, 1866, RLRC, FBR, RG 105, M752, reel 29. In another analysis of these records, Rebecca Scott argues that 80 percent of the children in 1865 and 70 percent in 1866 were over the age of seven and old enough to work (Scott, "Battle over the Child," 104–5).

12. Richard Boyle to "The President" [Abraham Lincoln], March 9, 1865, RLRC, FBR, RG 105, M752, reel 13.

13. George P. Rawick, ed., *The American Slave: A Composite Autobiography* (Westport, CT: Greenwood, 1941), 14:52, 75, 214, 248, 411.

14. Ibid., 14:46, 65, 163, 304, 372. Deborah Gray White provides a description of the life cycle of female slaves in *Ar'n't I a Woman? Female Slaves in the Plantation South* (New York: Norton, 1985), 91–118.

15. Rawick, *American Slave*, 14:329, 166, 197.

16. Marie Jenkins Schwartz, *Born in Bondage: Growing Up Enslaved in the Antebellum South* (Cambridge: Harvard University Press, 2000), 8–9, 14, 77–78, 93, 98–99, 155, 208 (quotation).

17. Rawick, *American Slave*, 14:262, 277, 377, 429.

18. R. T. Turner to Howard, March 30, 1866, RLRC, FBR, RG 105, reel 36. Reverend John L. Dennis to Judge H. L. Bond, ibid., reel 31. Brevet Major H. N. Foster to Brigadier General

Allan Rutherford, February 1, 1867. T. S. Watson, "Report of Harper's Plantation — Extract"; "Complaint of Abner Williams," June 4, 1866; "Deposition of R. J. Williams," May 22, 1866; and "Opinion of the Court," n.d., all in *Harper Williams v. Abner Williams Freed*, "Reports of Court Cases," FBR, RG 105, M843, reel 31.

19. "Contract between Jacob McCrory & wife & Mary A. Smith," June 6, 1865; John C. Barrett to Whittlesey, October 26, 1865; and Barrett to Whittlesey, November 15, 1865, all in LR, FBR, RG 105, M843, reel 7.

20. "Contract between Jacob McCrory & wife & Mary A. Smith," June 6, 1865; Barrett to Whittlesey, October 26, 1865; Barrett to Whittlesey, November 15, 1865; "Contract between Jacob McCrory and Daniel Ladd & Frederick Cartwright," November 21, 1865; Clinton A. Cilley to Whittlesey, December 3, 1865; and Cilley to Whittlesey, December 9, 1865, all in ibid.

21. "Affidavit of Martha Hill," June 29, 1866, Lumberton, NC; indenture of John, Betsey, Hannah, Sally, Aleck, and William, March 21, 1866, Sampson County; and indenture of Sammy, November 1865, Duplin County, all in "Register of Indentures."

22. Amos McCollough and Samuel High Smith to Howard, May 6, 1866, LR, FBR, RG 105, M843, reel 8.

23. "Chapter 5: Apprentices," *Revised Code*, 78; *Owens v. Chaplain*.

24. Mrs. R. C. Pritchard to General Sickles, April 1, 1867, LR, FBR, RG 105, M843, reel 12.

25. Ibid.; Daniel Russell to Lieutenant G. N. Tifton, October 9, 1866, RLRC, FBR, RG 105, reel 43.

26. Rebecca F. Mottley to Jacob F. Chur, September 7, 1867, LR, FBR, RG 105, M843, reel 11.

27. Edwards, *Gendered Strife and Confusion*, 39.

28. Catherine Ann Devereux Edmonston, May 13 and June 26, 1865, *"Journal of a Secesh Lady": The Diary of Catherine Ann Devereux Edmonston*, ed. Beth G. Crabtree and James W. Patton (Raleigh: North Carolina Division of Archives and History, Department of Cultural Resources, 1979), 711—13.

29. Eliza DeRosset to Lou DeRosset, April 8, 1866, DeRosset Family Papers, Southern Historical Collection, Wilson Library, University of North Carolina at Chapel Hill.

30. Mrs. J. D. E. Gregory to Major Henry Camp, April 25, 1867, LR, FBR, RG 105, M843, reel 13; Gregory to General Nelson A. Miles, May 20, 1867, ibid., reel 11.

31. Leon F. Litwack discusses the effect of slave sales on African American families and their efforts to reunite in *Been in the Storm So Long: The Aftermath of Slavery* (New York: Knopf, 1979), 229—39, quotation from p. 231. Eugene Genovese explains the ideology of paternalism behind southern slaveholders' justifications of and rationalizations for slave sales and separations in *Roll, Jordan, Roll: The World the Slaves Made* (New York: Vintage Books, 1972), 450—58; on slave family unity and perseverance see 482—523. Herbert Gutman found that in communities with fewer slave sales, families maintained large, cohesive households including both parents and children for many years in (*The Black Family in Slavery and Freedom, 1750—1925* [New York: Vintage Books, 1976], 220—27). Jacqueline Jones argues that freedwomen consciously accepted the sexual division of labor that defined them as wives and mothers in order to preserve the black family during freedom in *Labor of Love, Labor of Sorrow: Black Women, Work, and the Family from Slavery to the Present* (New York: Basic Books, 1985), 62—68. And Laura F. Edwards argues in *Gendered Strife and Confusion*, 24—54, that freedmen and women supported efforts to legalize their marriages,

fight apprenticeship of their children, and preserve their independence by forming their own households.

32. Samuel S. Ashley to Reverend James J. Woolsey, March 12, 1866, RLRC, FBR, RG 105, reel 29; "Deposition of Grace Jenkins," October 6, 1866, LR, FBR, RG 105, M843, reel 8.

33. Austin W. Fuller to Colonel Stephen Moore, entitled, "Enclosure #2: Final Action," [c. spring 1867], and Fuller to Howard, December 26, 1866, both in RLRC, FBR, RG 105, reel 37.

34. *Freedmen's Bureau v. B. M. Richardson,* March 21, 1866, in "Case Files Relating to the Administration of Justice," FBR, RG 105, M843, reel 31.

35. H. C. Percy to Howard, April 11, 1870, and Lilly Pryor to "My Dearest Father," April 1, 1870, both in RLRC, FBR, RG 105, reel 69.

36. Durrill, *War of Another Kind,* 186 – 89, 212 – 13. Otto Olsen briefly discusses the evolution of the Conservative Party in North Carolina in "North Carolina: An Incongruous Presence," in *Reconstruction and Redemption in the South,* ed. Olsen (Baton Rouge: Louisiana State University Press, 1980), 156 – 69.

37. William C. Harris, *William Woods Holden: Firebrand of North Carolina Politics* (Baton Rouge: Louisiana State University Press, 1987) 187 – 88; Escott, *Many Excellent People,* 124 – 26. For remarks by John Pool on the status of the freedpeople see *Raleigh Sentinel,* October 12, 1865.

38. Laura Edwards provides this analysis of the Black Codes and includes discussion of Moore in *Gendered Strife and Confusion,* 34 – 39. See also "Report on the Committee on Freedmen," January 22, 1866, *Executive and Legislative Documents Laid Before the General Assembly of North Carolina, Session 1865 – 1866,* doc. 9 (Raleigh: State Printer, 1866), 8 – 16.

39. *Raleigh Standard,* March 21, 1866; Alexander, *North Carolina Faces the Freedmen,* 40 – 49.

40. *Journal of the Senate of the General Assembly of the State of North Carolina at its Session of 1865 – 1866* (Raleigh: State Printer, 1866), 240 – 41.

41. *Raleigh Standard,* April 4, 1866; "Report on the Committee on Freedmen," 6; *Public Laws of the State of North Carolina, Passed by the General Assembly at the Session of 1866 – 67,* ch. 74 (Raleigh: William E. Pell, 1867), 197 – 98.

42. Johnson, *Ante-Bellum North Carolina,* 707; Alexander, *North Carolina Faces the Freedmen,* 115 – 17.

43. "List of names of White and Black bound as apprentices," 1867; "Ordered that the indentures of apprenticeship of the following named colored children by this court be and are hereby cancelled," Chowan County, August term 1867; and indentures, Franklin, Craven, Sampson, Mecklenberg, Duplin, and Carteret counties, 1867, all in "Register of Indentures."

44. Fanny J. Irving to the Freedmen's Bureau, August 3, 1866, LR, FBR, RG 105, M843, reel 8. No records exist of the fate of Irving or her son.

45. Mebrina Wolf to Governor Jonathan Worth, April 4, 1867, and William H. Bagley to Chur, April 13, 1867, both ibid.

46. *Raleigh Standard,* March 21, 1866.

47. Roberta Sue Alexander notes Whittlesey's and Cilley's discontent with the Freedmen's Code in Alexander, *North Carolina Faces the Freedmen,* 49 – 50; for Howard see Howard to John C. Robinson, November 21, 1866, LR, FBR, M843, RG 105, reel 13.

48. Thomas Devereux to Worth, October 20, 1866, *Executive and Legislative Documents Laid Before the General Assembly of North Carolina, Session 1866 – 1867,* doc. 17 (Raleigh: State Printer, 1867), 3, 5 – 6.

49. Ibid., 1–9.

50. Ibid. Indenture of Henderson and Westley, March 28, 1866, Sampson County; affidavit of Owen B. Morissey, April 3, 1866, Duplin County; and indenture of Susan, Diana, Jonas, Laura, Eliza, and Joshua, April 10, 1866, Duplin County, all in "Register of Indentures."

51. Message of Governor Jonathan Worth, *Executive and Legislative Documents, 1866–1867*, 17–20.

52. Ibid.; Worth to Russell, February 16, 1867, in *The Correspondence of Jonathan Worth*, ed. J. G. de Roulhac Hamilton (Raleigh: North Carolina Historical Commission and Edwards and Broughton, 1909), 2:890.

53. *Journal of the House of Commons of the General Assembly of the State of North Carolina at its Session of 1866–1867* (Raleigh: State Printer, 1867), 53, 66, 198. Though party affiliation for all House and Senate members is unavailable for this period, the committee was made up of six members who lived in eastern Piedmont counties and only two men who represented western counties. Of the six in the majority, two had formidable reputations. F. A. Thornton, of Warren County, was known as a "Fire-Eating Secessionist," and Joseph Johnson Davis was a Confederate veteran of the Battle of Gettysburg who later became a high-ranking official in the Ku Klux Klan. Of the two westerners only George Washington Logan possessed an illustrious record. Logan, a Unionist, was known for speaking out against the slaveholding aristocracy. Before this group of men lay the task of revising the apprenticeship code so as to meet the expectations of the U.S. Congress (see William S. Powell, ed., *Dictionary of North Carolina Biography*, 6 vols. [Chapel Hill: University of North Carolina Press, 1979–96], 4:298, 6:31, 2:36–37, 4:83; and "An Act to Amend the 5th Chapter of the Revised Code, Entitled 'Apprentices,'" *Public Laws of the State of North Carolina, Passed by the General Assembly at the Sessions of 1866–67* [Raleigh: William E. Pell, 1867], 10–11).

54. *Journal of the House of Commons, 1866–1867*, 236–37; "Act to Amend the 5th Chapter of the Revised Code," 10–11.

55. "Act to Amend the 5th Chapter of the Revised Code," 10–11.

CHAPTER THREE

FREE-LABOR IDEOLOGY, APPRENTICESHIP,
AND THE FREEDMEN'S BUREAU

1. Recent scholars have grappled with the Freedmen's Bureau's complex history. In *Yankee Stepfather* William S. McFeely argues that the Freedmen's Bureau failed its purpose (149–65, 267–87). Paul Cimbala argues that agents not only acted on biases and prejudices but also found themselves burdened with bureaucracy, confusion over policies, threats and violence from local whites, and even loneliness (Cimbala, *Under the Guardianship of the Nation*, 198–203. See also Scott, "Battle over the Child," 102–4; Alexander, *North Carolina Faces the Freedmen*, 112–20; and Edwards, *Gendered Strife and Confusion*, 50).

2. Whittlesey to Howard, January 15, 1866, RLRC, FBR, RG 105, reel 23.

3. *Raleigh Semi-Weekly Record*, September 9, 1865; *Wilmington Herald*, October 6, 1865.

4. McCollough and Smith to Howard, May 6, 1866, LR, FBR, RG 105, M843, reel 8; *Raleigh Standard*, October 5, 1867; Edwards, *Gendered Strife and Confusion*, 45–49.

5. Malone refutes previous scholarship by Eugene Genovese and Herbert Gutman to argue that neither matriarchal nor patriarchal family patterns existed in nineteenth-century slave families. She further argues that late nineteenth- and early twentieth-century scholars developed the "myth of the matriarchy" to reinforce racist images of the weak black family, irresponsible fathers, and dominant mothers (see Ann Patton Malone, *Sweet Chariot: Slave Family and Household Structure in Nineteenth-Century Louisiana* [Chapel Hill: University of North Carolina Press, 1992], 7, 8, 254–63). Brenda E. Stevenson has continued this debate by showing that women held significant power in slave families (see Stevenson, *Life in Black and White: Family and Community in the Slave South* [Oxford: Oxford University Press, 1996], 222, 227, 256, 326–27. See also Franklin, *Free Negro in North Carolina*, 37, 130, 184). Nancy Bercaw discusses African Americans' alternative households in *Gendered Freedoms: Race, Rights, and the Politics of Household in the Delta, 1861–1875* (Gainesville: University Press of Florida, 2003), 102–6.

6. Report of Assistant Commissioner Eliphalet Whittlesey, January 15, 1866, Reports of Operations: Statistics, FBR, RG 105, M843, reel 23. For statistics and a description of the camps see Mobley, *James City*, 29, 43. For a description of the New Bern and James City refugee camps see Karin Lorene Zipf, "Promises of Opportunity: The Freedmen's Savings and Trust Company in New Bern, North Carolina" (M.A. thesis, University of Georgia, 1994), 19–20.

7. On October 28, 1865, the Freedmen's Bureau reported that 165 men, 1,004 women, and 1,605 children received support from the federal government. By April 1866 the numbers had declined, but the proportion remained roughly the same. Whittlesey reported that 48 men, 558 women, and 1,235 children drew upon the government for support that month. The disproportion was not unique to the city of New Bern. That same month, 566 men, 2,013 women, and 2,792 children throughout North Carolina received assistance from Freedmen's Bureau agents (report of Assistant Commissioner Eliphalet Whittlesey, October 28, 1865, April 28, 1866, and May 13, 1866). For a discussion of the household, see Edwards, *Gendered Strife and Confusion*, 22–41; and Bercaw, *Gendered Freedoms*, 102–4. See also report of Vincent Colyer, May 25, 1863, and report of Horace James, July 1864, both in *The Wartime Genesis of Free Labor: The Upper South*, ed. Ira Berlin et al., ser. 1, vol. 2, of *Freedom: A Documentary History of Emancipation, 1861–1867* (Cambridge: Cambridge University Press, 1993), 123–26, 199–201; report of Captain Alex Goslin, December 31, 1865, Reports of Operations: Statistics, FBR, RG 105, M843, reel 23; and testimony of Lucy Chase, May 10, 1863, in Berlin et al., *Wartime Genesis of Free Labor: The Upper South*, 150–51.

8. Mobley, *James City*, 9; Circular #3, May 4, 1866, Circulars, FBR, RG 105, M843, reel 20; report of the head surgeon, M. K. Hogan, October 31, 1866, Reports of Operations: Statistics, ibid., reel 22.

9. Christine Stansell explains the relative independence of women who lived in New York's tenement neighborhoods before 1860 in Stansell, *City of Women: Sex and Class in New York, 1789–1860* (Urbana: University of Illinois Press, 1987), 41–52. Deborah Gray White argues that a unique culture evolved in slave communities where men and women redefined the notions of womanhood and manhood (see White, *Ar'n't I A Woman?* 142–60).

10. Zipf, "Promises of Opportunity," 26, 111, 117, 125. For information regarding state laws on women and property see Bynum, *Unruly Women*, 60–66; Suzanne Lebsock, *The Free Women of Petersburg: Status and Culture in a Southern Town, 1784–1860* (New York: Norton, 1984), 23; and idem, "Radical Reconstruction and the Property Rights of Southern Women," *Journal of Southern History*

43 (May 1977): 209–10. On women's political participation see Elsa Barkley Brown, "Negotiating and Transforming the Public Sphere: African American Political Life in the Transition from Slavery to Freedom," *Public Culture* 7 (Summer 1994): 107–46; and *Wilmington Herald,* September 27, 1865.

11. *Journal of Freedom* (Raleigh), October 7, 1865. Galloway's bill did not survive committee (see entries dated February 1 and 24, 1869, *Journal of the Senate of the General Assembly of the State of North Carolina at its Session of 1868–1869* [Raleigh: M. S. Littlefield, 1869], 223, 343; and entries dated January 31 and March 1, 1870, *Journal of the Senate of the General Assembly of the State of North Carolina at is Session of 1869–1870* [Raleigh: M. S. Littlefield, 1870], 264, 466). Nancy Bercaw discusses the boundaries of household politics in *Gendered Freedoms,* 158–63.

12. Albion Tourgée to Howard, July 29, 1865, RLRC, FBR, RG 105, reel 18.

13. Ibid.

14. McFeely, *Yankee Stepfather,* 78–83.

15. Whittlesey to Asa Teal, July 28, 1865, Letters Sent by the Assistant Commissioner (hereinafter referred to as LS), Records of the Assistant Commissioner for the State of North Carolina, FBR, 1865–1870, RG 105, M843, reel 1; Whittlesey to Cilley, November 16, 1865, ibid.

16. Whittlesey to Howard, January 1, 1866, RLRC, FBR, RG 105, reel 29; "Report of the Freedmen's Bureau in North Carolina," January 15, 1866, RLRC, FBR, RG 105, reel 23; Circular 1, February 16, 1866, Circulars, FBR, RG 105, M843, reel 20; Whittlesey to Howard, March 16, 1866, RLRC, FBR, RG 105, reel 29.

17. Circular #1.

18. Whittlesey to Howard, January 15, 1866, 39th Cong., 1st sess., House Executive Document 70, 242–43; "Report of the Bureau of Military Justice," August 9, 1866, General Court Martial Records for Brevet Brigadier General Eliphalet Whittlesey, Registers of the Records of the Proceedings of the U.S. Army Courts-martial, 1809–1890, RG 153, National Archives (hereinafter referred to as court-martial case #00-1682).

19. Howard to the Reverend George Whipple, May 8, 1866; deposition of Winthrop Tappan; and deposition of William Grimes, all in court-martial case #00-1682.

20. Deposition of Horace James, ibid.

21. McFeely, *Yankee Stepfather,* 78–83, 249–53; "Report of the Case of Brevet Brigadier General Eliphalet Whittlesey," August 9, 1866, court-martial case #00-1682.

22. See "Report of the Case of Brevet Brigadier General Eliphalet Whittlesey" (quotations); and McFeely, *Yankee Stepfather,* 253.

23. Circular #1.

24. Cilley to Whittlesey, November 19, 1865, LR, FBR, RG 105, M843, reel 7.

25. "Chapter 5: Apprentices," *Revised Code,* 78; Robinson to Howard, November 8, 1866, LS, FBR, RG 105, M843, reel 1; William A. Jenkins to Whittlesey, February 20, 1866, and Colonel A. G. Brady to Benjamin Evans, May 9, 1866, both in LR, FBR, RG 105, M843, reel 8.

26. *Raleigh Standard,* June 1866; Whittelsey to Barrett, October 30, 1865, and Cilley to Whittlesey, December 16, 1865, both in LR, FBR, RG 105, M843, reel 7; Nat Parker et al. to "The Head Commissioners of the Freedmen," April 4, 1866, and Joseph S. Cannon to Whittlesey, October 21, 1865, both in LR, ibid., reel 8.

27. Rutherford to Andrew Coats, September 11, 1866, LR, FBR, RG 105, M843, reel 12.

28. Ashley to Woolsey, March 12, 1866, and Whittlesey to Howard, April 10 and May 15, 1866, all in RLRC, FBR, RG 105, reel 29.

29. William Fowler to Robinson, June 22, 1866, LR, FBR, RG 105, M843, reel 9. Eugene Genovese argues the important role of slave fathers in *Roll, Jordan, Roll,* 486–93. Herbert Gutman also discusses the positive role of slave fathers in *The Black Family in Slavery and Freedom,* 190, 307–8.

30. Teal to Whittlesey, July 27, 1865, LR, FBR, RG 105, M843, reel 9; Whittlesey to Teal, July 27, 1865, LS, FBR, RG 105, M843, reel 1.

31. Parker et al. to "The Head Commissioners of the Freedmen," April 4, 1866.

32. Lieutenant George S. Hawley to Whittlesey, May 18, 1866, LR, FBR, RG 105, M843, reel 8.

33. Ibid.

34. Nat Parker et al. to "The Head Commissioners of the Freedmen," April 4, 1866; Hawley to Whittlesey, April 9, 1866, LR, FBR, RG 105, M843, reel 8.

CHAPTER FOUR

RECONSTRUCTING "FREE WOMAN"

1. Affidavit of Lucy Ross in the case of Lucy Ross and children, September 24, 1866, RLRC, FBR, RG 105, reel 43.

2. Ibid.; affidavit of William James in the case of Lucy Ross and her children, September 24, 1866, RLRC, FBR, RG 105, reel 43. Lucy Ross is not clear about the time of day or night that her children were kidnapped. Depositions made by other men and women document that often kidnappings were made in the night, at gunpoint.

3. Ibid. This interpretation of events is constructed from the affidavits of both Lucy Ross and William James. Freedmen's Bureau officials later included Lucy Ross's complaint with others in an appeal to the North Carolina Supreme Court, *In the Matter of Harriet Ambrose and Eliza Ambrose.* Laura Edwards examines this case from Wiley Ambrose's point of view. She argues that southern whites violated Ambrose's rights to control his dependents. By contrasting Lucy Ross's experience, which Edwards omits, to Ambrose's, historians will better understand black women's claims to womanhood and independence (see Edwards, *Gendered Strife and Confusion,* 42–54).

4. Lebsock, *Free Women of Petersburg,* 15–53; idem, "Radical Reconstruction and the Property Rights of Southern Women," 209–10; Bynum, *Unruly Women,* 88–103. Marylynn Salmon contrasts the rights and responsibilities of *feme covert* and *feme sole* in *Women and the Law of Property in Early America* (Chapel Hill: University of North Carolina Press, 1986), 14–57.

5. Lebsock, *Free Women of Petersburg,* 24; Bynum, *Unruly Women,* 103–13.

6. Elizabeth Fox-Genovese, *Within the Plantation Household: Black and White Women of the Old South* (Chapel Hill: University of North Carolina Press, 1988), 43, 49–51, 290–93; White, *Ar'n't I a Woman?* 28–31, 49–61.

7. In *Labor of Love, Labor of Sorrow,* 3–4, 52–68, Jacqueline Jones argues that southern whites refused to grant former slave women the privileges of white women. She asserts that whites expected former slave women to serve as domestics and field laborers. Laura Edwards discusses freedwomen's unique construction of womanhood in *Gendered Strife and Confusion,* 145–83, 198–210. See also Laura Edwards, "Sexual Violence, Gender, Reconstruction, and the

Extension of Patriarchy in Granville County, North Carolina," *North Carolina Historical Review* 68 (July 1991): 237–60; and Catherine Clinton, "Reconstructing Freedwomen," in *Divided Houses: Gender and the Civil War*, ed. Catherine Clinton and Nina Silber (New York: Oxford University Press, 1992), 306–19.

8. *The State v. Thomas Long*, 31 NC 488 (1849). Victoria Bynum provides a rich analysis of laws that constrained free black women's sexual and social behavior in *Unruly Women*, 35–58, 96–110.

9. A. G. Brady to Eliza Cook, July 9, 1866; Brady to James H. Cook, July 12, 1866; "Complaint of Eliza Cook," July 15, 1866; and R. G. Badger to T. D. McAlpine, July 26, 1866, all in RLRC, FBR, RG 105, reel 39.

10. "Complaint of Eliza Cook," July 15, 1866, and "Deposition of Eliza Cook," July 12, 1866, both in ibid.

11. "Complaint of Eliza Cook," July 15, 1866; McAlpine to Colonel J. V. Bomford, December 11, 1866; Bomford to Howard, December 13, 1866; and H. A. Bodham to Bomford, December 13, 1866, all in ibid. It is unknown whether Eliza Cook's children were apprenticed subsequent to her eviction. Since her family was evicted during the peak of apprenticeship (see above, ch. 2), it is likely.

12. Powell, *Dictionary of North Carolina Biography*, 1:237.

13. Edwards, *Gendered Strife and Confusion*, 45–65; *North Carolina Standard* (Raleigh), October 10, 1866.

14. Edwards, *Gendered Strife and Confusion*, 48, 161–82.

15. "Deposition of Grace Jenkins," October 6, 1866, LR, FBR, RG 105, M843, reel 8; C. H. Foster to Howard, December 11, 1866, ibid., reel 11; Captain Hannibal D. Norton to Colonel M. Cogswell, March 18, 1867, ibid., reel 12.

16. White, *Ar'n't I a Woman?* 133–41.

17. Jacqueline Jones argues in *Labor of Love, Labor of Sorrow*, 3–4, that black women forged a unique sense of womanhood that reconciled the notions of women's labor outside of the home and women's work within the domestic realm. Other studies that examine African American women's unique labor experiences include Susan A. Mann, "Slavery, Sharecropping, and Sexual Inequality," *Signs* 14 (Summer 1989): 774–98; Leslie A. Schwalm, "'Sweet Dreams of Freedom': Freedwomen's Reconstruction of Life and Labor in Lowcountry South Carolina," *Journal of Women's History* 9 (Spring 1997): 9–38; idem, *A Hard Fight for We: Women's Transition from Slavery to Freedom in South Carolina* (Urbana: University of Illinois Press, 1997); Noralee Frankel, "The Southern Side of 'Glory': Mississippi African-American Women during the Civil War," in *"We Specialize in the Wholly Impossible": A Reader in Black Women's History*, ed. Darlene Clark Hine, Wilma King, and Linda Reed (Brooklyn, NY: Carlson, 1995), 335–42; Edwards, "Sexual Violence, Gender, Reconstruction, and the Extension of Patriarchy"; and Thavolia Glymph, "'This Species of Property': Female Slave Contrabands in the Civil War," in *A Woman's War: Southern Women, Civil War, and the Confederate Legacy*, ed. Edward D. C. Campbell Jr. and Kym S. Rice (Charlottesville: University Press of Virginia, 1996), 55–72. For a discussion of African American women agricultural workers see Schwalm, "Sweet Dreams of Freedom," 1, 11–15. On African American women's political contributions in Reconstruction Richmond see Brown, "Negotiating and Transforming the Public Sphere," 108, 119–21. Other studies of black women in this period include Michelle A.

Krowl, "Dixie's Other Daughters: African-American Women in Virginia, 1861–1868" (Ph.D. diss., University of California, Berkeley, 1998); Tera W. Hunter, *To' Joy My Freedom: Southern Black Women's Lives and Labors after the Civil War* (Cambridge: Harvard University Press, 1997); and Marli F. Weiner, *Mistresses and Slaves: Plantation Women in South Carolina, 1830–80* (Urbana: University of Illinois Press, 1997).

18. William M. Robbins (attorney for Betsey Newsom) to Bomford, February 12, 1867; John R. Edie to Chur, December 8, 1866; and testimonies of Betsey Newsom and A. J. Newsom, February 16, 1867, Salisbury, NC, all in LR, FBR, RG 105, M843, reel 10.

19. Carole Pateman, *The Disorder of Women: Democracy, Feminism, and Political Theory* (Stanford: Stanford University Press, 1989), 43–46, 60–67.

20. Robbins to Bomford, February 12, 1867, LR, FBR, RG 105, M843, reel 10.

21. Lawrence Lee, *The History of Brunswick County, North Carolina* (Bolivia, NC: Brunswick County, 1980), 109–10; U.S. Bureau of the Census Manuscript Records, Population and Slave Schedules, Brunswick County, 1860. Russell's court orders for the twenty years that he served the Brunswick County Court are logged in the Minutes of the Court of Pleas and Quarter Sessions, Brunswick County, 1847–68, NCSA. Russell's 1866 indenture orders are compiled from the Minutes of the Court of Pleas and Quarter Sessions, Brunswick County, 1866, and Apprenticeship Bonds, 1866, Brunswick County.

22. Apprenticeship Bonds, 1865–66, New Hanover, Robeson, and Brunswick counties, NCSA.

23. Russell to Tifton, October 9, 1866, RLRC, FBR, RG 105, reel 43.

24. Edwards, *Gendered Strife and Confusion*, 67–69; Karin L. Zipf, "'The WHITES Shall Rule the Land or Die': Gender, Race, and Class in North Carolina Reconstruction Politics," *Journal of Southern History* 65 (August 1999): 499–503.

25. Lucy Ross to Howard, October 31, 1866, RLRC, FBR, RG 105, reel 43.

26. Ibid.; affidavits of William James, James Ross, and Charles Aubriden, all September 24, 1866, in RLRC, FBR, RG 105, reel 43.

27. Robinson to Miles, December 26, 1866, LR, FBR, RG 105, M843, reel 12; Howard to Robinson, November 21, 1866, ibid., reel 13.

28. Horace W. Raper examines the Reconstruction Acts and Holden's formative role in North Carolina's Republican Party in *William W. Holden: North Carolina's Political Enigma* (Chapel Hill: University of North Carolina Press, 1985), 59–126. See also Olsen, "North Carolina: An Incongruous Presence," in *Reconstruction and Redemption in the South*, 167.

29. Robinson to Bomford, December 26, 1866, and Robinson to Worth, October 30, 1866, both in RLRC, FBR, RG 105, reel 43.

30. "Chapter 5: Apprenticeship," *Revised Code*, 78. See also the legal arguments made by counsel in *In the Matter of Harriet Ambrose and Eliza Ambrose*, original court transcript 9020.

31. *In the Matter of Harriet Ambrose and Eliza Ambrose.*

32. Rutherford to Tifton, January 3, 1867, and Tifton to Rutherford, January 7, 1867, both in "Records of the Complaint Branch," Letters Received, Wilmington, NC, FBR, entry 2892, box 62, RG 105.

33. Howard to Robinson, November 21, 1866, LR, FBR, RG 105, M843, reel 13.

34. Worth to Robinson, November 1, 1866, ibid.; Tifton to Rutherford, January 7, 1867, "Records of the Complaint Branch," Letters Received, Wilmington, NC, FBR, entry 2892, box 62, RG 105; Russell to Tifton, October 9, 1866, RLRC, FBR, RG 105, reel 43.

35. Petition for *habeas corpus, In the Matter of Harriet Ambrose and Eliza Ambrose,* original court transcript 9020, 5–7.

36. Ibid., 8–9.

37. Powell, *Dictionary of North Carolina Biography,* 5:182–83.

38. Petition for *habeas corpus,* 6–7.

39. Ibid.; Edwards, *Gendered Strife and Confusion,* 42–45.

40. F. D. Sewell to Rutherford, January 26, 1867, RLRC, FBR, RG 105, reel 43; and Circular #5, February 16, 1867, Circulars and Broadsides, North Carolina Collection, Wilson Library, University of North Carolina at Chapel Hill.

41. John M. Foote to Whittlesey, July 31, 1867, LR, FBR, RG 105, M843, reel 11; "List of Names of White and Black bound as apprentices," 1865–66, "Register of Indentures."

42. Petition of citizens of Randolph County, June 12, 1867, LR, FBR, RG 105, M843, reel 11.

43. *Public Laws of the State of North Carolina, 1866–67,* 10–11. This law was ratified on February 26, 1867 (see LR, FBR, RG 105, M843, reel 10; and Sewell to Worth, n.d., RLRC, FBR, RG 105, reel 43). See also Bercaw, *Gendered Freedoms,* 161, 171–77.

44. Powell, *Dictionary of North Carolina Biography,* 5:225; "Ordinance on Apprentices," March 7, 1868, Constitutional Convention Ordinances, Records of the Secretary of State, NCSA.

45. Powell, *Dictionary of North Carolina Biography,* 5:244; "Ordinance on Apprentices."

46. Apprenticeship Bonds, 1867, Robeson and New Hanover counties; "Complaint of William French," October 21, 1867, Wilmington, North Carolina, "Records of the Complaint Branch," FBR, entry 2903, vol. 268, RG 105; "Complaint of Elsie Scott," January 24, 1868, ibid., vol. 270.

CHAPTER FIVE

PARENTS' RIGHTS OR CHILDREN'S BEST INTERESTS?

1. Anastasia Sims, *The Power of Femininity in the New South: Women's Organizations and Politics in North Carolina, 1880–1930* (Columbia: University of South Carolina Press, 1997), 40, 511–52, 56–57; Jacquelyn Dowd Hall, *Revolt against Chivalry: Jessie Daniel Ames and the Women's Campaign against Lynching,* rev. ed. (New York: Columbia University Press, 1993), 149–55; Glenda Elizabeth Gilmore, *Gender and Jim Crow: Women and the Politics of White Supremacy in North Carolina, 1896–1920* (Chapel Hill: University of North Carolina Press, 1996), 92–96.

2. Sims, *Power of Femininity,* 40, 160, 164–65; Gilmore, *Gender and Jim Crow,* 92–96.

3. Michael Grossberg, *A Judgement for Solomon: The D'Hauteville Case and Legal Experience in Antebellum America* (Cambridge: Cambridge University Press, 1996), 50; Bardaglio, *Reconstructing the Household,* 89.

4. Richard Dillon to Chur, May 2, 1868, LR, FBR, RG 105, M843, reel 13.

5. Dillon to Rutherford, March 16, 1868, and deposition of Helen Lomax, March 14, 1868, both in LR, FBR, entry 2892, box 62, RG 105.

6. *J. F. G. Spears and wife v. R. L. Snell,* 74 NC 210 (1876).

7. Ibid.

8. The General Assembly removed this provision prior to the publication of the 1883 North Carolina Revised Code (see "Chapter 3: Apprentices," *The Code of North Carolina enacted March 2, 1883*, 2 vols. [New York: Banks and Brothers, 1883], 1:4–5).

9. *Miles Mitchell v. Marina Mitchell and her children*, 67 NC 307 (1872).

10. Ibid.

11. Grossberg, *Judgement for Solomon*, 55; Bardaglio, *Reconstructing the Household*, 163–65.

12. Bardaglio, *Reconstructing the Household*, 137–39; *In Re Samuel Parker*, 144 NC 170 (1907).

13. "Complaint of Mary Scoggins," March 25, 1878, and "Affidavit of John M. Allen," April 6, 1878, both in *Mary Scoggins v. William Scoggins*, 80 NC 319 (1879), original court transcript 12,301, NCSCD.

14. "Chapter 35: Guardian and Ward," sec. 1565, *Code of North Carolina enacted March 2, 1883*, 1:609–10.

15. Ibid; "Chapter 169: An Act in Relation to Indigent and Other Apprentices," *Laws and Resolutions of the State of North Carolina* (Raleigh: Josephus Daniels, 1889), 138–39.

16. See *Ashby v. Page*, 108 NC 6 (1891), original court transcript 16,662, 6–10, NCSCD.

17. Ibid.; *Ashby v. Page*, 106 NC 328 (1890), original court transcript 16,210, 2–6, NCSCD.

18. *Ashby v. Page*, 108 NC 6 (1891), original court transcript 16,662, 1–6.

19. Ibid., 33–35, 37, 39.

20. Ibid., 20–28, 34–37.

21. Ibid., 20–24.

22. Ibid., 6–10, 28–32.

23. For McCorkle's decision see *Ashby v. Page*, 108 NC 6 (1891), original court transcript 16,662, 13–15. For the North Carolina Supreme Court judgment see *Ashby v. Page*, 108 NC 6 (1891).

24. "Petition of Guilford County in re Mrs. Emma Phillips," November 21, 1914; "Petition of Guilford County in re Mrs. John Parrish," October 26, 1914; and "Petition of Guilford County in re Susan Crisco," February 24, 1914, all in Apprenticeship Bonds, Guilford County.

25. Prince and Laura Jones's answer to the "Petition for Writ of Habeas Corpus in the Matter of Mary Jane Jones," March 1, 1910, and the judicial opinion, both in *In Re Habeas Corpus of Mary Jane Jones*, 153 NC 312 (1910), original court transcript 154, 7–8, NCSCD.

26. *In Re Habeas Corpus of Mary Jane Jones.*

27. Ibid.

28. *In Re Rosa Gray Hamilton*, 182 NC 44 (1921); "Respondents' brief on rehearing," n.d., *In Re Rosa Gray Hamilton*, original court transcript 9, 6, NCSCD. For a summary of the case, see *In Re Rosa Gray Hamilton.*

29. For the debate see the summary, majority opinion, and dissent of *In Re Rosa Gray Hamilton*. To bolster his argument, Justice Stacy cited another custody decision, *In Re Daisy Bell Warren*, 178 NC 43 (1919), in which the court rejected the petition of a mother, a former millworker who had once possessed a bad "reputation," for custody of her illegitimate child.

30. For Judge Walker's dissent see *In Re Rosa Gray Hamilton*. To bolster his point, Walker cited another custody case, *A. T. Newsome v. Q. T. Bunch*, 144 NC 15 (1907), which both recognized the validity of paternal rights and stressed the importance of the "best interests" doctrine. Rosa Gray Hamilton's case resurfaced in the next session, but the North Carolina Supreme Court dismissed

the petition (see *In Re Rosa Gray Hamilton*, 183 NC 57 [1922]). Among earlier cases in which the court established the "best interests" precedent is *In the matter of Elizabeth Lewis*, 88 NC 31 (1883).

31. *Annie McIntosh Clegg v. I. N. Clegg*, 186 NC 28 (1923); *Annie McIntosh Clegg v. I. N. Clegg*, 187 NC 730 (1924); "Testimony of the Plaintiff," c. February 23, 1924, *Clegg v. Clegg*, 187 NC 730 (1924), original court transcript 305, 1–2, NCSCD.

32. Testimony of the Plaintiff," c. February 23, 1924, *Clegg v. Clegg*, 187 NC 730 (1924), original court transcript 305, 1–2; "Defendant Appellant's Brief," June 15, 1923, *Clegg v. Clegg*, 186 NC 28 (1923), original court transcript 281, 18, NCSCD.

33. "Testimony of the Plaintiff," c. February 23, 1924, *Clegg v. Clegg*, 187 NC 730 (1924), original court transcript 305, 2.

34. Ibid., 4–6.

35. Ibid., 5–6. *Clegg v. Clegg*, 186 NC 28 (1923).

36. Nancy MacLean, *Behind the Mask of Chivalry: The Making of the Second Ku Klux Klan* (New York: Oxford University Press, 1994), xiii–xvi, 135–44.

37. Ibid., 32–33, 113–14.

38. *Papers Read at the Meeting of Grand Dragons Knights of the Ku Klux Klan At their First Annual Meeting held at Asheville, North Carolina, July 1923*, Joyner Library Special Collections, East Carolina University, Greenville, NC, 72, 124–25.

39. *Clegg v. Clegg*, 186 NC 28 (1923); *Papers Read at the Meeting of Grand Dragons Knights of the Ku Klux Klan, July 1923*, 81–89.

40. *Papers Read at the Meeting of Grand Dragons Knights of the Ku Klux Klan, July 1923*, 84, 91–93.

41. *Clegg v. Clegg*, 186 NC 28 (1923).

42. Ibid.

43. Ibid.

44. "Judgment," February 23 1924, *Clegg v. Clegg*, 187 NC 730 (1924), original court transcript 305, 3–6, NCSCD.

CHAPTER SIX

"THE DAY OF APPRENTICESHIP IS PAST"

1. *In Re Richard Watson*, 157 NC 340 (1911), original court transcript 454, 6, NCSCD; U.S. Bureau of the Census Manuscript Records, Population and Slave Schedules, Mecklenburg, 1910, 207; *The Uplift* 11, no. 11 (January 15, 1921), published by the printing class of the Stonewall Jackson Manual Training and Industrial School, Concord, NC, Dr. James Edward Smoot Collection, NCSA, 1.

2. In this chapter I do not attempt to provide a definitive analysis of progressive reform or child welfare. Rather, I examine progressivism and child welfare as they relate to apprenticeship and changing views of race, class, and gender.

3. "Apprentices," *The North Carolina Criminal Code and Digest* (Raleigh: Edwards and Broughton, 1892), 22–23.

4. Arthur E. Fink, "Changing Philosophies and Practices in North Carolina Orphanages," *North Carolina Historical Review* 48 (October 1971):336–37.

5. Ibid., 337–39; State Board of Agriculture, *North Carolina and Its Resources* (Winston: M. I. and J. C. Stewart, Public Printers and Binders, 1896), 242–45; Mary Elizabeth Barr, "Child-Caring Institutions," in *Child Welfare in North Carolina: An Inquiry by the National Child Labor Committee for the North Carolina Conference for Social Service*, ed. W. H. Swift (New York: National Child Labor Committee, 1918), 136–52.

6. Fink, "Changing Philosophies and Practices in North Carolina Orphanages," 349–50.

7. William A. Link, *The Paradox of Southern Progressivism, 1880–1930* (Chapel Hill: University of North Carolina Press, 1992), 58–68. For a more comprehensive discussion of the events that led to segregation and disfranchisement see Gilmore, *Gender and Jim Crow*. Betty Jane Brandon discusses McKelway's views in "Alexander Jeffrey McKelway: Statesman of the New Order" (Ph.D. diss., University of North Carolina at Chapel Hill, 1969), 29. See also *Charlotte Presbyterian Standard*, November 6, 1901, and November 25, 1903; and Joel Williamson, *The Crucible of Race: Black-White Relations in the American South since Emancipation* (New York: Oxford University Press, 1984), 110–11, 140–41, 177, 199–201.

8. Link, *Paradox of Southern Progressivism*, 58–62; *North Carolina Presbyterian*, March 10, 1898.

9. William A. Link explains McKelway's views towards childhood in Link, *Paradox of Southern Progressivism*, 162–63.

10. Steven Mintz and Susan Kellogg, *Domestic Revolutions: A Social History of Family Life* (New York: Free Press, 1988), 114–17; Viviana A. Zelizer, *Pricing the Priceless Child: The Changing Social Value of Children* (New York: Basic Books, 1985), 57, 70, 72; Joseph F. Kett, *Rites of Passage: Adolescence in America, 1790 to the Present* (New York: Basic Books, 1977), 143, 171, 211, 217.

11. Link, *Paradox of Southern Progressivism*, 166–68.

12. Sims, *Power of Femininity*, 120–22.

13. Ibid.; "Chapter 116a: Stonewall Jackson Manual Training and Industrial School," in *Revisal of 1908 of North Carolina*, ed. George P. Pell (Charleston, S.C.: Walker Evans & Cogswell Co., 1908), 2581–85.

14. Hubert Smith to J. P. Cook, March 29, 1892, quotation from scrapbook, James P. Cook Collection, NCSA; *The Uplift* 11, no. 11 (January 15, 1921): 2–5, 7, quotation from p. 5.

15. Ibid., 21–22.

16. *In Re Richard Watson*, original court transcript 454, 1–3.

17. Ibid., 2, 14, 17.

18. Mabel Brown Ellis, "Dependency and Delinquency," in Swift, *Child Welfare in North Carolina*, 36–28, 93–103; W. H. Swift, "Law and Administration," in ibid., 259, 313–14.

19. The quotation is from Link, *Paradox of Southern Progressivism*, 203. Examples of reform in school governance are found in ibid., 231–35.

20. Powell, *Dictionary of North Carolina Biography*, 1:149–50.

21. Thomas W. Bickett, *Public Letters and Papers of Thomas Walter Bickett: Governor of North Carolina, 1917–1921*, ed. R. B. House (Raleigh: Edwards and Broughton, State Printers, 1923), 28–31.

22. *Raleigh News and Observer*, February 13, 14, 15, 17, 1919. The conference program appeared on February 13, and Rondthaler's speech appeared on February 17, 1919.

23. Ibid., January 22, February 19, 27, 1919.

24. Ibid., January 28, February 3, March 5, 1919. For specifics on the bill's passage through the General Assembly see *Journal of the Senate of the General Assembly of the State of North Carolina* (Raleigh: Edwards and Broughton, State Printers, 1919), 89, 199, 297, 340, 554, 601; and *Journal of the House of the General Assembly of the State of North Carolina* (Raleigh: Edwards and Broughton, State Printers, 1919), 398, 567, 650.

25. *Journal of the Senate of the General Assembly* (1919), 113, 182, 211; *Journal of the House of the General Assembly* (1919), 235, 279; *Raleigh News and Observer*, February 1, 1919; "Article 3: Control Over Indigent Children," in "Chapter 90: Child Welfare," *Consolidated Statutes of North Carolina*, 2 vols. (Raleigh: Edwards and Broughton, 1920), 2:117.

26. Powell, *Dictionary of North Carolina Biography*, 5:287–88; *Raleigh News and Observer*, January 26 and February 16, 1919.

27. Bickett, *Public Letters and Papers*, 18–20. Shipman's sentiments and the full text of his bill are reproduced in *Raleigh News and Observer*, January 26, 1919.

28. Powell, *Dictionary of North Carolina Biography*, 5:287–88 (Saunders), 4:95–96 (Long).

29. *Raleigh News and Observer*, February 4, 1919.

30. Ibid.; *Journal of the House of the General Assembly* (1919), 278; *Raleigh News and Observer*, February 22, 23, March 3, 1919.

31. Joyner's remarks appeared in the *Raleigh News and Observer*, February 23, 1919. Bickett's letter is reprinted in ibid., February 27, 1919.

32. *Raleigh News and Observer*, February 6, 9, 1919.

33. Reports of the Neal bill's passage in the senate appeared in the *Raleigh News and Observer*, March 7, 8, 10, 11, 1919, and the *Charlotte Observer*, March 8, 1919; Livingston's comments appeared in "1919 Legislative Review," *Raleigh News and Observer*, March 11, 1919.

34. "Article 2: Juvenile Courts," in "Chapter 90: Child Welfare," *Consolidated Statutes of North Carolina*, 2:104–17.

35. Ibid., 2:106–16. Edward L. Ayers discusses class divisions among whites on issues such as disfranchisement and child labor at the turn of the twentieth century in *The Promise of the New South: Life after Reconstruction* (New York: Oxford University Press, 1992), 308–9, 415–17.

36. "Defendant's Case on Appeal," *Harry Starnes, by his next friend, W. S. Starnes v. Albion Manufacturing Co.*, 147 NC 556 (1908), original court transcript 23,313, 1–6, NCSCD.

37. "Article 47: General Compulsory Attendance Law" and "Article 48: Compulsory Attendance of Indigent Children," in "Chapter 95: Education," *Consolidated Statutes of North Carolina*, 2:329–30.

38. James L. Leloudis, *Schooling the New South: Pedagogy, Self, and Society in North Carolina, 1880–1920* (Chapel Hill: University of North Carolina, 1996), 22–24, 137–41, 182. Leloudis also explains that African American contributions and northern philanthropical institutions such as the Anna T. Jeanes Fund and the Rosenwald Fund sponsored southern blacks' education in North Carolina (186–91, 226–27).

39. Link, *Paradox of Southern Progressivism*, 270–73.

40. "Brief of Defendant," *State v. T. C. Johnson*, 188 NC 591 (1924), original court transcript 418, 1–2, NCSCD.

41. Ibid., 5; *State v. T. C. Johnson*, 188 NC 591 (1924). For more on community resistance to smallpox vaccinations see Judith Walzer Leavitt, "Be Safe. Be Sure": New York City's

Experience with Epidemic Smallpox," in *Hives of Sickness: Public Health and Epidemics in New York City,* ed. David Rosner (New Brunswick, NJ: Rutgers University Press, 1995), 104–6.

42. *State v. M. S. Lewis,* 194 NC 620 (1927), original court transcript 482, 14–15, NCSCD.

43. W. H. Swift, introduction to Swift, *Child Welfare in North Carolina,* 6–7.

CONCLUSION

1. *In Re Richard Watson,* original court transcript 454, 13–14, NCSCD. The Pennsylvania case referenced here is *Ex Parte Crouse,* 4 Whart. 9 (1839).

2. These and other modern examples of cases that involve the "best interests" argument are discussed in Joel R. Brandes, "Judging the 'Best Interests' of the Child," *New York Law Journal,* February 23, 1999; Jason G. Adess, "Grandparents Given Edge in Custody Case," *Chicago Daily Law Bulletin,* September 26, 2001; and "Mother Is Barred from Smoking in Her Son's Presence," *New York Law Journal,* March 27, 2002, all at http://www.lexis-nexis.com/.

BIBLIOGRAPHY

PRIMARY SOURCES

Archival and Manuscript Collections

National Archives, Southeast Region, East Point, GA.

Records of the Adjutant General's Office, 1780s–1917. RG 94.

Records of the Assistant Commissioner for the State of North Carolina, Bureau of Refugees, Freedmen and Abandoned Lands, 1865–1870. RG 105. M843.

Records of the Bureau of Refugees, Freedmen and Abandoned Lands. RG 105.

Records of the Office of the Judge Advocate General (Army). RG 153.

U.S. Bureau of the Census. Manuscript Records. Population and Slave Schedules, 1850, 1860, 1870.

National Archives, Washington, DC.

Registers and Letters Received by the Commissioner of the Bureau of Refugees, Freedmen and Abandoned Lands, 1865–1872. RG 105. M752.

Registers of the Records of the Proceedings of the U.S. Army General Courts-martial, 1809–1890. RG 153.

North Carolina Collection, Wilson Library, University of North Carolina at Chapel Hill.

Circulars and Broadsides.

North Carolina State Archives, Raleigh.

Apprenticeship Bonds. Brunswick, Duplin, Guilford, Mecklenburg, New Hanover, Orange, Robeson, Wake, and Wilkes counties.

Cook, James P., Collection.

Mial, Alonzo T. and Millard, Papers.

Minutes of the Court of Pleas and Quarter Sessions. Brunswick County. 1847–68.

Minutes of the Court of Common Pleas and Quarter Sessions. Mecklenburg County, 1810–1860.

North Carolina General Assembly Session Records. 1800.

Records of the Secretary of State.

Smoot, Dr. James Edward, Collection.

Southern Historical Collection, Wilson Library,
University of North Carolina at Chapel Hill.

DeRosset Family Papers.

Russell, Daniel L., Papers.

Special Collections Library, Duke University, Durham.

Tillinghast Family Papers.

PUBLISHED GOVERNMENT DOCUMENTS

The Code of North Carolina enacted March 2, 1883. 2 vols. New York: Banks and Brothers, 1883.

The Colonial Records of North Carolina, Published under the Supervision of the Trustees of the Public Libraries, By order of the General Assembly. Edited by William L. Saunders. 30 vols. Wilmington, NC: Broadfoot, 1993–94.

Consolidated Statutes of North Carolina. 2 vols. Raleigh: Edwards and Broughton, 1920.

Constitution of the State of North Carolina, Together with the Ordinances and Resolutions of the Constitutional Convention Assembled in the City of Raleigh, Jan. 14, 1868. Raleigh: Joseph W. Holden, Convention Printer, 1868.

Executive and Legislative Documents Laid Before the General Assembly of North Carolina, Session 1865–1866. Raleigh: State Printer, 1866.

Executive and Legislative Documents Laid Before the General Assembly of North Carolina, Session 1866–1867. Raleigh: State Printer, 1867.

Fifth Census or, enumeration of the inhabitants of the United States. Washington, DC: D. Green, 1832.

Journal of the Constitutional Convention of the State of North Carolina at Its Session, 1868. Raleigh: State Printer, 1868.

Journal of the House of Commons at its Special Session of 1866. Raleigh: State Printer, 1865.

Journal of the House of Commons of the General Assembly of the State of North Carolina at its Session of 1866–1867. Raleigh: State Printer, 1866.

Journal of the House of the General Assembly of the State of North Carolina. Raleigh: Edwards and Broughton, State Printers, 1919.

Journal of the Senate of the General Assembly of the State of North Carolina. Raleigh: Edwards and Broughton, State Printers, 1919.

Journal of the Senate of the General Assembly of the State of North Carolina at its Session of 1865 – 1866. Raleigh: State Printer, 1866.

Journal of the Senate of the General Assembly of the State of North Carolina at its Session of 1868 – 1869. Raleigh: M.S. Littlefield, 1869.

Journal of the Senate of the General Assembly of the State of North Carolina at its Session of 1869 – 1870. Raleigh: M.S. Littlefield, 1870.

Laws and Resolutions of the State of North Carolina. Raleigh: Josephus Daniels, 1889.

The North Carolina Criminal Code and Digest. Raleigh: Edwards and Broughton, 1892.

North Carolina: The 1850 Cumberland County Census. Edited by Dorothy Anderson Askea. N.p., n.d.

North Carolina Government, 1585 – 1979: A Narrative and Statistical History. Edited by John L. Cheney Jr. Raleigh: Department of the Secretary of State, 1981.

Population of the United States in 1860; compiled from the original returns of the Eighth Census. Washington, DC: GPO, 1864.

Public Laws of the State of North Carolina, Passed by the General Assembly at the Session of 1866. Raleigh: William E. Pell, 1866.

Public Laws of the State of North Carolina, Passed by the General Assembly at the Sessions of 1866 – 67. Raleigh: William E. Pell, 1867.

Records of the Executive Council, 1755 – 1775. Edited by Robert J. Cain. 9 vols. Raleigh: North Carolina Department of Cultural Resources, 1994.

Return of the Whole Number of Persons Within the Several Districts of the United States . . . Second Census. New York: Norman Ross, 1990.

Revisal (Code) of 1908 of North Carolina. Charleston, SC: Walker Evans and Cogswell, 1908.

Revised Code of North Carolina, enacted by the General Assembly at the Session of 1854. Boston: Little, Brown, 1855.

The Revised Statutes of the State of North Carolina, Passed by the General Assembly at the Session of 1836 – 7. 2 vols. Raleigh: Turner and Hughes, 1837.

State Board of Agriculture. *North Carolina and Its Resources.* Winston: M. I. and J. C. Stewart, Public Printers and Binders, 1896.

The State Records of North Carolina. Edited by Walter Clark. Vols. 11 – 26. Goldsboro, NC: Nash Brothers, 1904.

North Carolina Supreme Court Cases

In the Matter of Harriet Ambrose and Eliza Ambrose. 61 NC 91.

Chaney Ashby v. James H. Page. 106 NC 328.

Chaney Ashby v. James H. Page. 108 NC 6.

James W. Bell v. Caleb L. Walker, et al. 50 NC 43.

Annie McIntosh Clegg v. I. N. Clegg. 186 NC 28.

Annie McIntosh Clegg v. I. N. Clegg. 187 NC 730.

Ex Parte Crouse. 4 Whart. 9.

Loveless Doggett et al. v. David Moseley. 52 NC 587.

Cornelius Dowd v. Stephen Davis. 15 NC 61.

Den ex dem Hines Drake, et al. v. Henry Drake, et al. 15 NC 110.

Den on Demise of J. C. B. Ehringhaus v. Marmaduke Cartwright. 30 NC 480.

William Fairly v. Archibald Priest and others. 56 NC 383.

Fanny Frolick v. James T. Schonwald. 52 NC 427.

Elizabeth L. Goodrum v. James Goodrum and Al. 43 NC 313.

Grant, an orphan, by his Guardian, v. Whitaker, from Halifax. 5 NC 231.

In Re Rosa Gray Hamilton. 182 NC 44.

Nancy Harris & Al. v. Herbert Harris & Al. 42 NC 111.

John G. Hooks and Al. v. Blackman Lee and Al. 43 NC 157.

William Hooks v. William T. Perkins. 44 NC 21.

In Re Habeas Corpus of Mary Jane Jones. 153 NC 312.

John F. Lee et al. v. Abraham Shankle, et al. 51 NC 313.

In the matter of Elizabeth Lewis. 88 NC 31.

In Re Mary v. Means, Infant. 176 NC 307.

Nancy Midgett v. Willoughby McBryde. 48 NC 21.

Mills v. McAllister. 2 NC 303.

Miles Mitchell v. Marina Mitchell and her children. 67 NC 307.

Haywood Musgrove v. Wm. J. Kornegay, et al. 52 NC 71.

A. T. Newsome v. Q. T. Bunch. 144 NC 15.

Harriet Owens v. Jasper Chaplain. 48 NC 323.

Prue v. Hight. 51 NC 265.

Harry Starnes, by his next friend, W. S. Starnes v. Albion Manufacturing Co. 147 NC 556.

In Re Samuel Parker. 144 NC 170.

Samuel R. Potter v. Sterling B. Everitt & Al. 42 NC 152.

Mary Scoggins v. William Scoggins. 80 NC 319.

J. F. G. Spears and wife v. R. L. Snell. 74 NC 210.

The State v. Thomas Long. 31 NC 488.

State v. M. S. Lewis. 194 NC 620.

State v. T. C. Johnson. 188 NC 591.

In Re Constance Turner. 151 NC 474.

Isaac Waggoner & Wife v. Henry Miller. 26 NC 480.

In Re Daisy Bell Warren. 178 NC 43.

In Re Richard Watson. 157 NC 340.

Newspapers and Journals

Charlotte Observer. 1919.

Charlotte Presbyterian Standard. 1901–3.

Journal of Freedom (Raleigh). 1865.

New Bern Republican. 1867–68.

News and Observer (Raleigh). 1919.

North Carolina Observer (Raleigh). 1876–80.

North Carolina Presbyterian (Fayetteville). 1898.

North Carolina Standard (Raleigh). 1866–67.

Raleigh Register. 1867–68.

Raleigh Semi-Weekly Record. 1865.

Raleigh Sentinel. 1865.

Wilmington Herald. 1865–66.

Wilmington (Daily) Post. 1867.

SECONDARY SOURCES

Adess, Jason G. "Grandparents Given Edge in Custody Case." *Chicago Daily Law Bulletin,* September 26, 2001. http://www.lexis-nexis.com/.

Alexander, Roberta Sue. *North Carolina Faces the Freedmen: Race Relations during Presidential Reconstruction.* Durham: Duke University Press, 1985.

Anderson, Eric. *Race and Politics in North Carolina, 1872–1901.* Baton Rouge: Louisiana State University Press, 1981.

Anscombe, Francis C. *I Have Called You Friends: The Story of Quakerism in North Carolina.* Boston: Christopher, 1959.

Ayers, Edward L. *The Promise of the New South: Life after Reconstruction.* New York: Oxford University Press, 1992.

Bailyn, Bernard. *Education in the Forming of American Society.* Chapel Hill: University of North Carolina Press, 1960.

Balanoff, Elizabeth. "Negro Legislators in the North Carolina General Assembly, July 1868–February 1872." *North Carolina Historical Review* 49 (January 1972): 21–32.

Bardaglio, Peter W. *Reconstructing the Household: Families, Sex, and the Law in the Nineteenth-Century South.* Chapel Hill: University of North Carolina Press, 1995.

Barr, Elizabeth. "Child-Caring Institutions." In Swift, *Child Welfare in North Carolina,* 136–52.

Bederman, Gail. *Manliness and Civilization: A Cultural History of Gender and Race in the United States, 1880–1917.* Chicago: University of Chicago Press, 1995.

Bellows, Barbara L. "'My Children, Gentlemen, Are My Own': Poor Women, the Urban Elite, and the Bonds of Obligation in Antebellum Charleston." In *The Web of Southern Social Relations: Women, Family, and Education,* ed. Walter J. Fraser Jr., R. Frank Saunders Jr., and Jon L. Wakelyn, 52–71. Athens: University of Georgia Press, 1985.

Bender, Thomas. *Community and Social Change in America.* Baltimore: Johns Hopkins University Press, 1978.

Bercaw, Nancy. *Gendered Freedoms: Race, Rights, and the Politics of Household in the Delta, 1861–1875.* Gainesville: University Press of Florida, 2003.

Berlin, Ira, Barbara J. Fields, Thavolia Glymph, Joseph P. Reidy, and Leslie S. Rowland, eds. *Freedom: A Documentary History of Emancipation, 1861–1867.* Ser. 1, vol. 1, *The Destruction of Slavery.* New York: Cambridge University Press, 1985.

Berlin, Ira, Thavolia Glymph, Steven F. Miller, Joseph P. Reidy, Leslie S. Rowland, and Julie Saville, eds. *Freedom: A Documentary History of Emancipation, 1861–1867.* Ser. 1, vol. 3, *The Wartime Genesis of Free Labor: The Lower South.* New York: Cambridge University Press, 1991.

Berlin, Ira, Steven F. Miller, Joseph P. Reidy, and Leslie S. Rowland, eds. *Freedom: A Documentary History of Emancipation, 1861–1867.* Ser. 1, vol. 2, *The Wartime Genesis of Free Labor: The Upper South.* New York: Cambridge University Press, 1993.

Berlin, Ira, Steven F. Miller, and Leslie S. Rowland. "Afro-American Families in the Transition from Slavery to Freedom." *Radical History Review* 42 (Fall 1988): 89–121.

Berlin, Ira, Joseph P. Reidy, and Leslie S. Rowland, eds. *Freedom: A Documentary History of Emancipation.* Ser. 2, *The Black Military Experience.* New York: Cambridge University Press, 1982.

Bickett, Thomas W. *Public Letters and Papers of Thomas Walter Bickett: Governor of North Carolina, 1917–1921.* Edited by R. B. House. Raleigh: Edwards and Broughton, 1923.

Billings, Dwight B., Jr. *Planters and the Making of a "New South": Class, Politics, and Development in North Carolina, 1865–1900.* Chapel Hill: University of North Carolina Press, 1979.

Blassingame, John W. *Black New Orleans, 1860–1880.* Chicago: University of Chicago Press, 1973.

———. *The Slave Community: Plantation Life in the Antebellum South.* New York: Oxford University Press, 1972.

Bloch, Ruth. "The Gendered Meanings of Virtue in Revolutionary America." *Signs* 13 (Autumn 1987): 37–58.

Blount, John Gray. *The John Gray Blount Papers.* Edited by Alice Barnwell Keith. 4 vols. Raleigh: North Carolina Department of Archives and History, 1959.

Boydston, Jeanne. *Home and Work: Housework, Wages, and the Ideology of Labor in the Early Republic.* New York: Oxford University Press, 1990.

Brandes, Joel R. "Judging the 'Best Interests' of the Child." *New York Law Journal,* February 23, 1999. http://www.lexis-nexis.com/.

Brandon, Betty Jane. "Alexander Jeffrey McKelway: Statesman of the New Order." Ph.D. diss., University of North Carolina at Chapel Hill, 1969.

Brown, Elsa Barkley. "African-American Women's Quilting: A Framework for Conceptualizing and Teaching African-American Women's History." *Signs* 14 (Summer 1989): 921–29.

———. "Negotiating and Transforming the Public Sphere: African American Political Life in the Transition from Slavery to Freedom." *Public Culture* 7 (Summer 1994): 107–46.

————. "Polyrhythms and Improvisation: Lessons for Women's History." *History Workshop Journal* 31 (Spring 1991): 85–90.

————. "'What Has Happened Here': The Politics of Difference in Women's History and Feminist Politics." *Feminist Studies* 18 (Summer 1992): 295–312.

Brown, Kathleen M. *Good Wives, Nasty Wenches, and Anxious Patriarchs: Gender, Race, and Power in Colonial Virginia.* Chapel Hill: University of North Carolina Press, 1996.

Brown, Letitia Woods. *Free Negroes in the District of Columbia, 1790–1846.* New York: Oxford University Press, 1972.

Butler, Lindley S., and Alan D. Watson, eds. *The North Carolina Experience: An Interpretive and Documentary History.* Chapel Hill: University of North Carolina Press, 1984.

Bynum, Victoria E. "Reshaping the Bonds of Womanhood: Divorce in Reconstruction North Carolina." In Clinton and Silber, *Divided Houses,* 320–33.

————. *Unruly Women: The Politics of Social and Sexual Control in the Old South.* Chapel Hill: University of North Carolina Press, 1992.

Campbell, Edward D. C., Jr., and Kym S. Rice. *A Woman's War: Southern Women, Civil War, and the Confederate Legacy.* Charlottesville: University Press of Virginia, 1996.

Carby, Hazel. *Reconstructing Womanhood: The Emergence of the Afro-American Woman Novelist.* New York: Oxford University Press, 1987.

Censer, Jane Turner. "A Changing World of Work: North Carolina Elite Women, 1865–1895." *North Carolina Historical Review* 73 (January 1996): 28–55.

————. *North Carolina Planters and Their Children, 1800–1860.* Baton Rouge: Louisiana State University Press, 1984.

————. "'Smiling through Her Tears': Ante-Bellum Southern Women and Divorce." *American Journal of Legal History* 25 (January 1982): 114–34.

Cimbala, Paul A. *Under the Guardianship of the Nation: The Freedmen's Bureau and the Reconstruction of Georgia, 1865–1870.* Athens: University of Georgia Press, 1997.

Clinton, Catherine. "Bloody Terrain: Freedwomen, Sexuality, and Violence during Reconstruction." *Georgia Historical Quarterly* 76 (Summer 1992): 310–32.

————. *The Plantation Mistress: Woman's World in the Old South.* New York: Pantheon Books, 1982.

————. "Reconstructing Freedwomen." In Clinton and Silber, *Divided Houses,* 306–19.

Clinton, Catherine, and Nina Silber, eds. *Divided Houses: Gender and the Civil War.* New York: Oxford University Press, 1992.

Collins, Patricia Hill. *Black Feminist Thought: Knowledge, Consciousness, and the Politics of Empowerment.* Boston: Unwin Hyman, 1990.

Cott, Nancy F. *The Bonds of Womanhood: "Woman's Sphere" in New England, 1780–1835.* New Haven: Yale University Press, 1977.

Crouch, Barry A. "Seeking Equality: Houston Black Women during Reconstruction." In *Black Dixie: Afro-Texan History and Culture in Houston,* ed. Howard Beeth and Cary D. Wintz, 56–59. College Station: Texas A&M University Press, 1992.

Crow, Jeffrey J., and Robert F. Durden. *Maverick Republican in the Old North State: A Political Biography of Daniel L. Russell.* Baton Rouge: Louisiana State University Press, 1977.

Crow, Jeffrey J., and Flora J. Hatley, eds. *Black Americans in North Carolina and the South.* Chapel Hill: University of North Carolina Press, 1984.

Cullen, Jim. "'I's a Man Now': Gender and African American Men." In Clinton and Silber, *Divided Houses,* 76–91.

Davidoff, Leonore, and Catherine Hall. *Family Fortunes: Men and Women of the English Middle Class, 1780–1850.* Chicago: University of Chicago Press, 1980.

Davis, Angela. *Women, Race, and Class.* New York: Random House, 1981.

Dennett, John Richard. *The South as It Is, 1865–1866.* 1965. Reprint. Athens: University of Georgia Press, 1986.

Drago, Edmund L. *Black Politicians and Reconstruction in Georgia: A Splendid Failure.* Baton Rouge: Louisiana State University Press, 1982.

DuBois, W. E. B. *Black Reconstruction: An Essay toward a History of the Part Which Black Folk Played in the Attempt to Reconstruct Democracy in America, 1860–1880.* New York: Russell and Russell, 1935.

———. *The Souls of Black Folk.* New York: Signet, 1969.

Durrill, Wayne K. *War of Another Kind: A Southern Community in the Great Rebellion.* New York: Oxford University Press, 1990.

Edmondston, Catherine Ann Devereux. *"Journal of a Secesh Lady": The Diary of Catherine Ann Devereux Edmonston.* Edited by Beth G. Crabtree and James W. Patton. Raleigh: North Carolina Division of Archives and History, Department of Cultural Resources, 1979.

Edwards, Laura F. *Gendered Strife and Confusion: The Political Culture of Reconstruction.* Urbana: University of Illinois Press, 1997.

———. "Sexual Violence, Gender, Reconstruction, and the Extension of Patriarchy in Granville County, North Carolina." *North Carolina Historical Review* 68 (July 1991): 237–60.

Ellis, Mabel Brown. "Dependency and Delinquency." In Swift, *Child Welfare in North Carolina.*

Escott, Paul D. *Many Excellent People: Power and Privilege in North Carolina, 1850–1900.* Chapel Hill: University of North Carolina Press, 1985.

Evans, William McKee. *Ballots and Fence Rails: Reconstruction on the Lower Cape Fear.* New York: Norton, 1966.

Faler, Paul. *Mechanics and Manufacturers in the Early Industrial Revolution: Lynn, Massachusetts, 1780–1860.* Albany: State University of New York Press, 1981.

Faust, Drew Gilpin. "Altars of Sacrifice: Confederate Women and Narratives of War." *Journal of American History* 76 (March 1990): 1200–1228.

———. *Mothers of Invention: Women of the Slaveholding South in the American Civil War.* Chapel Hill: University of North Carolina Press, 1996.

————. "'Trying to Do a Man's Business': Slavery, Violence, and Gender in the American Civil War." *Gender and History* 4 (Summer 1992): 197–214.

Ferguson, Herman W. *Mecklenburg County, North Carolina: Minutes of the Court of Common Pleas and Quarter Sessions: Volume IV: 1831–1840.* Rocky Mount: Herman W. Ferguson, 2002.

Fields, Barbara J. "Ideology and Race in American History." In *Region, Race, and Reconstruction: Essays in Honor of C. Vann Woodward*, ed. J. Morgan Kousser and James M. McPherson, 143–77. New York: Oxford University Press, 1982.

————. *Slavery and Freedom on the Middle Ground: Maryland during the Nineteenth Century.* New Haven: Yale University Press, 1985.

————. "Slavery, Race, and Ideology in the United States of America." *New Left Review*, no. 181 (May–June 1990): 95–118.

Fink, Arthur E. "Changing Philosophies and Practices in North Carolina Orphanages." *North Carolina Historical Review* 48 (October 1971): 333–58.

Foner, Eric. "Black Reconstruction Leaders at the Grass Roots." In *Black Leaders of the Nineteenth Century*, ed. Leon Litwack and August Meier, 219–34. Urbana: University of Illinois Press, 1988.

————. *Freedom's Lawmakers: A Directory of Black Officeholders during Reconstruction.* New York: Oxford University Press, 1993.

————. *Free Soil, Free Labor, Free Men: The Ideology of the Republican Party before the Civil War.* New York: Oxford University Press, 1993.

————. *Nothing But Freedom: Emancipation and Its Legacy.* Baton Rouge: Louisiana State University Press, 1983.

————. *Reconstruction: America's Unfinished Revolution, 1863–1877.* New York: Harper and Row, 1988.

————. *Tom Paine and Revolutionary America.* New York: Oxford University Press, 1976.

Fox-Genovese, Elizabeth. *Feminism without Illusions: A Critique of Individualism.* Chapel Hill: University of North Carolina Press, 1988.

————. *Within the Plantation Household: Black and White Women in the Old South.* Chapel Hill: University of North Carolina Press, 1988.

Frankel, Noralee. "The Southern Side of 'Glory': Mississippi African-American Women during the Civil War." In Hine, King, and Reed, *"We Specialize in the Wholly Impossible,"* 335–41.

Frankenburg, Ruth. *White Women, Race Matters: The Social Construction of Whiteness.* Minneapolis: University of Minnesota Press, 1993.

Franklin, John Hope. *The Free Negro in North Carolina, 1790–1860.* New York: Norton, 1943.

Frederickson, George M. *The Black Image in the White Mind: The Debate on Afro-American Character and Destiny, 1817–1914.* New York: Harper Torchbooks, 1972.

————. *White Supremacy: A Comparative Study in American and South African History.* Oxford: Oxford University Press, 1981.

Friedman, Jean E. *The Enclosed Garden: Women and Community in the Evangelical South, 1830–1900.* Chapel Hill: University of North Carolina Press, 1985.

Genovese, Eugene D. *The Political Economy of Slavery: Studies in the Economy and Society of the Slave South.* New York: Pantheon Books, 1965.

———. *Roll, Jordan, Roll: The World the Slaves Made.* New York: Vintage Books, 1976.

———. *The Slaveholders' Dilemma: Freedom and Progress in Southern Conservative Thought, 1820–1860.* Columbia: University of South Carolina Press, 1992.

———. *The World the Slaveholders Made: Two Essays in Interpretation.* New York: Pantheon Books, 1969.

Giddings, Paula. *When and Where I Enter: The Impact of Black Women on Race and Sex in America.* New York: Bantam, 1984.

Gilmore, Glenda Elizabeth. *Gender and Jim Crow: Women and the Politics of White Supremacy in North Carolina, 1896–1920.* Chapel Hill: University of North Carolina Press, 1996.

Glymph, Thavolia. "Freedpeople and Ex-Masters: Shaping a New Order in the Postbellum South, 1865–1868." In *Essays on the Postbellum Southern Economy,* ed. Glymph and John J. Kushma, 48–72. College Station: Texas A&M Press for the University of Texas at Arlington, 1985.

———. "'This Species of Property': Female Slave Contrabands in the Civil War." In Campbell and Rice, *A Woman's War,* 55–72.

Gordon, Linda. "Black and White Visions of Welfare Reform: Women's Welfare Activism, 1890–1945." *Journal of American History* 78 (September 1991): 539–50.

———. "Social Insurance and Public Assistance: The Influence of Gender in Welfare Thought in the United States, 1890–1935." *American Historical Review* 97 (February 1992): 19–54.

Greene, Lorenzo J., et al. *Missouri's Black Heritage.* Columbia: University of Missouri Press, 1993.

Grossberg, Michael. *Governing the Hearth: Law and the Family in Nineteenth-Century America.* Chapel Hill: University of North Carolina Press, 1985.

———. *A Judgement for Solomon: The D'Hauteville Case and Legal Experience in Antebellum America.* Cambridge: Cambridge University Press, 1996.

Gutman, Herbert. *The Black Family in Slavery and Freedom, 1750–1925.* New York: Vintage Books, 1976.

———. "Work, Culture, and Society in Industrializing America, 1815–1919." In *Work, Culture, and Society in Industrializing America,* 3–78. New York: Knopf, 1976.

Hale, Grace Elizabeth. *Making Whiteness: The Culture of Segregation in the South, 1890–1940.* New York: Pantheon Books, 1997.

Hall, Jacquelyn Dowd. "'The Mind That Burns in Each Body': Women, Rape, and Racial Violence." In *Powers of Desire: The Politics of Sexuality,* ed. Ann Snitow, Christine Stansell, and Sharon Thompson, 328–49. New York: Monthly Review Press, 1983.

————. "O. Delight Smith's Progressive Era: Labor, Feminism, and Reform in the Urban South." In *Visible Women: New Essays on American Activism*, ed. Nancy A. Hewitt and Suzanne Lebsock, 166–98. Urbana: University of Illinois Press, 1993.

————. "Private Eyes, Public Women: Images of Class and Sex in the Urban South, Atlanta, Georgia, 1913–1915." In *Work Engendered: Toward a New History of American Labor*, ed. Ava Baron, 243–72. Ithaca: Cornell University Press, 1991.

————. *Revolt against Chivalry: Jessie Daniel Ames and the Women's Campaign against Lynching.* Rev. ed. New York: Columbia University Press, 1993.

Hall, Jacquelyn Dowd, James Leloudis, Robert Korstad, Mary Murphy, LuAnn Jones, and Christopher Daly. *Like a Family: The Making of a Southern Cotton Mill World.* Chapel Hill: University of North Carolina Press, 1987.

Hamilton, J. G. de Roulhac. *Life of Andrew Johnson: Seventeenth President of the United States.* Greeneville: East Tennessee Publishing, 1928.

————. *Reconstruction in North Carolina.* New York: Columbia University Press, 1914.

Harley, Sharon. "For the Good of Family and Race: Gender, Work, and Domestic Roles in the Black Community, 1880–1930." *Signs* 15 (Winter 1990): 336–49.

Harris, William C. *Presidential Reconstruction in Mississippi.* Baton Rouge: Louisiana State University Press, 1967.

————. *William Woods Holden: Firebrand of North Carolina Politics.* Baton Rouge: Louisiana State University Press, 1987.

Herndon, Ruth Wallis, and John E. Murray, eds. "Bound to Labor: Varieties of Apprenticeship in Early America." In review.

Hewitt, Nancy A. "Beyond the Search for Sisterhood: American Women's History in the 1980s." *Social History* 10 (October 1985): 229–321.

————. "Compounding Differences." *Feminist Studies* 18 (Summer 1992): 313–26.

————. "Reflections from a Departing Editor: Recasting Issues of Marginality." *Gender and History* 4 (Summer 1992): 3–9.

Higginbotham, Evelyn Brooks. "African-American Women's History and the Metalanguage of Race." *Signs* 17 (Winter 1992): 251–74.

————. "Beyond the Sound of Silence: Afro-American Women in History." *Gender and History* 1 (Spring 1989): 50–67.

————. "Negotiating and Transforming the Public Sphere: African American Political Life in the Transition from Slavery to Freedom." *Public Culture* 7 (1994): 107–46.

————. *Righteous Discontent: The Women's Movement in the Black Baptist Church, 1880–1920.* Cambridge: Harvard University Press, 1993.

Hill, Samuel S., Jr. *Southern Churches in Crisis.* New York: Holt, Rinehart and Winston, 1967.

Hine, Darlene Clark, Wilma King, and Linda Reed, eds. *"We Specialize in the Wholly Impossible": A Reader in Black Women's History.* Brooklyn, NY: Carlson, 1995.

Hodes, Martha. "The Sexualization of Reconstruction Politics: White Women and Black Men in the South after the Civil War." *Journal of the History of Sexuality* 3, no. 3 (1993): 402–17.

———. "Wartime Dialogues on Illicit Sex: White Women and Black Men." In Clinton and Silber, *Divided Houses*, 230–42.

Holt, Sharon Ann. "Making Freedom Pay: Freedpeople Working for Themselves, North Carolina, 1865–1900." *Journal of Southern History* 60 (May 1994): 229–62.

hooks, bell. *Ain't I a Woman: Black Women and Feminism.* Boston: South End, 1981.

Hudson, Larry E., Jr. *To Have and to Hold: Slave Work and Family Life in Antebellum South Carolina.* Athens: University of Georgia Press, 1997.

Huebner, Timothy S. *The Southern Judicial Tradition: State Judges and Sectional Distinctiveness, 1790–1890.* Athens: University of Georgia Press, 1999.

Hull, Gloria T., Patricia Bell Scott, and Barbara Smith, eds. *All the Women Are White, All the Blacks Are Men, but Some of Us Are Brave: Black Women's Studies.* Old Westbury, NY: Feminist Press, 1982.

Hume, Richard L. "Negro Delegates to the State Constitutional Conventions of 1867–69." In *Southern Black Leaders of the Reconstruction Era*, ed. Howard N. Rabinowitz, 129–53. Urbana: University of Illinois Press, 1982.

Hunter, Tera W. "Domination and Resistance: The Politics of Wage Household Labor in New South Atlanta." *Labor History* 34 (Spring–Summer 1993): 205–20.

———. *To 'Joy My Freedom: Southern Black Women's Lives and Labors after the Civil War.* Cambridge: Harvard University Press, 1997.

Inscoe, John. *Mountain Masters: Slavery and the Sectional Crisis in Western North Carolina.* Knoxville: University of Tennessee Press, 1989.

Janiewski, Dolores E. *Sisterhood Denied: Race, Gender, and Class in a New South Community.* Philadelphia: Temple University Press, 1985.

Jennings, Thelma. "'Us Colored Women Had to Go through a Plenty': Sexual Exploitation of African American Slave Women." *Journal of Women's History* 1 (Winter 1990): 45–74.

Johnson, Guion Griffis. *Ante-Bellum North Carolina: A Social History.* Chapel Hill: University of North Carolina Press, 1937.

Johnson, Michael, and James Roark. *No Chariot Let Down: Charleston's Free People of Color on the Eve of the Civil War.* Chapel Hill: University of North Carolina Press, 1984.

Jones, Jacqueline. *Labor of Love, Labor of Sorrow: Black Women, Work, and the Family from Slavery to the Present.* New York: Basic Books, 1985.

Jordan, Winthrop. *White over Black: American Attitudes toward the Negro, 1580–1812.* Chapel Hill: University of North Carolina Press, 1968.

Joyner, Charles. *Down by the Riverside: A South Carolina Slave Community.* Urbana: University of Illinois Press, 1984.

Kerber, Linda K. "The Paradox of Women's Citizenship in the Early Republic: The Case of *Martin vs. Massachusetts, 1805.*" *American Historical Review* 97 (April 1992): 349–78.

———. "Separate Spheres, Female Worlds, Woman's Place: The Rhetoric of Women's History." *Journal of American History* 75 (June 1988): 9–39.

———. *Women of the Republic: Intellect and Ideology in Revolutionary America.* Chapel Hill: University of North Carolina Press, 1980.

Kett, Joseph F. *Rites of Passage: Adolescence in America, 1790 to the Present.* New York: Basic Books, 1977.

Kousser, J. Morgan. *The Shaping of Southern Politics: Suffrage Restriction and the Establishment of the One-Party South.* New Haven: Yale University Press, 1974.

Krowl, Michelle A. "Dixie's Other Daughters: African-American Women in Virginia, 1861–1868." Ph.D. diss., University of California, Berkeley, 1998.

Ladd-Taylor, Molly. *Mother-Work: Women, Child Welfare, and the State, 1890–1930.* Urbana: University of Illinois Press, 1994.

Landes, Joan B. *Women and the Public Sphere in the Age of the French Revolution.* Ithaca: Cornell University Press, 1988.

Lane, Joan. *Apprenticeship in England, 1600–1914.* Boulder, CO: Westview, 1996.

Lasch, Christopher. *The World of Nations: Reflections on American History, Politics, and Culture.* New York: Knopf, 1973.

Lebsock, Suzanne. *The Free Women of Petersburg: Status and Culture in a Southern Town, 1784–1860.* New York: Norton, 1984.

———. "Radical Reconstruction and the Property Rights of Southern Women." *Journal of Southern History* 43 (May 1977): 195–216.

———. "Woman Suffrage and White Supremacy: A Virginia Case Study." In *Visible Women: New Essays on American Activism,* ed. Nancy A. Hewitt and Suzanne Lebsock, 62–100. Urbana: University of Illinois Press, 1993.

Lee, Lawrence. *The History of Brunswick County, North Carolina.* Bolivia, NC: Brunswick County, 1980.

Lefler, Hugh T., and William S. Powell. *Colonial North Carolina: A History.* New York: Scribner, 1973.

Leloudis, James L. *Schooling the New South: Pedagogy, Self, and Society in North Carolina, 1880–1920.* Chapel Hill: University of North Carolina Press, 1996.

Link, William A. *The Paradox of Southern Progressivism, 1880–1930.* Chapel Hill: University of North Carolina Press, 1992.

Litwack, Leon. *Been in the Storm So Long: The Aftermath of Slavery.* New York: Knopf, 1979.

Logan, Frenise A. "Black and Republican: Vicissitudes of a Minority Twice Over in the North Carolina House of Representatives, 1876–1877." *North Carolina Historical Review* 61 (July 1984): 311–46.

MacLean, Nancy. *Behind the Mask of Chivalry: The Making of the Second Ku Klux Klan*. New York: Oxford University Press, 1994.

Malone, Ann Patton. *Sweet Chariot: Slave Family and Household Structure in Nineteenth-Century Louisiana*. Chapel Hill: University of North Carolina Press, 1992.

Manarin, Louis H. *Guide to Military Organization and Installations: North Carolina, 1861–1865*. Raleigh: North Carolina Confederate Centennial Commission, 1961.

Mann, Susan A. "Slavery, Sharecropping, and Sexual Inequality." *Signs* 14 (Summer 1989): 774–98.

McCurry, Stephanie. *Masters of Small Worlds: Yeoman Households, Gender Relations, and the Political Culture of the Antebellum South Carolina Low Country*. New York: Oxford University Press, 1995.

———. "The Politics of Yeoman Households in South Carolina." In Clinton and Silber, *Divided Houses*, 22–38.

———. "The Two Faces of Republicanism: Gender and Proslavery Politics in Antebellum South Carolina." *Journal of American History* 78 (March 1992): 1245–64.

McFeely, William S. *Yankee Stepfather: General O. O. Howard and the Freedmen*. 1968. Reprint. New York: Norton, 1994.

McGee, David. "'Home and Friends': Kinship, Community, and Elite Women in Caldwell County, North Carolina, during the Civil War." *North Carolina Historical Review* 74 (January 1997): 363–88.

Mintz, Steven, and Susan Kellogg. *Domestic Revolutions: A Social History of Family Life*. New York: Free Press, 1988.

Mitchell, Reid. *The Vacant Chair: The Northern Soldier Leaves Home*. New York: Oxford University Press, 1993.

Mobley, Joe A. *James City: A Black Community in North Carolina, 1863–1900*. Raleigh: North Carolina Department of Cultural Resources, 1981.

Mohanty, Chandra Talpade. "Cartographies of Struggle: Third World Women and the Politics of Feminism." In *Third World Women and the Politics of Feminism*, ed. Mohanty, Ann Russo, and Lourdes Torres, 1–47. Bloomington: Indiana University Press, 1991.

———. "Under Western Eyes: Feminist Scholarship and Colonial Discourses." In *Third World Women and the Politics of Feminism*, ed. Mohanty, Ann Russo, and Lourdes Torres, 51–80. Bloomington: Indiana University Press, 1991.

Mohr, Clarence. *On the Threshold of Freedom: Masters and Slaves in Civil War Georgia*. Athens: University of Georgia Press, 1986.

Montgomery, David. *Beyond Equality: Labor and the Radical Republicans, 1862–1872*. New York: Knopf, 1967.

———. *Citizen Worker: The Experience of Workers in the United States with Democracy and the Free Market during the Nineteenth Century*. New York: Cambridge University Press, 1993.

Morgan, Edmund S. *American Slavery, American Freedom: The Ordeal of Colonial Virginia*. New York: Norton, 1975.

"Mother Is Barred from Smoking in Her Son's Presence." *New York Law Journal*, March 27, 2002. http://www.lexis-nexis.com/.

Nicholson, Linda, ed. *Feminism/Postmodernism*. New York: Routledge, 1990.

———. *Gender and History: The Limits of Social Theory in the Age of the Family*. New York: Columbia University Press, 1986.

Nieman, Donald G. *To Set the Law in Motion: The Freedmen's Bureau and the Legal Rights of Blacks, 1865–1868*. Millwood, NY: KTO, 1979.

Norton, Mary Beth. *Founding Mothers and Fathers: Gendered Power and the Forming of American Society*. New York: Knopf, 1996.

———. *Liberty's Daughters: The Revolutionary Experience of American Women, 1750–1800*. Boston: Little, Brown, 1980.

O'Brien, Gail. *The Legal Fraternity and the Making of a New South Community, 1848–1882*. Athens: University of Georgia Press, 1986.

Olsen, Otto H. *A Carpetbagger's Crusade: The Life of Albion Winegar Tourgee*. Athens: University of Georgia Press, 1986.

———. *Reconstruction and Redemption in the South*. Baton Rouge: Louisiana State University Press, 1980.

Papers Read at the Meeting of Grand Dragons Knights of the Ku Klux Klan At their First Annual Meeting held at Asheville, North Carolina, July 1923. Joyner Library Special Collections. East Carolina University. Greenville, NC.

Pateman, Carole. *The Sexual Contract*. Stanford: Stanford University Press, 1988.

———. *The Disorder of Women: Democracy, Feminism, and Political Theory*. Stanford: Stanford University Press, 1989.

Potter, Henry, et al., eds. *Laws of the State of North Carolina*. Vol. 2. Raleigh: J. Gales, 1821.

Powell, William S. *Dictionary of North Carolina Biography*. 6 vols. Chapel Hill: University of North Carolina Press, 1979–96.

———. *North Carolina through Four Centuries*. Chapel Hill: University of North Carolina Press, 1989.

Quarles, Benjamin. *The Negro in the Civil War*. New York: Da Capo, 1989.

Quimby, Ian M. G. *Apprenticeship in Colonial Philadelphia*. New York: Garland, 1985.

Rable, George C. *Civil Wars: Women and the Crisis of Southern Nationalism*. Urbana: University of Illinois Press, 1989.

Raper, Horace W. *William W. Holden: North Carolina's Political Enigma*. Chapel Hill: University of North Carolina Press, 1985.

Rapport, Sara. "The Freedmen's Bureau as a Legal Agent for Black Men and Women in Georgia: 1865–1868." *Georgia Historical Quarterly* 73 (Spring 1989): 26–53.

Rawick, George, ed. *The American Slave: A Composite Autobiography*. Ser. 2, vols. 14–15. Westport, CT: Greenwood, 1972.

Reeve, Tapping. *The Law of Baron and Femme, of Parent and Child, Guardian and Ward, Master and Servant, and of the Powers of Courts of Chancery*. Burlington, VT: Chauncey Goodrich, 1846.

Reid, Richard. "A Test Case of the 'Crying Evil': Desertion among North Carolina Troops during the Civil War." *North Carolina Historical Review* 58 (July 1981): 243–62.

Robinson, Armstead. "Beyond the Realm of Social Consensus: New Meanings of Reconstruction for American History." *Journal of American History* 68 (May 1981): 276–97.

Robinson, Blackwell P., and Alexander R. Stoesen. *The History of Guilford County, North Carolina, U.S.A. to 1980, A.D.* Guilford County: Guilford County Bicentennial Commission, 1971.

Rodgers, Daniel T. "Republicanism: The Career of a Concept." *Journal of American History* 79 (June 1992): 11–38.

Rorabaugh, W. J. *The Craft Apprentice: From Franklin to the Machine Age in America.* New York: Oxford University Press, 1986.

Rose, Willie Lee. *Rehearsal for Reconstruction: The Port Royal Experiment.* New York: Knopf, 1964.

Rosner, David, ed. *Hives of Sickness: Public Health and Epidemics in New York City.* New Brunswick, NJ: Rutgers University Press, 1995.

Ruffin, Thomas. *The Papers of Thomas Ruffin.* Edited by J. G. de Roulhac Hamilton. 4 vols. Raleigh: North Carolina Historical Commission and Edwards and Broughton, 1920.

Ryan, Mary P. *The Cradle of the Middle Class: The Family in Oneida County, New York, 1790–1865.* New York: Cambridge University Press, 1981.

Salmon, Marylynn. *Women and the Law of Property in Early America.* Chapel Hill: University of North Carolina Press, 1986.

Saville, Julie. *The Work of Reconstruction: From Slave to Wage Laborer in South Carolina, 1860–1870.* New York: Cambridge University Press, 1994.

Schwalm, Leslie A. *A Hard Fight for We: Women's Transition from Slavery to Freedom in South Carolina.* Urbana: University of Illinois Press, 1997.

———. "'Sweet Dreams of Freedom': Freedwomen's Reconstruction of Life and Labor in Lowcountry South Carolina." *Journal of Women's History* 9 (Spring 1997): 9–38.

Schwartz, Marie Jenkins. *Born in Bondage: Growing Up Enslaved in the Antebellum South.* Cambridge: Harvard University Press, 2000.

Scott, Anne Firor. *The Southern Lady: From Pedestal to Politics, 1830–1930.* Chicago: University of Chicago Press, 1970.

Scott, Joan Wallach. *Gender and the Politics of History.* New York: Columbia University Press, 1988.

Scott, Joan Wallach, ed. *Feminism and History.* Oxford: Oxford University Press, 1996.

Scott, Rebecca. "The Battle over the Child: Child Apprenticeship and the Freedmen's Bureau in North Carolina." *Prologue* 10 (Summer 1978): 101–13.

Seybolt, Robert Francis. *Apprenticeship and Apprenticeship Education in Colonial New England and New York.* New York: Arno Press and the New York Times, 1969.

Simon, Bryant. *A Fabric of Defeat: The Politics of South Carolina Millhands in State and Nation, 1920–1945.* Chapel Hill: University of North Carolina Press, 1998.

Sims, Anastasia. *The Power of Femininity in the New South: Women's Organizations and Politics in North Carolina, 1880–1930.* Columbia: University of South Carolina Press, 1997.

Skocpol, Theda. *Protecting Soldiers and Mothers: The Political Origins of Social Policy in the United States.* Cambridge: Harvard University Press, 1992.

Smith-Rosenberg, Carroll. *Disorderly Conduct: Visions of Gender in Victorian America.* New York: Knopf, 1985.

Stansell, Christine. *City of Women: Sex and Class in New York, 1789–1860.* Urbana: University of Illinois Press, 1987.

Steinfeld, Robert J. *The Invention of Free Labor: The Employment Relation in English and American Law and Culture, 1350–1870.* Chapel Hill: University of North Carolina Press, 1991.

Stevenson, Brenda E. *Life in Black and White: Family and Community in the Slave South.* Oxford: Oxford University Press, 1996.

Still, William. *The Underground Rail Road.* Philadelphia: William Still, 1883.

Swift, W. H., ed. *Child Welfare in North Carolina: An Inquiry by the National Child Labor Committee for the North Carolina Conference for Social Service.* New York: National Child Labor Committee, 1918.

Tate, Claudia. *Domestic Allegories of Political Desire: The Black Heroine's Text at the Turn of the Century.* New York: Oxford University Press, 1992.

Thomas, Emory M. *The Confederate Nation, 1861–1865.* New York: Harper and Row, 1979.

Trefousse, Hans Louis. *Andrew Johnson: A Biography.* New York: Norton, 1989.

Tushnet, Mark V. *The American Law of Slavery, 1810–1860: Consideration of Humanity and Interest.* Princeton: Princeton University Press, 1981.

Ulrich, Laurel Thatcher. *A Midwife's Tale: The Life of Martha Ballard, Based on Her Diary, 1785–1812.* New York: Knopf, 1990.

Watson, Alan D. *History of New Bern and Craven County.* New Bern: Tryon Palace Commission, 1897.

———. "Orphanages in Colonial North Carolina: Edgecombe County as a Case Study." *North Carolina Historical Review* 70 (April 1975): 105–19.

———. "Public Poor Relief in Colonial North Carolina." *North Carolina Historical Review* 69 (October 1977): 347–63.

Weiner, Marli F. *Mistresses and Slaves: Plantation Women in South Carolina, 1830–80.* Urbana: University of Illinois Press, 1997.

White, Deborah Gray. *Ar'n't I A Woman? Female Slaves in the Plantation South.* New York: Norton, 1985.

Whites, LeeAnn. "The Civil War as a Crisis in Gender." In Clinton and Silber, *Divided Houses,* 3–21.

———. *The Civil War as a Crisis in Gender: Augusta, Georgia, 1860–1890.* Athens: University of Georgia Press, 1995.

Wiley, Bell I. *Southern Negroes, 1861–1865.* New York: Rinehart, 1953.

Williams, William H. *Slavery and Freedom in Delaware, 1639–1865.* Wilmington, DE: Scholarly Resources, 1996.

Williamson, Joel. *The Crucible of Race: Black-White Relations in the American South since Emancipation.* New York: Oxford University Press, 1984.

Wilson, Charles Reagan, ed. *Religion in the South.* Jackson: University Press of Mississippi, 1985.

Wilson, Joan Hoff. *Law, Gender, and Injustice: A Legal History of U.S. Women.* New York: New York University Press, 1991.

Wilson, Theodore Brantner. *The Black Codes of the South.* University: University of Alabama Press, 1965.

Winston, Robert W. *Andrew Johnson: Plebian and Patriot.* New York: Holt, 1928.

Wood, Betty. *Women's Work, Men's Work: The Informal Slave Economies of Lowcountry Georgia.* Athens: University of Georgia Press, 1995.

Woodward, C. Vann. *Origins of the New South, 1877–1913.* Baton Rouge: Louisiana State University Press, 1951.

————. *The Strange Career of Jim Crow.* 3d rev. ed. New York: Oxford University Press, 1974.

Worth, Jonathan. *The Correspondence of Jonathan Worth.* Edited by J. G. de Roulhac Hamilton. 2 vols. Raleigh: North Carolina Historical Commission and Edwards and Broughton, 1909.

Zelizer, Viviana A. *Pricing the Priceless Child: The Changing Social Value of Children.* New York: Basic Books, 1985.

Zipf, Karin Lorene. "Promises of Opportunity: The Freedman's Savings and Trust Company in New Bern, North Carolina." M.A. thesis, University of Georgia, 1994.

————. "Reconstructing 'Free Woman': African-American Women, Apprenticeship, and Custody Rights." *Journal of Women's History* 12 (Spring 2000): 8–31.

————. "'The WHITES Shall Rule the Land or Die': Gender, Race, and Class in North Carolina Conservative Reconstruction Politics." *Journal of Southern History* 65 (August 1999): 499–534.

INDEX

Abandonment, 21–23, 120, 127

Adultery, 22, 116

African Americans: alleged dependence of, 53, 54, 58, 59, 63, 74, 78, 80, 94; and child custody, 136; court testimony by, 59, 69; and education, 149; and marriage, 59; and parental rights, 2, 67, 69, 70, 79–81, 98–100, 102, 104, 108, 111, 155; and Republican Party, 96, 103; and suffrage, 69, 96; as threat to white society, 132; and weapons, 37, 59. *See also* Free blacks; Freedpeople; Freedwomen; Slaves

Alamance County, 18

Albemarle County, 12

Alexander, Roberta Sue, 61

Allen, James, 108

Allen, William R., on child custody, 136, 153

Ambrose, Eliza, 1, 97. See also *In the Matter of Harriet Ambrose and Eliza Ambrose*

Ambrose, Harriet, 1, 97. See also *In the Matter of Harriet Ambrose and Eliza Ambrose*

Ambrose, Wiley, 1, 97, 98, 106

Anson, NC, 50

Anson County, 150

Apprenticeship: and abuse, 55, 56; and age, 45, 47, 60, 66, 75, 79, 96; in antebellum North, 40, 41; bonds, 17, 18, 26, 29, 31–33, 45, 79; and character, 52; during Civil War, 41, 42; and class, 5, 25–27; in colonial America, 9, 10; complaints concerning, 17, 18, 31, 52, 53; defined, 4; demographics of, 29, 33, 34 (table 2), 35, 36, 41, 45, 46 (table 4), 47, 61; documentation of, 3; and economics, 6, 47; English origin of, 9; escape from, 57; formal, 4; and gender, 3, 5, 37, 39, 47, 60, 66, 79, 102; informal, 4, 32; involuntary, 1, 2, 4, 11, 51, 55, 56, 62, 69, 73, 74, 79, 80–82, 84, 85, 89, 90, 92–95, 98, 101, 103, 106; and masters' responsibilities, 12, 16, 17, 27, 31, 93, 130; and race, 2, 5, 26–29, 33, 35, 37, 39, 51, 60–62, 66, 67; and notification of parties, 90, 99–101, 110; in postbellum South, 44; and social control, 5, 7, 28, 29, 33, 35, 38, 40, 61, 64, 67, 104, 106, 155; and terms of service, 10, 15, 16, 29, 31, 64; voluntary, 31–33, 50, 51. *See also* Indenture

Apprenticeship code, 4, 11, 18, 26, 59, 110, 114, 142, 147; racial distinctions in, 65, 66, 102

Apprenticeship law: in antebellum NC, 21, 22, 25–28, 33, 106, 107; changes in, 2, 3, 59, 60, 65, 66, 79, 102, 103, 110, 114, 130, 154, 155; in colonial America, 9, 10; in colonial NC, 10–12, 15, 16; in England, 9; replaced, 147

Artificers, Statute of (1563), 9

Artis, Thomas, 17, 18, 38

Ashby, Chaney Calhoun, 114–17. See also *Ashby v. Page*

Ashby, James, 114; character of, 115, 116

Ashby v. Page (1890, 1891), 118, 119, 127, 139, 155

Ashe, Bell, 31

Ashe, Thomas S., 112

Ashe County, 62

Asheville, NC, 124, 125

Ashley, Samuel S., 55, 80

Aubriden, Charles, 95

Augusta, GA, 42

Augustus, Sarah Louise, 48

Avery, John, 12

Aycock, Charles Brantley, 149

Bagley, Daniel, 56

Baker, Elsy, 90, 91

Barbour, Charlie, 47

Bardaglio, Peter, 112

Barrett, John C., 50

Bastardy laws, 86–89, 99, 138–40

Bead, William, 12

Beadle, William H. H., 44, 56

Beard, David, 36

Beaufort County Juvenile Court, 120

Bell, James W., 32

Bell v. Walker et al., 32

Bennett, James, Jr., 115

Bennett, James, Sr., 115

Berry, Charles, on orphan act (1755), 14

Bertie County, 79, 81, 82

Bethania, NC, 62

Bickett, Thomas Walter, 143; and child welfare reforms, 138, 139; on Connor-Saunders Bill, 145

Black Codes, 44, 63, 89. See also Freedmen's Code

Blount, William, on African American apprentices, 16

Boger, Charles E., 135, 136

Bomford, J. V., on apprenticeship, 101

Boyle, Richard, 47

Boyles, R. R., 116

Brady, A. G., 88

Bribery, 50, 116

Brooks, George Washington, 89

Brown, Mabel Ellis, 137

Brunswick County, 1, 29, 32, 33, 35, 37, 38, 41, 45, 55, 93

Brunswick County Court, 1, 25, 79

Buncombe County Children's Home, 131

Bureau of Refugees, Freedmen and Abandoned Lands. See Freedmen's Bureau

Burnet, Lydia, 17, 38

Burns, Robert L., and child welfare, 140

Cabarrus County, 151

Cabarrus County Superior Court, 109

Caldwell, Tod R., on orphanages, 130

Calhoun, John, 115

Calhoun, Mary Etta Margaret, 114–17

Cannon, Joseph S., 79

Carney, Reddick, 55

Carteret County, 37, 61, 62

Carthage, NC, 140

Cartwright, Frederick, 50

Cary, Lorin Lee, 10

Charlotte, NC, 35, 129

Chavers, Temperance, 25

Chavis, Betsey, 31

Chavis, John, 31

Cherokee County, 150

Child, Thomas, on orphan act (1755), 14

Child labor laws, 3, 139, 142, 147, 155; manufacturers' opposition to, 143, 144, 146, 147; violation of, 148

Child support, 86, 88, 138, 140

Child welfare, and apprenticeship, 130, 137

Child Welfare Act (1919), 3, 147, 151, 152, 155

Childhood, 133, 139

Children: and adolescent behavior, 133; and "best interests," 3, 106, 113, 119–21, 126–28, 136, 137, 139, 140, 153–55; destitute, 68, 75, 78, 82, 98; free black, 10, 15–18, 26–29, 33, 38, 78, 93, 97, 102, 107; and free labor ideology, 75, 96; of freedpeople, 44, 47, 49–57, 59–61, 63–65, 69–72, 75, 77, 85, 89, 98–100, 117; hired out by parents, 32, 49, 50, 148; illegitimate, 10, 16, 17, 25, 27, 28, 33, 51, 60, 66, 78, 86, 87, 89, 92, 97–99, 102, 109, 114, 116, 119, 138, 140; indigent, 141, 142, 147; and inherited property, 12, 25, 109, 110; of mixed race, 2, 13, 16, 27, 28; and orphanages, 131; as public wards, 141; and qualifications for apprenticeship, 17, 21, 22, 24, 25, 27, 28, 44, 46, 51, 60, 65, 66, 75, 78, 79, 82, 86, 87, 89, 93, 96, 97, 102, 106, 107, 110, 114; rights of, 3, 100, 110, 117, 138, 139; of single parents, 70, 78, 79, 82, 93, 97, 107, 111, 117; of slaves, 47–49, 54

Chowan Council (precinct court), on apprenticeship dispute, 12, 13

Chowan County, 62

Chur, Jacob F., 92

Cilley, Clinton A., 50, 92; on apprenticeship, 78, 79; on Freedmen's Code, 63

Citizenship, 74, 85, 86, 94, 100

Civil Rights Act (1866), 63, 65, 67, 76, 88, 89, 96, 98

Clark, Walter J., 117; and women's suffrage, 107

Clarkson, Heriot, on child custody, 125, 126

Clegg, Annie McIntosh, 121–27

Clegg, Isaac N., 121–27

Clegg v. Clegg (1923, 1924), 127

Climer, Nancy E., 31

Cofer, Betty, 48

Coggin, John, 48

Coleman, W. M., 69

Colored Orphan Asylum (Oxford, NC), 131

Connor, Henry G., 142

Connor-Saunders Bill (1919): opposition to, 143, 144; and organized labor, 145; praised, 145; provisions of, 143; resurrected, 146

Conscription (Confederate), 41

Consent: and apprenticeship, 29, 33, 51, 66, 69, 74–76, 80, 82, 83, 90, 92, 93, 96, 98, 99, 101, 102; and political theory, 92; and reformatory commitments, 136; and women's property rights, 20, 21

Conservatives, 58, 98

Constitutional conventions, 96; (1865), 58, 69, 100; (1868), 103

Contracts and contractual agreements, 4, 11, 28, 32, 44; for child care, 114; for exhibit of children, 50; for labor, 49, 70, 76, 77

Cook, Eliza, 87–89, 91

Cook, James H., 88

Coon, Charles L., 137

County courts: and apprenticeship, 16–18, 24, 26, 27, 35, 36, 44, 45, 47, 51, 55, 59, 60, 65–67, 74, 75, 79, 80, 84, 85, 94, 97–102, 106–7, 110, 114, 117, 118; and child custody, 119; and guardianship, 21; and orphans, 14, 21; and reformatories, 136. *See also names of county courts*

Courts (precinct), and apprenticeship, 12

Coverture, 20, 21

Craven County, 62

Crisco, Susan, 118

Cumberland County, 61

Currie, Archibald B., 108

Currituck County, 27, 39

Custody: and apprenticeship, 114; and patriarchy, 108, 113

Daniels, Josephus, on child welfare, 140

Davidson County, 92

Debro, Sarah, 47

DeRosset, Eliza, 54

Devereux, Thomas P., on freedpeople and apprenticeship, 63–65

Devin, W. A., 125

Dillon, Richard, 109; on filial responsibility, 108

District of Columbia, 28, 29

Divorce, 19, 22, 108, 112, 124

Dixon, Thomas, 132

Dobbs, Arthur, on colonial authority, 13, 14

Dower rights, 20, 86, 87

Duplin County, 29, 33, 35, 44, 62, 69

Duplin County Court, 51

Edgecombe County, 61

Edmonston, Catherine, 53, 54

Education: for African Americans, 149; for apprentices, 17, 27; compulsory, 3; for freedpeople, 58, 69; for orphans, 12

Edwards, Laura F.: on *Ambrose* case, 100, 101; on apprenticeship and parental rights, 53; on dependence of women, 89, 90

Elections: and county government, 20; gubernatorial, 58

Elizabeth City, NC, 142

Emancipation Proclamation, 99

Escott, Paul D., 19

Family relationships: of African Americans, 69, 70, 80; and apprenticeship, 2; brother, 24, 38, 70, 114, 115, 122, 127; daughter, 1, 28, 50, 51, 54, 94, 111, 121, 122; father, 4, 17, 21, 24, 25, 27, 28, 31, 32, 49, 53–55, 57, 68, 69, 79–82, 84–87, 92, 97, 100, 106, 108–14, 116, 118–20, 123, 125–29, 136, 138–40, 147; grandfather, 109; grandmother, 114, 124, 129; grandparents, 120, 121; husband, 1, 19–23, 47, 52, 55, 70–72, 80, 86, 89, 114, 122, 123, 125–27; mother, 9, 17, 21, 23–25, 38, 47, 49, 53, 54, 65, 67, 79, 80, 82, 84–86, 90, 93, 97, 104, 106, 108–15, 117–20, 122, 126, 128, 129, 136, 139–41, 147, 150; restored, 54, 55; and separation, 54, 55; sister, 70, 122, 125, 127; son, 24, 25, 51–53, 55, 62, 72, 79–81, 92, 110, 111, 123, 125, 129; and state intervention, 2, 3, 70, 130, 147–49, 152–54; stepfather, 12, 99, 109; uncle, 52, 109, 118, 119; widow, 2, 3, 21–24, 62, 67, 107, 113, 114, 119, 140, 141; wife, 1, 19–23, 38, 49, 50, 55, 70, 72, 82, 86, 89, 108, 113, 116, 120, 121, 125, 126

Faucette, Lindsey, 48

Fayetteville, NC, 127, 133
Feme covert, 23, 86
Feme sole, 20, 22–24, 86
Fields, Barbara, 44
Fines. *See* Punishment: fines
Fisher, H. H., 44
Foner, Eric, 10
Foote, John M., 101
Forsyth County, 62
Fourteenth Amendment, 96, 151
Fowler, William, on parental rights, 80, 81
Fox, John, 12
Franklin, John Hope: on free blacks, 37; on interracial marriage, 16
Franklin County, 62
Franklin County Court, 18, 26
Frazier, W. R., 102
"Free base born children," 15, 25, 27, 28, 60, 66, 87, 99, 100. *See also* Children: illegitimate
Free blacks: and apprenticeship, 33, 35, 38, 39, 79; demographics of, 29, 30 (table 1), 34 (table 2); join Union army, 42; and marriage, 70; and parental rights, 15, 26; regulation of, 28, 29, 37, 38; as threat to antebellum society, 19. *See also* Children: free black
Free labor ideology, 40, 41, 75, 78
Free Masons, Grand Lodge of the Order of, 131
"Free woman" concept, 88, 89, 92; defined, 86
Freedmen's Bureau: and *Ambrose* case, 97–99, 101; and apprenticeships, 3, 45, 56, 61, 66, 74, 75, 78–83, 94, 97, 98, 101; assists freedwomen, 88, 89; cancels apprenticeships, 45, 52, 61, 62, 79, 92, 96, 101, 102; complaints to, 50–52, 54–56, 62, 69, 79–81, 85, 92, 95, 102, 104; criticized, 81, 82, 94, 96; and cus-

tody disputes, 109; investigated, 77; records of, 45, 57, 92, 93; and refugee camps, 71
Freedmen's Bureau circulars: #1, 75, 76, 78, 80, 81; #5, 101
Freedmen's Code, 60; criticized, 63; expansion of, 60, 61; provisions of, 59; racial discrimination in, 98
Freedmen's conventions, 58, 69, 70, 72
Freedmen's Savings and Trust Company, 72
Freedpeople: and apprenticeship, 44, 50–52, 55, 66, 73, 89, 100; and citizenship, 74, 100; and free labor ideology, 78; and labor of children, 49, 50; and labor contracts, 76, 77; and labor shortages, 43, 44, 52; and marriage, 55, 89; petition for rights and revision of state laws, 58, 69; in refugee camps, 43, 70, 71; and reuniting families, 54, 55; in Union army, 70. *See also* Children: of freedpeople
Freedwomen: challenge apprenticeship, 90–97; compared with free black women, 87; and "free woman" concept, 85–87; independence of, supported, 95; and labor issues, 91; legal status of, 85; and political involvement, 91; and womanhood, 86, 87, 90, 91
French, William, 104
French and Indian War, 13, 14
Frolick, Fanny, 28, 39. See also *Frolick v. Schonwald*
Frolick v. Schonwald (1859–60), 2, 28, 155
Fullerton, James Scott, 77

Galloway, Abram H.: on rights of former slaves, 69; on women's suffrage, 72, 73

Gaston, William, on apprenticeship indentures, 17
Gates County, 20, 79, 81, 82
Goldsboro, NC, 43
Granville County, 18, 26
Green, Nancy (Nannie) Jones, 118–20
Green, Simon, 118–20
Greene County, 20
Greensboro, NC, 29, 36
Gregory, Mrs. J. D. E., 54
Grimes, William, 76, 77
Guardianship, 12, 15, 21, 25, 98, 154
Guilford County, 27, 29, 31, 33, 35, 36, 41, 45
Guilford County Court, 118

Habeas corpus, 99, 104, 106, 108, 115, 118, 123, 129
Hall, G. Stanley, 133
Hamilton, Hatton, 120, 121
Hamilton, Rosa, 120
Harris, Sarah, 49
Harvey, Thomas, 12
Hawley, George, on apprenticeship, 81, 82
Herrington, Jesse, 32
Hertford County, 66, 79, 81, 82
Hertford County Court, 110, 111
High, Joe, 47
Hight, Herbert H., 18, 26
Hill, Martha, 51
Hoke, William A., 118; on child custody, 119, 120
Holden, William W.: appointed provisional governor, 58; chairs constitutional convention, 59; on Freedmen's Code and apprenticeship, 63; and Republican Party, 96
Hooks, William, 17, 18
Howard, O. O., 3, 51, 66, 69, 74, 77, 78,

102; on apprenticeship, 95, 96, 98; on employment of freedpeople, 76; on Freedmen's Code, 63

Illegitimacy, defined, 6, 25. See also Children: illegitimate
Imprisonment. See Punishment: imprisonment
In loco parentis, 32, 55, 154
In Re Habeas Corpus of Mary Jane Jones (1910), 119
In Re Richard Watson (1911), 153, 154
In the Matter of Harriet Ambrose and Eliza Ambrose (1867), 61, 99–102, 155
Indenture (apprentice agreement), 56, 67; amended, 27; terms of, 12, 17, 31, 32, 64
Indentured servitude, distinguished from apprenticeships, 10, 11
Inferior courts. See County courts
Inheritance. See Children: and inherited property; Dower rights; Orphans: and their estates
Interstate Commerce Act (1916), provisions of, 142, 143
Irving, Fanny J., 62
Irving, Washington, on women, 126
Ivey, Steward P., 32

James, Horace: and model farm, 76, 77; and refugee camps, 70, 71
James, William, 84
James City, NC, 43
Jamestown, VA, 10
Jenkins, Grace, 55, 90
Jenkins, William A., 59, 60, 79
Johnson, Andrew, 8, 24, 38, 58, 66
Johnson, Guion, 37, 61
Johnson, T. C., 150, 151
Johnson, William, 8, 24

Johnston, Rachel, 23
Jones, Betsey, 90
Jones, Mary Jane, 118–20
Jones, Prince, 118, 119
Joyner, J. Y., on Connor-Saunders Bill, 145
Justices of the peace, 17; and apprenticeship, 93, 94; influence of, 20
Juvenile courts, 3, 137, 139, 141, 147–49, 155

Kay, Marvin L. Michael, 10
Keel, Alsbury, 77
Kidnapping, 55, 93, 94
King, B. F., 115, 116
King's Daughters, 134
Kirk, Charles, 109
Ku Klux Klan, 122–25

Labor shortages, 43, 44
Ladd, Daniel, 50
Law: on children and inherited property, 12; on "enticing servants," 60, 61; on guardianship, 113; on labor, 10, 11; on orphans, 12, 14, 15, 25; on women's property rights, 20, 21, 23, 24. *See also* Apprenticeship law; Black Codes; Child labor laws; Freedmen's Code
Lawwell, Elizabeth, 23
Lawwell, Samuel, 23
Leloudis, James L., 149
Lewis, M. S., 151
Link, William A., 150
Littleton, NC, 52
Livingston, John A., on child labor law, 146
Local government, in antebellum North Carolina, 19, 20
Lomax, Helen, 109

Long, William Lunsford, and child labor law, 143, 146
Lumberton, NC, 51, 123
Lynching, 132, 133

Malone, Ann Patton, 69, 70
Manly, M. E., 28
Marriage, 87; interracial, 15, 16, 70. *See also* Freedpeople: and marriage; Women: and remarriage
Maryland, 28, 29, 44
Massachusetts Bay colony, 9
McBryde, Willoughby, 17, 27, 39. See also *Midgett v. McBryde*
McCollough, Amos, 51, 69
McCrory, Jacob, 50
McCrory, Milly and Christina (conjoined twins), 50
McDonough, Mary, 9, 24
McDowell County, 143
McKelway, Alexander: on child labor, 133, 134; on lynching, 132, 133; on social order, 132
McLaurin, Dan, 123
Mecklenburg County, 29, 35, 45, 62, 136, 148
Mecklenburg County Court, 35
Midgett, Nancy, 17, 27, 28, 38, 39. See also *Midgett v. McBryde*
Midgett v. McBryde (1855), 2, 27, 28, 155
Miles, Nelson A., 102
Mills, Richard, 79, 80
Misdemeanor, 61, 130, 143, 149, 151
Mississippi, 44
Missouri, 28, 29
Mitchell, Marina, 110–12. See also *Mitchell v. Mitchell*
Mitchell, Miles, 110, 111. See also *Mitchell v. Mitchell*
Mitchell v. Mitchell (1872), 118, 119, 127

Monroe County, GA, 44
Moore, Bartholomew F., and Freedmen's Code, 59
Moore, Godwin Cotton, 66
Moore County, 38, 108
Moore County Court, 17
Morehead, John Motley, 4
Morgan, Edmund, 10
Mottley, Ned, 52, 53
Mottley, Rebecca F., 52, 53
Murphy, Archibald D., 4

National Child Labor Committee, 137
Neal, W. W., 143
Neal Bill and Substitute (1919), 143, 144, 148; amended, 146; opposition to, 144, 145; provisions of, 144
New Bern, NC, 43, 47, 69–72
New Hanover County Court, 93, 104
New Orleans, LA, 42
Newsom, Betsey, 91–93
Norfolk, VA, 57
North Carolina Conference for Social Service, 137, 139
North Carolina Equal Rights League, 58, 72
North Carolina Federation of Women's Clubs, 134
North Carolina General Assembly: and child welfare reforms, 140–42, 144, 146, 147; and divorce, 22; election to, 19, 20; and Freedmen's Code, 60, 61; influence of slaveholding families in, 20; and revision of colonial laws, 14; on women, 22–24
North Carolina Manumission Society, 36
North Carolina Supreme Court, 2; and Ambrose case, 99, 100; and apprenticeship, 17, 18, 27, 39; and child labor law violation, 148; on custody, 28, 120, 121; and guardianship, 21; on school attendance, 148, 151; and women's property rights, 20, 22, 23; and women's rights to children, 109, 115, 117
Northampton County, 143

Officeholding, qualifications for, 20
Old Fort, NC, 127
Onslow County, 61, 62, 101, 102
Orange County, 37, 61
Orphanages, 130, 131
Orphans, 12, 17, 24, 25, 65, 68, 69, 75, 78, 93, 96, 98, 111; and their estates, 14, 15, 21; legal definition of, 15
Owensby, Robert, 116
Oxford Orphan Asylum, 131

Page, James H., 114–17. See also Ashby v. Page
Page, L. Berry, 114
Parens patriae, 31, 136, 137, 154
Parental rights, 4, 7, 13, 52, 53, 66, 67, 75, 80, 94, 103, 106, 119, 139, 147, 148, 153–55; maternal, 23, 24, 54, 65, 79, 85, 92, 106, 109–14, 118, 120–22, 126; paternal, 4, 15, 32, 53, 54, 69, 81, 100, 102, 108, 112, 118, 120–22, 126, 127, 136, 140
Parker, Nat, 81, 82
Parrish, Mrs. John, 118
Pasquotank County, 37, 61
Patriarchy, in antebellum North Carolina, 18, 19
Paul, George, 120
Pearson, Richmond M.: on apprenticeship, 27, 28; on child custody, 109, 119; on free blacks, 19
Perkins, William T., 17, 18
Perquimans County, 20, 143
Perry, Lily, 48

Philadelphia, PA, 9, 10
Phillips, Emma, 118
Pitt County, 76
Pollard, John, 31
Pollard, Rhonda, 31
Pool, Betsey, 31
Pool, John, on freedpeople, 58, 59
Poor relief, 12, 17, 22
Possessive individualism, 11, 91
Pritchard, Mrs. R. C., 51–53
Property rights. *See* Dower rights;
    Women: and property rights
Prue, Alfred, 18, 26
Pryor, Lilly, 56, 57
Punishment: confinement at reforma-
    tory, 129, 136; fines, 16, 61, 130, 143; im-
    prisonment, 61, 88, 129, 130, 140, 143,
    149; lashing, 10

Quakers: and apprenticeship, 36, 37; and
    slavery, 36

Raleigh, NC, 24, 29, 36, 58, 69, 72, 139
Raleigh Gazette, 8
Raleigh News and Observer, 139–41, 144–46
Randolph County, 102, 108
Reade, Edwin Godwin, 99, 100; on *Am-
    brose* case, 100, 101, 106; on child cus-
    tody, 111, 118
Reconstruction Acts (1867), 96
Reeve, Tapping, on women and
    guardianship, 21
Reform movement: and apprenticeship,
    137; and class, 132, 149; and paternal-
    ism, 130, 132–34; and race, 132, 133, 135,
    149; and schools, 137, 138
Reformatories, 129, 137; and race, 135
Republican Party, 96
Richardson, B. M., 56
Richmond, VA, 91, 122–24

Roanoke Island, 39, 43, 47
Roanoke Rapids, NC, 143
Robbins, Parker David, 103
Robeson County, 29, 33, 35, 41, 45, 141
Robeson County Court, 45, 93, 95, 96,
    104
Robeson County Superior Court, 125,
    127
Robinson, Jackson, 32, 38
Robinson, John, Sr., 32
Robinson, John C., 98, 99; on appren-
    ticeship, 3, 95, 96
Rodman, William B., 103
Rondthaler, Howard E.: on child wel-
    fare, 139; on "Children's Code," 140
Ross, Delia, 84, 85, 94, 104
Ross, James, 95
Ross, Lucy, 84, 85, 91, 93–98, 103, 104
Ross, Maria, 84, 85, 94, 104
Ross, William, 84, 95
Rowan County, 23
Rowland, NC, 121, 127
Ruffin, Thomas: on apprenticeship, 18,
    26; on patriarchal authority, 18, 19
Ruger, Thomas, 77, 95
Russell, Daniel L., Sr., 1, 52, 53, 106; and
    apprenticeship, 84, 85, 93–98, 103,
    104; defends actions, 94, 98, 99;
    influence of, 93, 95
Rutherford, Allan, 79, 80, 95, 96, 99
Rutherford County Court, 112, 113

Salisbury, NC, 57
Sampson County, 44, 62, 69
Sampson County Court, 45, 51, 55, 65, 80
Saunders, Hepsey, 1, 97, 98
Saunders, William Oscar, 142, 143, 146;
    on Neal Substitute, 144
Schonwald, James T., 28. See also *Frolick
    v. Schonwald*

School attendance, compulsory, 144, 148–50, 155
School reform, 149
Schwartz, Marie Jenkins, 48, 49
Scoggins, Mary, 112, 113. See also *Scoggins v. Scoggins*
Scoggins, William, 113. See also *Scoggins v. Scoggins*
Scoggins v. Scoggins (1879), 127
Scott, Elsie, 104
Scott, William, 49
Selby, James J., 8
Sewell, F. D., 101
Shipman, M. L., and labor legislation, 142, 143
Simmons, Furnifold, 132
Skipper, Daniel, 55, 90
Slaveholders (former), and apprenticeship, 59, 60, 67, 85
Slaves: and apprenticeship, 32; demographics of, 29, 30 (table 1); duties of, 47, 48; laws governing, 10; and masters' rights, 19; and paternalism, 48, 49; and separation of families, 54; and Union army, 43. See also Quakers: and slavery
Smith, Hubert, 135
Smith, John, 49
Smith, Mary A., 50
Smith, Samuel High, 51, 69
Snell, Cyrus, 109, 110
Snell, R. L., 109
Society of Friends. See Quakers
South Carolina, 44, 50, 91
South Mills, NC, 54
Spears, Margaret, 109, 111, 119
Spears v. Snel (1876), 109, 110, 119
Stacy, H. E., and juvenile courts, 141
Stacy, W. P., on child custody, 120, 121
Starnes, W. S., 148

State Board of Charities and Public Welfare, 131
State v. Jowers (1850), 19
Steedman, John, 77
Steinfeld, Robert J., 11
Stokes County, 114
Stokes County Superior Court, 114, 115
Stonewall Jackson Manual Training and Industrial School (Concord, NC), 129, 153; founding of, 134, 135; life in, 135, 136
Suffrage. See African Americans: and suffrage; Women: and suffrage
Suicide, 56, 57
Superior courts: on apprenticeship, 17, 18; and child custody, 109, 120; and delinquent children, 141, 147; and orphans, 14; and paternity cases, 140. See also names of superior courts
Surls, Berry, 31
Surry County, 67
Swift, W. H.: on apprenticeship, 137; on child welfare, 151, 152

Tappan, Winthrop, 76
Teal, Asa, 81
Tillinghast, Eliza, 44
Tillinghast, Sarah, 43
Tourgée, Albion, on freedpeople, 73, 74
Turner, Nat, 37
Tyrrell County Court, 101

Union army: in coastal NC, 42, 43; and former slave children, 47; and refugee camps, 70, 71
Unionists, 58, 63, 96, 100; African American, 102
United Daughters of the Confederacy, 108, 134
United States District Court, 88, 89

Vagrancy, 28, 129, 136
Vance, Zebulon B., 58, 100
Vance County Court, 119
Voting, 19, 20

Waddell, Alfred Moore, 132
Wages: for children, 49, 51, 77, 110, 111;
    for freedmen, 70, 77; for women, 77
Wake County, 29, 31, 33, 35, 36, 41, 45
Walker, Caleb L., 32
Walker, David, 37
Walker, Platt D., on custody and judicial
    discretion, 121
Warren County, 20, 23, 59, 79
Washington County, 43, 55
Washington County Superior Court, 32
Watson, Richard, 129, 136, 137, 153
Watson, Samuel S., 129, 136
Waugh, H. M., 67
Wayne County, 38
Whigs, 57, 58
White supremacy, 6
Whittlesey, Eliphalet, 45, 56, 66, 81, 82;
    on apprenticeship, 3, 40, 68, 74–76,
    80, 95; court-martialed, 77, 78; on
    Freedmen's Code, 63; on freedpeople,
    74; and model farm, 76–78; praised,
    78; on sanitation in refugee camps, 71
Whitworth, Elizabeth, 23
Wiggins, Starkey, 55
Wilkes County, 29, 35, 62
Williams, Abner, 49, 50
Williams, Catherine, 48
Williams, Harper, 49, 50

Wilmington, NC, 58, 84
Womanhood, 86, 87, 90, 91, 107, 114, 117,
    118, 127
Women: abused, 122; and apprenticeship,
    2, 3, 15, 24–29, 31, 39, 62, 67, 104, 105,
    107, 117; character of, 22, 54, 65, 107,
    117, 118; and charity, 42; and child
    custody, 86, 95, 109, 111–13, 118, 120,
    121, 125, 127, 128, 136; and child rear-
    ing, 80; and children's estates, 110; in
    Civil War, 42; and concept of "lady,"
    107, 108; as dependent on men, 86, 90,
    97; elite, 43, 44, 52; and "good char-
    acter," 114, 118, 155; and guardianship,
    15, 21, 24, 25, 106, 113, 128; and judicial
    authority, 113; and Ku Klux Klan,
    122–25; and political involvement, 72;
    and property rights, 20–24, 73, 86,
    122; and public involvement, 107, 108,
    127; in refugee camps, 70–72; and re-
    marriage, 109, 119; as single parents,
    82, 90, 93, 97, 102, 103; and suffrage,
    72, 73, 107, 125; unable to provide for
    children, 75, 82, 102, 114; and work,
    72. *See also* Family relationships:
    daughter, grandmother, sister, widow,
    wife; Freedwomen; Parental rights:
    maternal
Worth, Jonathan, 58, 79; appeal to, 62;
    on Freedmen's Code and apprentice-
    ship, 65, 98

Yellady, Dilly, 49
Young, Matthew, 31